HUNTING WISDOM

Hunting Wisdom

A Bacchic Orphic Diviner's Manual

H. JEREMIAH LEWIS

Nysa Press

Thrasyllos stayed with Polemaenetos as guest-friend for a while and became so intimate with him that the soothsayer, upon his death, left to Thrasyllos his books on divination and bequeathed to him a portion of the property which is now in question. Thrasyllos, with these books as his capital, made the art of divination his profession and this shameless itinerant soothsayer carried on numerous affairs with women in many cities.

(Isokrates, *Aiginetikos* 5-6)

I propose a re-examination of the ancient evidence that takes seriously the model, proposed by Burkert and others, of itinerant religious specialists competing for religious authority among a varying clientele. Rather than looking for a coherent set of sacred texts canonical to people who considered themselves Orphics, texts expressive of doctrines pertaining to sin, salvation, and the afterlife, we should look for the products of bricolage, pieced together from widely available traditional material to meet the demand of clients looking for extra-ordinary solutions to their problems. If the texts and rituals are products of bricolage, however, and their creators bricoleurs competing for authority, we cannot expect to find either consistency of texts or doctrines, merely a loose family resemblance between composites of the same traditional elements. A redefinition of ancient Orphism requires a polythetic definition that accommodates the complexities of the ancient contexts rather than the sort of monothetic definition that identifies Orphism by its scriptures and doctrines. Nevertheless, the attempt to force the evidence into this preconceived modern construct has created unnecessary confusions in interpretation, as, e.g., the debate over the Orphic status of the author of the Derveni papyrus shows.

(Radcliffe G. Edmonds III, *Redefining Ancient Orphism*)

Also in the 1950s, painter and writer Brion Gysin more fully developed the cut-up method after accidentally re-discovering it. He had placed layers of newspapers as a mat to protect a tabletop from being scratched while he cut papers with a razor blade. Upon cutting through the newspapers, Gysin noticed that the sliced layers offered interesting juxtapositions of text and image. He began deliberately cutting newspaper articles into sections, which he randomly rearranged. The book *Minutes to Go* resulted from his initial cut-up experiment: unedited and unchanged cut-ups which emerged as coherent and meaningful prose. Gysin introduced Burroughs to the technique at the Beat Hotel. The pair later applied the technique to printed media and audio recordings in an effort to decode the material's implicit content, hypothesizing that such a technique could be used to discover the true meaning of a given text. Burroughs also suggested cut-ups may be effective as a form of divination saying, "When you cut into the present the future leaks out."

(Wikipedia, s.v. "Cut-up technique")

This book is dedicated to

those who served him
as Oracles, Prophets, Diviners,
Boukoloi, Bakchoi, Mainades,
Priests and Hierophants
down through the ages.

As well as:

Abaris
Aeschines
Akoites
Paculla Annia
Antheus
Apollon
Apollonios
Apuleius
Archilochos
Arion
Aristeas
Aristoxenos
Arlecchino
Antonin Artaud
Bakis
Georges Bataille
Charles Baudelaire
William Blake
Jorge Luis Borges
David Bowie
William Burroughs
Edward Butler
Lewis Carroll
Chaeremon
Cheiron
Cicero
Clement
The Comedic Poets
Aleister Crowley
Scott Cunningham
Daidalos
Salvador Dalí
Ernesto De Martino
Philip K. Dick

Diotima
E. R. Dodds
Dver
Radcliffe G. Edmonds, III
Empedokles
Epimenides
Arthur Evans (I)
Arthur Evans (II)
Galeotes
W. K. C. Guthrie
H.D.
Jane Ellen Harrison
The Headless Ones
Jim Henson
Heraïskos
Herakleitos
Herakles
Hermotimus
Iamblichos
Ikarios
John the Baptist
John of Inverkeithing
Sarah Iles Johnston
Karpokrates
Carl Kerényi
Kerinthos
Kleia
Kosko, Baubo, and Thettale
Galina Krasskova
Charles Godfrey Leland
P. Sufenas Virius Lupus
David Lynch
Charles Manson
The Nymphai

Martino and Pietro
Medeia
Melampos
Jim Morrison
Thomas Morton
Mousaios
Friedrich Nietzsche
Nonnos
Numenius
Olympias
Onomokritos
Orpheus
The Orpheotelestai
Walter Otto
Parmenides
St. Paul
Pharnobazos
Phemonoe
Pherekydes
Philip the Orpheotelest
Phryne
Pindar
The Pythiai
Sylvia Plath

Plato
Plutarch
Polemaenetos
Polyidus
Porphyry
Vettius Agorius Praetextatus
Proklos
Pythagoras
François Rabelais
Rhesos
Rhinthon
Arthur Rimbaud
Sarapio
The Sibyls
Sokrates
Spartacus' Wife
Tages
Thaïs
Theophrastos
Thespis
Thrasyllos
Tieresias
The Tragic Poets

And all the rest who, collectively, have taught me what it is
to be a Bacchic Orphic diviner.

I dedicate it as well to my assistants-in-the-work:

Amanita muscaria
Caffeine
Marijuana
The Psilocybes
Salvia divinorum
Tobacco
and all the many wonderful alcohols.

To
my elders,
my students,
my initiates,
my colleagues,
my clients,

my community
and all who will come after.

But most of all this book is dedicated to
Dionysos, Hermes, Arachne
and all the Gods and Spirits of the Starry Bull tradition.

Thank you.

May this humble book be pleasing to you all,
and serve well the purpose it was created for.

CONTENTS

FOREWORD: To Hold and Pour Forth (by Neve Antheus).......................ix
PREFACE: All Things Flow xi

PREPARATION
Is That You, Dionysos? 1
An Equal Share 5
Cleansing the Doors of Perception 7
Why We Do What We Do..12
Why Is the Starry Bull Strain of Bacchic Orphism So Horrific? 15
What To Do When Bad Things Happen To You 19
Spiritual Discernment 21
Some Things You Can Do When It Gets Intense 29
More on Spiritual Discernment..34
The Ethics of *Mantike*...39
Confirmation Bias..48
Problematic Oracles..50
How To Worship the Starry Bull Way 54
A Starry Bull Offering Rite..57
A Starry Bull Sacrament..59
Fireless Bacchic Chernips...61
Bacchic Orphic Chernips, Greco-Egyptian Style 63
Dionysian Purity 69
Cleanliness Is Next To Godliness..76
Cleansing and Consecration of the Diviner 81

THE ORACLE BOOK OF SANNION THE ORPHEOTELEST
Proteleia...83
The Net of Zagreus...84
The Olbian Oracle..85
The Oracle of the Coins...86
The Oracle of Meilichios and Bakcheios 87
The Oracle of Many Names..88
Katharmoi...89
Starry Bull Alphabet Oracle 91
The Leaves of Dionysos...96
How To Make Your Very Own Bibliomantic System 108
The Oracle of Dionysos Bakcheios 113
The Oracle of the Doors 119
The Oracle of the Masks 125

The Lots of Dionysos the Bridegroom 131
The Oracle of Dionysos Mousegetes 135
The Tablets of Orpheus 143
The Head of Orpheus 144
The Oracle of the Story 148
The Oracle of the Tree 149
Grape Leaf Oracle 151
Pithomanteia 152
Oomancy 155
Melamancy 156
The Oracle of the Wheel and Key 157
Cloth Divining 159
The Mirror of the Moon 162
Doll Divination 163
Starry Bull Astragalomancy 165
The Top of Destiny 194
Discovering the Weather 195
Kottabos Oracle 196
Diagnosing the Evil Eye With an Egg 199
The Walnut 200
The Oracle of the Stars 201
Prognostic for Thunder by Hours of the Day 202
Another Method of Divination by Thunder 204
The Oracle of Flame 205
The Diagnostic of Philolâus of Tarentum 208
The Oracle of Smoky Words 210
The Oracle of Ash 211
Phallomanteia 213
The Grace of Elais, Spermo and Oino 214
Thusthla 215
Catoptromancy 217
Oracle of Phanes 218
Oracle of the Threads 220
The Bronze 221
How To Make Your Very Own Telesterion 223
Analysis of the Toys 226
The Consecration Ceremony 229
Proper Care of Your Toys 230
The Toys as Divination Tools 232

APPENDIX: Miscellaneous Sources on Bacchic Orphic Purity
   Regulations 237
About the Author 269

FOREWORD:
To Hold and Pour Forth

3-3-6: As Zeus' oracle declares.
4-3-6: a mere mortal daring to fight a god.
1-4-3: abandon your city for barbarian lands.
2-1-1: The tasks that have been specially set for you.
3-2-1: you too must endure your lot.

I began this introduction as I begin all works for Dionysos: with divination. I divine first because our God, who is *polymorphos* and *polyonomos*, defies my conception. The confrontation between the divine and we mere mortals always poses certain dangers. Dionysos himself was born from the fires of one mortal's encounter with her God unmediated. Wrapt in ivy and secreted away by his messenger brother, he was raised among the Nymphs, raised as living embodiment of the divine coupled with the yearning-for-the-divine. A God of wild animals and of plants, of expansive life and of the underworld, of night and starry sky, he is everywhere at once and yet is also of the void. The paradox of Dionysos' immanence and simultaneous ineffability demands translation on the part those who would serve him.

Snakes kissed Melampos' ears and thereafter he could hear the whispering of the God in the wildness around him. He carried the secrets of the trees and beasts and went mad and wandered until his God released him. Akoites too recognized that terrible power when none of his comrades could. Spartacus' wife, subject to the Dionysiac frenzy, prophesied war in serpentine twists. Even Tiresias, that blind old man, could read the signs and counseled Pentheus in vain to keep holy the rites of Bakcheios.

In the retinue of Dionysos, the role of *mantis* is undeniably sacred. The myths report that the dark stranger comes in the company of mad-prophets and priests. These oft maligned ranters form the meshwork upon which the spider crawls. To receive and cleanly transmit the good counsel of the Lord is not a task for the faint of heart. He tells terrible truths and tears down walls. His words come as the serpent's rattle and as the raging bull, as dithyramb and as earthquake. Dionysos is a God who breaks and makes-again. Those who have been pieced together may serve as vessels, so that the sweet wine might reach the lips of others. To hold and pour him forth is an all-consuming pleasure. To hold and pour forth is simultaneous self-effacement and self-affirmation. To hold and pour forth these revelations requires his mediums to commit themselves to training as specialists.

This training insists upon purification, sacrifice, discernment, piety, and above-all, ecstasy. To wear the mask of *mantis* one must be worn as a mask in turn.

Would you come before the Gods in search of knowledge? This book contains powerful tools and rites. Here, drink this. Look into this basket. There are things you must see.

- Neve Antheus

PREFACE:
All Things Flow

Like all of my books, this one began with an idea — and also like all of my books, what you hold in your hands bears almost no resemblance to that initial idea.

I had just finished putting together a new divination system when it struck me — why not collect all of these into a booklet so Starry Bull folks could have easy access to them? After all, ours is a tradition founded and promulgated by itinerant diviners and religious specialists, so we really should have better resources available for those who feel called to serve their Gods and community in this way. That got me thinking about what, bare minimum, Bacchic Orphic *manteis* (Greek for "diviners") ought to know to do their job right and...well, before I realized it this manual had morphed from 40 to almost 300 pages. Some of the material has seen previous publication but a lot of it was written specifically for this book.

Don't just skip ahead to the shiny new divination systems, tempting as that may be — or if you do, be sure to go back and give the introductory material a good, thorough read before you hang up your *mantis* shingle. We're not doing this for shits and giggles (even if some folks are forced to sign "for entertainment purposes only" waivers before practicing publicly) — no, we are taking up one of the oldest and most sacred professions known to mankind. The diviner straddles the gulf between the hidden and the seen and makes known to their community the sage counsel of the Gods and Spirits. When everything is out of balance, illness and misfortune afflict the people, the holy has been profaned and the land cries out for justice — that is when the *mantis* steps in and untangles the threads so that all may enjoy felicitous relations once more. That can be a heavy burden of responsibility to bear, especially since the learning curve is pretty steep, the terrain utterly unforgiving and the consequences of fucking up can be irreversible and severe, especially for the client and their family. So read — and consider — carefully what follows.

This book is not intended as a complete training manual for the prospective *mantis*, and in fact it presumes some basic familiarity on the part of the reader with the art and science of divination. Instead we'll cover the deeper philosophy and ethics of the craft, how to deal with problematic oracles and clients, how to work with altered states of consciousness and practice spiritual discernment as well as other relevant topics.

Additionally, since *manteis* are often called upon to answer questions about purification and miasma, prescribe rituals and other devotional practices, help navigate taboos and sacred regulations and act as amateur spiritual counselors, I have included material on that as well as an Appendix with a miscellany of sources on ancient Bacchic Orphism which serves as the basis for our emergent Starry Bull tradition. These are not so much a list of rules to be followed as examples of our religious specialists and diviners in action, and from which we can draw in dealing with our own clients today.

I have included material on regular devotional practice not just so that the *mantis* will have something to share with a client when they ask how they should honor the Starry Bull Gods and Spirits, but also for the health and well-being of the *mantis.* You're only as good as your connection to your Gods and Spirits, and as with every relationship it requires constant diligence and upkeep to ensure things continue running smoothly. I strongly recommend performing the Starry Bull Offering Rite on a weekly basis, and the Starry Bull Sacrament monthly (preferably on the Noumenia, or feast of the New Moon) or whenever you want an extra oomph to your devotions. If you don't have this, or some regular practice of your own, in place you risk getting gunked up by taking upon yourself the miasma of your clients or having your signal clarity compromised — not to mention the fact that you should never go before the Gods and Spirits with empty hands. This will also ensure that your spiritual batteries stay charged and you don't suffer burnout, which is an all too common consequence of this kind of intensive work.

Finally, when you do get to the Dionysian divination systems I've included, have fun with them! Experiment and see what works for you and what doesn't. Don't hesitate to tweak them if needed (I've certainly taken and adapted systems beyond those that come from ancient Greece, Italy or Egypt in keeping with the ancestral traditions of my people; if you had culture, we Romans appropriated — and perfected — it) just know why you're making the changes you are, how that will alter the mechanics of the system and that whoever you're dedicating it to is down with using such a system, as well as similar concerns. Bricolage is not a license for indiscriminate eclecticism! Spend some time really getting to know the system before deciding to include it in your divination kit or tinkering with it.

Especially when you're first learning I highly recommend acquiring a journal and writing everything down. The results of your sessions, random thoughts and associations you get while working with the systems, the results of any special exercises I've provided, or dreams, visions, encounters you have, the product of any research you do, etc. Not only is it helpful to write things out (there's some brain chemistry involved I won't bother getting into) but it makes it a lot easier to spot evolving patterns especially when one has as piss poor a memory as I do. However, if you write down the results of divination sessions with clients use a codename for them so you don't inadvertently betray their confidence.

Whenever possible, craft the systems yourself. Yeah, yeah, I know, I'm shit at handicrafts too, but it really helps build up a strong connection between you and the system. Once you've made yours, take good care of them, keeping them properly stored and out of the hands of random people. Some *manteis* let clients handle their systems, some don't. If you do, make sure the client has gone through appropriate protocols, including cleansing with *chernips*, and be sure that this is never done in a casual and unfocused setting and cleanse the system each time after it's handled. You should cleanse and feed your systems regularly to keep them in good working order — at least once a month, and more frequently if you see lots of clients. (I feed mine on alcohol, blood and incense smoke, usually on the Noumenia.)

And the rest, as they say, can be found in the book.

Cheers!

- Sannion, (H. Jeremiah Lewis)
The Scenic Hudson Valley,
October 31st, 2016 e.v.

NB: Throughout this book I tend to use the terms "divination" and "oracle" interchangeably, in part to remain faithful to the original sources from antiquity, such as those from the *PGM*. In actuality, there are many significant differences between performing mechanical divination versus prophetic oracles – although the techniques can also be blended together. The divination methods I present here can be used within an oracular context or on their own.

PREPARATION

Is That You, Dionysos?

When I first encountered my God in early adolescence I knew nothing about him beyond what he showed me through dreams, visions and direct communication. Later in my early teens when I sought to reconnect with him I didn't have a whole lot to go on, especially since that initial revelation had faded to a dim and corrupt memory over time. I spent the next few years chasing his shadow through various religious and philosophical systems, attracted to a number of figures like Siva, Jesus, Odin, the Wiccan Horned God, Nietzsche's Zarathustra, etc., who bore a certain superficial similarity to that strange, earthy, sensual and mysterious deity I had encountered as a child. Although some were very close indeed, possessing many of the qualities that had initially drawn me to him, none proved a perfect match until I happened upon Dionysos himself through a series of not-so-random coincidences. The more I came to learn of this God's history, mythology and cultus the more I came to realize that he and only he was my God. This, in turn, filled me with a yearning to know everything that I could about him from the past so that I would better understand who he is today.

And I have pursued that goal with a single-minded devotion that borders on the obsessive ever since. Oh, who am I kidding? I left the merely obsessive behind long ago! In the early days of my involvement in the online Hellenic polytheist community I earned a reputation as the king of sources for my encyclopedic knowledge of Dionysian lore and ability to come up with dozens of quotes on the spot on the most arcane of topics. Mind you, this was far more impressive in the days before theoi.com and the plentiful electronic databases of ancient literature that subsequent waves of Hellenic polytheists have had access to. Back in the day you actually had to read the corpus of Classical writings as well as all of the scholarly books and articles for yourself if you wanted to glean any significant information about the Gods and their religion. Somehow I managed to do this through the shitty Everett and Marysville public libraries and what I could find at Borders, Barnes & Noble and the smattering of used bookstores in the area. I still remember the excitement of finally laying my hands on a dog-eared copy of Farnell's *Cults of the Greek States*, long out of print at the time, which mysteriously showed up at the used bookstore where I worked.

But I digress.

My point is that when we hear the name Dionysos, the first thing that occurs to most of us is that he is an ancient Greco-Roman deity. We know him through his myths. He is the son of the immortal Zeus and the mortal

Semele. (Or Zeus and Persephone, or Zeus and Demeter, or Ammon and Rheia or so on and so forth, depending on which account you give priority to.) He was raised by the Nymphs and Satyrs on the distant mount Nysa, was pursued and tormented by the jealous Goddess Hera, released from madness by Kybele, traveled the earth teaching men his mysteries and the art of viticulture, redeemed and married Ariadne, brought his mother up out of Haides and accomplished many other fabulous deeds. Alongside this mythic conception of him there is also the Dionysos of cultus. The God of the winepress and the theater, the God who drives the women out of their homes to dance on the mountain and hunt the creatures of the forest, the God of Anthesteria, Lenaia, Liberalia, Oschophoria and the Bacchanalia, the God of Alexander the Great, the Ptolemies, and Marcus Antonius.

Herakleitos, Herodotos, Diodoros, Euripides, Aristophanes, Livy, Plutarch, Nonnos and numerous other poets, historians and philosophers have indelibly shaped our image of this God to the point where we are often not even conscious of our indebtedness to them. (To this list I would also add more contemporary voices such as Friedrich Nietzsche, Jane Ellen Harrison, Walter Otto, Carl Kerényi, Walter Burkert, Jim Morrison, Arthur Evans, and Donna Tartt.) Even those who have never bothered to crack open the books of these illustrious authors remain influenced by their conceptions since others have, and that is reflected in the writing we produce and the casual conversations we have on the various websites, blogs, e-mail lists and fora that primarily constitute the modern Hellenic, Neopagan and Dionysian communities. This information may be picked up second or third hand (or even further removed) in an elaborate game of telephone, but it always goes back to the originals, whether credited or not.

Even when we have direct and personal encounters with the God in complete isolation from the community at large, it is often filtered through this body of tradition, this conglomerate of cultus, history, myth and literature. We find parallels between what we are experiencing and what came before. We fashion a mental picture of him from the words of others, their epithets, their stories. This does not diminish what we see and feel — rather it lends depth to it, gives it a greater resonance and vitality. Helps us to understand the immensity of this God, that he has been with us all this time and active in our world. He existed long before we came into being and will be here long after we shuffle off this mortal coil. In a very real sense this body of tradition is what makes him an immortal God, and what's more, the specific God that he is — Dionysos and not, say, Odin or Cernunnos.

And yet it can be useful sometimes to temporarily strip all of this away, necessary though it may be for a true understanding of him, and to contemplate the Dionysos of my heart, the God I feel in the frenzy of worship. If everything that has ever been known about this God in the past were to suddenly vanish he would still exist and it would still be possible to encounter him. This, too, is what makes him a true and immortal God.

So what is this God, my personal Dionysos, like?

He is dark and strange, like a man and yet so very different from one. There is always something Other about him. Sometimes he appears young and beautiful, with a softness to his features that is almost feminine. Long-haired with sultry, pouting lips and skin like mocha, clothed in flowing, exotic and colorful fabrics. He is joyous and sensual, warm and inviting. But his eyes — there is something cold and unnerving about those eyes. They have seen too much of the world and the suffering it contains to belong to such a sweet and innocent face. Other times he has a countenance to match those eyes — wild and bearded, hard and whorled like the bark of an ancient tree. He wears no clothing but a verdant crown of ivy torn fresh from the earth and a heavy snake draped across his broad shoulders. He holds a bunch of plump grapes in his hands, squeezing them so that their juice stains his fingers. Large and savage cats recline at his feet eyeing you with lethal curiosity, but they will make no move unless he wills it. His smile is terrifying. And sometimes he is fat and jolly, laughing drunkenly at the absurd antics of his bestial companions while he gropes some busty maiden perched precariously on his knee.

Sometimes he doesn't appear human at all. A masculine presence lurking in the trees, the quiet stillness of a dark, damp cave, thunder rolling across the heavens and a sudden shower of rain, a somber madness and the excited clamor of a dancing, screaming crowd, fire, bull, ecstasy. It is in such an impersonal form that I most often encounter him.

During ritual Dionysos usually comes across as a *presence*, a conscious-ness that gradually rises up around me, within me until it becomes difficult to tell where he begins and I end. I feel him along the periphery of my awareness at first, and I know it's him by how everything is affected. He simultaneously heightens all of my senses and makes the world fluid and strange. The quality of light changes, becoming brighter and more intense. Sounds are distorted, as if I'm hearing them across a great distance. I feel a recklessness, a boldness take hold of me, freeing me to say and think and do things I would not ordinarily permit myself to. I become acutely aware of my body — the muscle and bone and blood beneath my skin, sometimes even the individual hairs on my head and he a divine breath flowing through me. I feel too full of him and may find it difficult to remain in place. Without even realizing it I will begin to sway or dance or be overcome by an urge to run around screaming at the top of my lungs. Other times the opposite happens. Something presses heavily upon me, as if the ground is holding me firm where I stand, as if I'm rooted deep, deep down below. Everything grows dark and still, the world outside of me disappearing in the silent gloom of the dead God. I become catatonic with no thoughts except for a dim awareness of the slow and steady rhythmic beating of the earth's heart. Still other times it is as if too much has been poured into the cup of my mind, sending my thoughts spilling out in a wine-scented gush. My thoughts take on the form of his myths, his poetry and I experience it all as if it is happening to me though these things took place long, long ago. I am gripped by a fury to write, to get it all out on paper and it is everything I can do to keep up with the frenzy of his inspiration.

My experiences of him takes many other forms as well — but this should suffice to give an impression of what it is like to feel the presence of this strange and wonderful God whom I know as Dionysos.

The Dionysian spirit is one of expansion. He lifts us out of our everyday confines, broadens our horizons, opens us to the fullness of life and dissolves whatever obstacle may be impeding our path. With all of this we should not be surprised to discover that prophecy was closely linked with Dionysos by the ancients — for it is only our limited sight which perceives past, present, and future as three distinct categories instead of merely parts of a single stream, a river that can twist, turn and flow back upon itself, as it becomes when viewed through divine eyes. Plutarch called Dionysian madness a secret knowledge, and Euripides explicitly called the God *mantis*, or seer and "prophet of the Thracians." Herodotos tells us that Dionysos shared the oracle at Delphi, while Pausanias testifies to one at Amphikleia and Aristotle tells us that just as the Apollonian seers prophesied at Klaros after drinking from a sacred spring, so Thracian prophets gained inspiration from Dionysos after drinking large quantities of wine.

What sort of prophecy did Dionysos preside over in antiquity? We have evidence of a number of different types. First, there are what have been called "mechanical" forms of divination, since they required a tool of some sort to communicate the divine will. This is the sort of divination that we see employed at the Villa of the Mysteries. In one of the scenes (see cover), a young Satyr, assisted by two companions, is gazing into the depths of a vessel. This sort of divination or scrying had a long history and is found in numerous places in the Greek Magical Papyri. This may also be what is indicated in the Orphic myth when the Titans creep up on the child Zagreus who is lost in meditation on his reflection in a mirror. The cup or bowl would be filled with water, wine, oil or some other substance, and the diviner would gaze into its depths to behold visions. The shimmering reflection of light and shadows on the surface (this operation would have been performed in a darkened room lit only by guttering oil lamps) would distract the conscious portions of his mind, allowing the images and a deeper, intuitive knowledge to rise to the surface. The visions that the diviner beheld could be symbolic (e.g., if he saw a flowering tree it meant renewal), more concrete (such as an actual scene from the future), or more along the lines of a monition, as we see from the Greek Magical Papyri which describe the magician actually holding conversations with a Spirit inside a bowl. Another form of mechanical divination associated with Dionysos was the interpretation of the lees left in a glass of wine. Unfortunately, we have no evidence of how these were interpreted, although we can surmise that the process was probably not unlike that used by modern readers of tea leaves or coffee grounds. We have evidence of a third form of mechanical divination associated with Dionysos from the *Alexander Romance* of Pseudo-Kallisthenes and the *Indika* of Arrian. According to the tradition represented in these texts, when Alexander the Great visited India he met with and spoke to the God Dionysos who lived in a pair of sacred trees. This brings to mind the oracle of Zeus at Dodona, where the barefoot priests discerned his will through the rustling of leaves. Unfortunately, history has provided us with no clues as to how the priests interpreted the rustling of leaves or how Alexander spoke with Dionysos.

The most common form of Dionysian divination, however, required no tools and was actually possession and prophecy in the proper sense of the term. At the height of Dionysian worship the spirit of the God can enfold and entwine with that of the worshiper, the two uniting in the most intimate form of communion. The Greeks called this *enthousiasmos* or literally "a God is within" and the individual was thereafter known as a Bakchos (m) or Bakches (f) signifying their unity with Dionysos Bakcheios. In addition to being filled with the God's spirit, made whole and new, they were granted prophetic gifts, imperviousness to pain and extreme conditions such as heat and cold, as well as the ability to perform miraculous deeds such as the Mainades who caused wine, milk, and oil to flow, or Akoites loosening the chains that bound him. (We find similar phenomena in Haiti where Vodouisants are "ridden" by the *lwa*.) In such a state it is not the individual's personality that is foremost but the God's. They have greater understanding and speak things that they would not otherwise know, in words they would not normally use. Often there is not just a change in personality but also in voice — as we see from the Greek tradition of Engastrimuthoi or "belly-talkers," women who in trance spoke with deep, gravelly voices that seemed to emanate from somewhere deep within their stomachs.

Of course, Dionysos could also inspire visions and prophetic under- standing without fully possessing an individual. We see this in Euripides' *Bakchai* when Kadmos utters wise speech which Teiresias attributes to the God and even proclaims an oracle at the end of the play, without ever having experienced direct *enthousiasmos*. The Athenian playwright Aischylos attributed his poetry to Dionysos' inspiration after the God visited him and commanded him to compose dramas in his honor. Alexander the Great was visited by Dionysos in a dream, who gave him advice regarding the military engagement that was to take the place the following day. Alexander followed his improbable advice and saved his army, which would have been soundly defeated had he followed his original course of action. So clearly, as Plutarch astutely observed, Dionysos had an equal share in the prophetic arts which guided the ancient Greeks and Romans.

In Plato's *Phaidros* Sokrates is made to say that "our greatest blessings come to us by way of madness." The madness that he is speaking of is telestic, initiatory and prophetic madness, where one is lifted out of their normal self and filled with something higher, more divine. The Greeks had a number of words to describe these states. *Ekstasis* meant literally to be taken out of one's self, a state similar to *ekphron* meaning "out of one's senses." *Katokoche* was their word for possession, a concept closely allied with *enthousiasmos,* which meant to be filled with a God, or literally "a God is within." When someone is *theoleptos,* they are "seized by a God," which can also be described as being *mainomenos,* or enmaddened, a title shared by Dionysos and his worshipers alike. All of this could also be called simply *epipnoia* or inspiration.

A helpful way to understand this is to imagine yourself as a pool of water. Usually the water is murky and dark so that all you can see within is the grime and detritus that has floated up to the surface. But at other times the water clears and upon its crystal surface one can see the wonders of heaven revealed — or mysterious things peering up from the depths. The murkiness of the water is caused by our ego-consciousness, our fears and anxieties, our wants and needs, the trivial concerns of our daily lives, our societal conditioning, the expectations that both we and others have for us — the white noise that's constantly going on in the back of our heads. For the average person this is what constitutes their self, the face which they present to the world and the part of their being which takes up so much of their time that they may not even be aware that there is anything more. But Dionysos teaches us otherwise, shows us the immensity of our spirits and offers us a path to reconnection with those hidden, shadowy parts of ourselves. To do so, we must simply let go — stop associating ourselves with that ego-consciousness and come into contact with a more vital, authentic, and powerful level of being, transforming ourselves into a vessel through which beautiful visions can flow.

These visions can come from one of two directions. In the first instance they can come from within, or to return to our original metaphor of the pool, from below. Such things consist of symbols, dreams, fantasies, other aspects of our personalities and even our higher selves, our Agathos Daimon in Greek parlance. Each of us has a complex internal world woven of images, memories, desires, dreams, etc. When we have access to this dark, nourishing realm of the imagination we find ourselves creative, whole and vital individuals. But this world can be uncomfortable for many, and society does its best to close off access to it by telling us that it is frightening, dirty, violent, irrational and impractical. All of which it most certainly can be. But it is a part of us and if we are to become whole people we must not be afraid to walk within this world, to give voice to that part of ourselves, to manifest the numinous within our lives, to heed what messages it may have for us — regardless of how "crazy" this may make us appear in the eyes of outsiders.

But the phenomena that we're discussing are not simply internal and psychological. In such states we can open ourselves to influences that lay outside of ourselves, to beings that are normally quite distinct from us such as Spirits, natural forces, Daimones, Gods, etc., all of which can influence, merge with, speak to and through us. There are varying levels of contact and communion with these external beings during trance states — the lowest, perhaps being inspiration, wherein one experiences themselves in conversation with the being but is still in full possession of their faculties and conscious self. At the other end of the spectrum the conscious self is fully submerged and the Spirit or God takes complete possession of one's body, compelling its movement and speaking through one like an actor wearing a mask:

> There are many oracles among the Greeks, and many, too, among the Egyptians, and again in Libya and in Asia there are many too. But these speak not, save by the mouth of priests and prophets: this one is moved by its own impulse, and carries out the divining process to the very end. The manner of his divination is the following: When he is desirous of uttering an oracle, he first stirs in his seat, and the priests straightway raise him up. Should they fail to raise him up, he sweats, and moves more violently than ever. When they approach him and bear him up, he drives them round in a circle, and leaps on one after another. At last the high priest confronts him, and questions him on every subject. The God, if he disapproves of any action proposed, retreats into the background; if, however, he happens to approve it, he drives his bearers forward as if they were horses. It is thus that they gather the oracles, and they undertake nothing public or private without this preliminary. This God, too, speaks about the symbol, and points out when it is the due season for the expedition of which I spoke in connexion therewith. (Lucian, *The Syrian Goddess* 36)

Between these two poles are a whole range of phenomena, with varying degrees of awareness and bodily control.

Now, while it is convenient to draw a distinction between these two types of trance — the inner and outer — there are also times when they seem to overlap, when the lines blur and we cannot tell if a dream might have originated outside of ourselves, or if a Spirit may be speaking from somewhere deep within us. Mystics from many traditions would have us believe that such a distinction serves only a limited, pragmatic purpose anyway, and that upper and lower worlds penetrate and bleed through each other until all is united in the harmony of creation. But you know how untrustworthy those mystics can be.

The ancient Greeks recognized a number of different methods for triggering and achieving these altered states of consciousness, all of which relate in some way to the world of Dionysos. Perhaps the most characteristically Dionysian of these was through dance and music. In the *Ion* Plato informs us that the *mainades* had special dances and responded only to particular types of music: "they have a sharp ear for one tune only, the one which belongs to the God by whom they are possessed, and to that tune they respond freely in gesture and speech, while they ignore all others." What information we have about this special mainadic type of dance indicates that it is very similar to the dances performed by modern-day Vodouisants — wild, rhythmic, with a strong backward tossing of the head. Euripides in *The Bakchai* describes them as dancing "with head tossed high to the dewy air," and has Pentheus say, "I was tossing my head up and down like a Bacchic dancer." Of Dionysos it is said that he will "bring his whirling *mainades,* with dancing and with feasts." We have evidence of this particular type of dancing not just from literature but depicted on a great number of vase paintings. Always the *mainad* is shown with a strong backward bend to her head. Whipping one's head about like this can cause disorientation in the inner ear and vertigo-like dizziness. It can also lead to a powerful shift in consciousness and possession by the God.

When attempting to induce a trance state it is important to pay attention to your surroundings. These can play a very important role, either making it a lot easier or stopping it outright. For instance a setting which is away from the city in some wild place like a desert or forested mountain — under the open night sky, with a crackling bonfire, the scent of pine and incense strong in the air, the droning sound of cicadas surrounding you — is going to make entering a trance very easy. Sitting on the couch in your overly hot living room while your husband watches professional wrestling and your daughter slams her juice cup repeatedly into the wall will make trancing rather more difficult. Not impossible, of course — sometimes trance-states can come upon us spontaneously, regard-less of our surroundings or what we're doing — but it's certainly not conducive to such states. Another important aid would be austerities — sleep deprivation, fasting, physical exertion, etc., which all help loosen the rational mind's control and assists our souls in attaining *ekstasis.* Additionally, there is the most quintessentially Dionysian method: alcohol and drugs, particularly entheogens, have a longstanding history of reliably inducing ecstatic trance states.

One tool that is often helpful in reaching a trance state (and has next to no negative side effects) is meditation and visualization. Meditation may seem like a practice that is completely antithetical to the Dionysian *bios* as it probably conjures images of New Age hippies doing strange things with crystals as they chant meaningless syllables or Buddhist monks in rigid *zazen* postures, quietly contemplating the nothingness that lies behind their navels. And yeah, that doesn't really fit in with the realm of the wild and rapturous God of life who is hailed by the dancing, singing, maddened crowd passionately crying "Euoi!" — or what he teaches about how we must be engaged in life, active, fiercely claiming our joy from the world. And yet, we must not forget that Dionysos is always a paradox and that stillness is as much characteristic of him as motion. Remember, Dionysos' supreme symbol is the mask which hangs serenely from the pillar, peering out onto the world around him. Before Dionysos manifests in the riot of colorful new growth he is the empty vine branch, pruned almost to the point of death, slumbering in the world below. He is the calmness at the center of the storm and the silence between notes in a song. He is also Zagreus, the Great Hunter, which requires action to catch his prey — but also great concentration and focus. And so meditation can indeed play an important role in your relationship with the God, serving as a way to quiet your raging emotions, to connect you with his somber, still, quiet vegetative aspects, to give you focus generally, to ground you and bring about awareness of the moment and of our bodies and as a means of opening the doors within us.

There is no one right way to meditate. The important thing is to bring about calmness within yourself and a growing awareness of things, both internally and in the world around you. If you are so caught up in how you're meditating that you can never find this serenity you're just wasting your time. But here are some tips that I've found personally helpful.

First I recommend finding a quiet place where you won't be interrupted. Sit in relaxing position — don't even try yoga poses unless this is something that you've already been working with — and start to breathe deeply and rhythmically. Focus on your breathing, how your breath circulates through your body and the effect this has on you. Direct your thoughts to a specific end so that they don't chase themselves around in your head or add to the cluttered white noise of your mind. This may be contemplation of one of Dionysos' names or myths, a particular idea, image, symbol, color, scent, etc., music you have playing in the background, or just stillness and emptiness if you wish. Stay like this for as long as you feel necessary, alternating focused thoughts with free-flowing mental tangents. Play around in your head. Try directing your thoughts, creating scenarios and images, thinking of only one thing — and absolutely nothing else — for as long as you can and then stretching that time further and further until you are completely absorbed by that single thought for 24 hours or longer. (Aleister Crowley had difficulty with this, so don't get discouraged if you fail at it your first time out, as there are benefits to even attempting this practice.) Try not thinking at all, but just *being*, soaking in the sensations around you. Anything and everything, as long as you're not ruminating over your problems for the millionth time that day or contemplating what color you want to paint the kitchen come spring. Regular meditation will make it easier to enter trance states and expand your consciousness, just as it's easier to navigate through a forest when you've been there plenty of times before.

There is, of course, one thing that we haven't really discussed so far: and that's why trance (and especially meditation) are important. And it's definitely not for shits and giggles, to see pretty lights and bullshit with the Spirits, or because you're looking for some kind of badge of honor for doing it, as if you are somehow a better *bakchai* than your sisters because it's easier for you to enter trance than it is for them. Simply put, not everyone can do it. Some people's psyches aren't elastic enough, they're too grounded in the material world or easily agitated or something in the past caused them so much trauma that they aren't able to relinquish control or they may have ADHD or etc. etc. etc. That doesn't mean that they love Dionysos any less, that they lack dedication in the performance of their pieties or that they haven't fully integrated the Dionysian philosophy into their lives. It simply means that they can't trance. So, if these aren't the reasons that we should do it — what are?

Simply put, Dionysian trance brings healing, wholeness, integration, and revitalization. The ancients were most emphatic about this. Plato describes the Bacchants as *ekphrones*, out of their senses, and says that it is the combined action of music and dance that restores them to their senses so that they are *emphrones*. In other words, Dionysian trance heals the afflicted, taking them from a dangerous madness to a gentler, divine madness. It allows us to access those parts of ourselves that are normally submerged, hidden, and repressed, so that we can work with the vital, creative, ecstatic energy that lies at our center, burning bright as the stars in heaven. When we cannot access our internal world, when the ideas, images, and fantasies that make up that world lay dormant, untouched and repressed they stagnate, grow hard and dead, and bleed through into our waking world in the form of unhealthy psychoses, destructive drives, violent madnesses. But when we immerse ourselves in them, learn to manipulate them, listen to their wisdom, we transform them, transform ourselves — and find wholeness through them. We also — and this is important — become a means through which the divine can act in our world, giving voice to that which has no voice, form to that which is formless.

Most of us today in the West operate under a fairly simplified conception of what constitutes *Ho Anthropos*, The Man. Man is a body and a mind with the mind subdivided into its conscious and unconscious halves. Many further postulate the existence of a spirit or soul that survives beyond the grave and is regarded as the true essence of a man. This nebulous organ of consciousness may be conceived of as independent of both mind and body or arising from the unconscious depths of mind.

The reductiveness of this model is strikingly apparent when you compare it to the ones that proliferate among most traditional polytheist cultures and indeed throughout much of Christian Europe until quite recently. Although I suspect it would prove fruitful to compare the various spiritual bodies and local and non-localized organs of intellect and power among the Greeks, Celts, Norse, Egyptians and other philosophical and religiomagical systems such as Qaballah and Buddhism, that is not my intent here.

What I intend to do instead is discuss why I believe that dance and music play a cathartic role in Dionysiac religion.

Ancient Dionysians held to the majority view that man consists of more than a mind, body and soul or spirit. In fact the impetus for this conception may have come from the Dionysian currents that swept through Greek religion with the God's arrival from abroad — up to that point there is little said on the subject. But with the enraptured rupture of the personality brought about by the God's unique form of worship characterized as it is by the experience of *ekstasis* (literally "stepping out of one's self") and *enthousiasmos* ("being filled with a divinity") the Greeks began to think hard about what they were made up of and what was going on within them. This sort of speculation became so widespread that it ended up as a significant plot point in the epics of Homer and was the constant obsession of philosophers, particularly those who claimed descent from Pythagoras. Much attention was spent on sorting out where these parts were located and how they operated together and whether there was any material component to them.

With regard to the last question I tend to think that there is, with the understanding that "material" encompasses a far wider degree of density than we are capable of perceiving with our ordinary senses. Meaning that even things that we think of as purely insubstantial such as emotion and thought possess a physicality that enables them to act and be acted upon by other objects. Those familiar with the theory of optics and harmonics developed by the school of Demokritos will understand.

For the most part thoughts are fluid and constantly in motion, bouncing off of each other and merging with other thoughts into something new. But what happens when too many thoughts collect in the chamber of our mind and congeal into a viscous blob that clogs the pipes and impedes the passage of other thoughts? Or when the flow of thoughts become agitated and erratic, chaotic and impossible to calm? This is madness, and in both cases the cure lies in Dionysiac ritual, especially with its strong emphasis on music and dance and striking imagery.

The point of these things is to get us flowing properly again, harmoniously. The vibrations from the music effect particular agitations on our thoughts, rather like the influence the moon holds over the tides or the force of magnetism, so that one could conjure quite specific moods out of thin air through the simple arrangement of a handful of notes. Likewise specific configurations of movement can radically alter our mental state. Imagine if I grabbed the child from your arms and started shaking it violently; undoubtedly you would feel an elevation of annoyance as a result — especially when that movement is aligned with rhythm and melody, as in the dance. Seriously, next time you're feeling blue do the Twist. Five hours of that will have you grinning like Gwynplaine.

Our thoughts are influenced by what we see, often at a level far below rational awareness and beyond our cultural and personal associations. Dionysian religion, with its penchant for theatricality, manipulated this to great effect through its choice of color and objects laden with symbolism such as the egg and cup but also objects capable of triggering powerful unconscious responses such as the snake or mask or bloody victim handled in an unconventional manner. Thought was even put into the order of presentation so that one's responses would build upon themselves and the individual could be lead through a series of experiences and understandings that resulted in epiphany and catharsis. This is what makes art such a powerful force in our lives and why true art and ritual are indistinguishable from each other.

And that's why whenever I'm feeling angry or depressed or like nothing is quite synching up right I resort to acts of creativity and ritual. Doing so helps focus my mind on my Gods and Spirits and that connection alone can help me get over the hump — but more than that I believe that there is efficacy in the rites themselves since I can feel their benefit even when I am unable to establish contact with my divinities. Even if I don't feel immediately better after doing it, I often find that in the aftermath my mind becomes more fluid and I am able to let go of unpleasant emotions I had been obsessively clinging to.

Now obviously the primary reason for doing these rituals is not therapeutic but devotional, however if this stuff is left unattended it can get in the way of pure devotion so I consider putting my mental house in order to be part of the work. But I also strongly believe that Dionysos is Lusios, the Loosener of Cares who has come to soothe men's suffering hearts and that it was he himself who taught us these sacred techniques, so it is only proper to use them in the way that he intended.

The great thing about working with altered states of consciousness is that you don't have to understand how or why it works in order to receive the benefits of this type of ritual. Everything you need to know to do this can be found on the side of an amphora or a description of Maenads and Satyrs from Greek literature.

What do you do?

Surround yourself with his imagery.

Pray.

Speak from the heart.

Sing.

Let the music move you.

Repetition is key.

Repetition is key.

Repetition is key.

Shake that shit loose!

Dance.

Run.

Scream.

Laugh.

Cry.

Don't hold back.

Go where it takes you.

Do what feels right, even if it doesn't make sense. *Especially then.*

Praise him with all you have. If all you have is broken, filthy and empty — give that to him. If you are his, it belongs to him anyway. He will restore it and make it better.

Open yourself up to him.

And dance.

Discover him in the dance.

If you do this enough you'll find the right way, what works and what does not.

You'll find the harmony that your component parts naturally seek.

You'll find his grace in the ritual.

Why Is the Starry Bull Strain of Bacchic Orphism So Horrific?

No one contests that Starry Bull mythology is horrific. Its central figure is a God who was torn apart as an infant or a young man in his prime, and this deed was performed either by the divine figures who had been appointed to guard him or the women most devoted to him. This God goes on to suffer madness and mockery and many of his closest circle are violently persecuted. His prophets are imprisoned, tortured and torn to pieces. Many of his women are suicides, with hanging being the commonest cause of death. He brings healing, release and justice to the victims of unthinkably terrible crimes. He leads his retinue of frenzied Spirits in the hunt and rules a portion of hell.

This is the stuff of nightmares. Who in their right mind would worship such a God? And for that matter how can one claim that this is an accurate portrayal of Dionysos, the mirthful lord of wine and freedom?

It isn't meant to be.

The Starry Bull tradition is a modern expression of a strain of Bacchic Orphism, itself but one of the many forms that the religion of Dionysos took in antiquity. This influences both the choice of source material that we draw upon and even more importantly how that material is interpreted. At no time do we deny that there are other faces which the God may show his devotees, nor that there are other avenues which open unto him. On the contrary, the beliefs and practices which shape the Starry Bull tradition are best seen as supplementary to more conventional forms of religiosity, with the tension between them a necessary component.

Let me explain what I mean by way of an example. Meet Hermagenes, son of Dolion of the Oineis tribe, a fairly average middle child born into a moderately well-off family in the Athens of Demetrios Poliorketes. Considering the tumultuous times he finds himself in, Hermagenes is not an ambitious man and uses the leisure provided by his father's estate to devote himself primarily to religious and social endeavors. Not only does he maintain cultus for the Gods of his household and honor his illustrious ancestors as he was raised from infancy to do, but unlike a lot of his contemporaries he devotes himself to the Gods and heroes of his *deme* and *phyle*. He has an important role in several of the larger civic festivals, belongs to a couple religious guilds and observes their calendars of monthly sacrifices, has served as *choregos* and *gymnasiarch* in the past, visits a specialist in Orphic rites once a month for purifications, attends lectures in Platonic theology at the Academy, and goes to the various temples strewn throughout his city when the need arises. He has made pilgrimage to Delphi, Eleusis and Samothrace, and also received initiation into the mysteries of Meter, Pan, Sabazios and two separate Bacchic cults.

All of these various threads, together, weave the tapestry of Hermagenes' religious life. No one of them is more important than the others, though each provide him with different benefits and make different demands on his time, resources and mental energy.

Ideally things should be no different today. An adherent of the Starry Bull tradition is free to honor as many other Gods and Spirits as they are called to, and even to honor the members of our loose pantheon in different forms and through different ways alongside their Starry Bull practice. This is not just permitted, it is strongly encouraged.

After all, this tradition was never intended to be all things for all people. We have carved off a small portion of that which is Dionysian for our own and intend to explore it to the fullest. It is a fragment and cannot provide you with all you need for a full and rich religious life any more than eating only grapes and figs will lead to a whole and healthy existence.

Our piece is bloody and trembling, and that's why it's ours.

You see, we aren't well. No one in this fucked up society is, but unlike the majority we recognize this all-important fact about ourselves. We each come to this path with different ailments of different degrees of severity but our common bond is madness. Madness that can be cured by the God, and madness that is sent by him. All the greatest blessings of the Gods may arrive by way of madness, but madness will also destroy you if you let it. And so we learn to dance with our madness. Instead of hiding from it, locking it away, suppressing it until it morphs into something far more dangerous, we let it out to play, try it on like a costume, see all the beautiful and ugly things it has to show us about the world, and about ourselves.

In a walnut shell, that's what the Starry Bull tradition is. It's giving yourself permission to go a little mad sometimes, to look at things through insane eyes.

Why? Isn't madness bad for individuals and communities?

Sure, but so is not making space for madness. In fact, far more social ills stem from repression than cutting loose.

Think about how much we lose by being divided and in conflict with ourselves.

When was the last time you played with finger paints? When was the last time you sang or danced, regardless of who might be around? When was the last time you ate something just because it tasted good and fuck the calories? When was the last time you just walked or drove in a random direction, with nowhere particular to be? When was the last time you plaited a flower crown or hugged a tree? When was the last time you cried at a movie? When was the last time you screamed or broke something because you were angry — or even better, when you weren't? When was the last time you felt truly alive?

Judging by the prevalence of zombies and convention-breaking anti-heroes in pop culture, I'm guessing not for a while. These tropes wouldn't have the appeal they do if folks were living vital and authentic lives. But that's really hard to do at the dawn of the 21st century in the West. From the cradle we're bombarded with messages carefully crafted to keep us complacent, conformist, unhappy, and striving to meet impossible and contradictory standards that wouldn't even be fulfilling if we could. And the really fucked up thing is that this conditioning is so pervasive and runs so deep within us that even if you choose not to buy into it and are a pretty introspective and conscientious soul you've still got issues in need of working out. Some of them are just part and parcel of the human condition. Hell, even chimps have anxiety disorders.

And that's why the Starry Bull tradition is such a horror show.

This shit's buried deep, deep down inside us and if you want to root it out you're going to need more than to just lie on some dude's couch and talk at him for an hour.

Terror, hunger, savagery, disgust — real primal emotions that get the heart racing and blood pumping — these things help you step out of your small, conditioned self and cleanse the wounds of ages past. You must descend into the abyss if you would attain catharsis; then and only then are you able to rise up in wholeness and joy. There is no true freedom that you have not suffered for.

And yet there's something else, a subtler and in some ways more important process that goes along with this. Nietzsche called it *Coincidentia oppositorum*, the unification through reconciliation of opposites, by which we discover the true nature of things, ourselves included. A small portion of man rises above the surface, like the barest tip of the iceberg — and he mistakes this for his personality. All the dreams and fears and fantasies and cravings that he does not associate with himself, considers unreal, unacceptable, inconsequential and does his damndest to lock up and never let see the light of day — those things don't just go away. They become twisted, sick or withered to nothing. Either he becomes psychically impotent or lashes out unexpectedly, irrationally and violently, destroying all he's worked so hard to build up. Why? Because he cannot reconcile his notions of himself as a "good" person with the monstrous urges he feels, because he's running from the pain and disappointment in his past. And he rips apart the whole world in the same fashion, seeing things as pure and filthy, desirable and repugnant, heavenly and diabolical, rational and mad.

Most things are not one or the other — they're both, and more, and our horrible mythology forces us to confront that artificial dichotomy and every other false notion we've got rattling around in our heads.

Like that the world's fair and nothing bad ever happens to good people.

17

Our God was ripped to bloody shreds and the ones who loved him most did it!

Fucking let that sink in for a second — *even the Gods can suffer affliction.* Makes what you're going through kinda small potatoes, huh? And yet here's the great part. The God who has suffered most in this tragic fucking universe wants only for us to be happy. To him, what you're going through isn't tiny and irrelevant. He suffers through it along with you, and rejoices in your triumph.

That's why we focus so much on gruesome and bizarre stories of violence, madness and sex. We do not flinch from seeing the worst in our Gods and Spirits because they have earned our trust and our devotion and what's more because we are driven by passionate longing to know them in their entirety, without judgment or expectation. And if you can look at a God with that kind of pure, unconditional love what's stopping you from seeing yourself that way too? From that comes the most important freedom — the freedom to truly be you. Once you know who you are and what you're capable of you can wear any mask you want and reveal only select portions of yourself to the world as the situation requires without the risk of losing yourself or becoming what you pretend.

But not everyone needs that, or needs it all the time. The Starry Bull tradition makes no exclusive demands — indeed, for every story we put forth, we put forth another in contradistinction to it. And another, and another. Because it's the Story behind the stories and the way those stories are told that defines our tradition. Understanding comes through comparison, which necessitates something other than the Starry Bull. Which is why most of our members are involved in numerous other communities and religious traditions as well.

If all of that doesn't make sense, don't worry, it wasn't meant for you. If it does, you probably *should* worry as you're on your way to becoming one of us.

Who are you?

Why, you're a mix of mud and stars, with blood of the Titans in your veins, a devotee of the mad God. And don't you ever forget it.

What To Do When Bad Things Happen To You

I would like to discuss an important issue within polytheism — namely what do you do when bad things happen to you, especially when it's a series of bad things and not just an isolated occurrence. This is especially pertinent for diviners and religious specialists, as we mostly deal with clients who are in crisis states, sometimes chronic ones.

My first recourse is always divination. When problems arise I read for myself and I also turn to respected colleagues since it's good to get a fresh, outside perspective on things. (Plus if I'm under some kind of attack I may not be able to trust my signal clarity.) The questions I tend to ask are: what is happening? What is causing it to happen? Can anything be done to turn the situation around?

Going in, I try to assume nothing. Just because I have a fairly close relationship with my Gods and Spirits and they've been extraordinarily kind and generous to me in the past doesn't mean that they are going to shield me from all affliction, or that I'm automatically on their good side, or that they're necessarily even capable of stopping this. (Olympian politics can be every bit as nasty and tangled as our own.) After all, these bad things could be part of my personal fate, the result of spiritual attack, a necessary obstacle to overcome in order to learn something valuable or acquire certain powers, just recompense for past crimes (whether my own or those of my ancestors), part of a larger pattern or merely some random thing that happened.

Once I've determined what's going on to the best of my ability (keeping in mind that my signal clarity may be compromised, I may be intentionally being misled by some God or Spirit for any number of reasons, or there may be too many moving parts to get a satisfactory read on the situation at the present time — all reasons why I turn to other diviners instead of relying solely on my own results in such situations), I come up with a strategy for handling things.

This begins by asking questions such as: do I need to make offerings, and if so, to whom and of what sort? Do I need to beef up my luck and personal protections? Do I need to modify my behavior or attitude, either by eliminating or adding certain things? Do I need to go on the offensive? What practical considerations need to be taken care of?

And it ends by actually following through with the advice that I'm given. There is no surer recipe for disaster than consulting the Gods and Spirits and then completely ignoring what they tell you. Mind, you may not always be in a position to heed their advice — at which point you just have to suck it up and accept what happens or see if there are offerings you can make to minimize the consequences of that decision.

I also use this as an opportunity to take stock of my life choices and internal constitution. Specifically I analyze my emotional responses to the event and any unexamined assumptions that may be influencing them. For instance, if I am angry I ask myself where is this anger coming from and who is it directed at? Myself, my Gods and Spirits, my loved ones, the world at large? Why? Have they actually done something to deserve that or am I just making them an easy target, deflecting so I don't have to deal with the true root which most often lies within myself? Do I feel that I am somehow deserving of special treatment, and if so what have I done recently to warrant this felicity? How is it unfair when illness, injury, want and frustration are part of the universal mortal condition — and hell, even the Gods and Spirits experience vicissitudes? Besides, fairness is a human value unfittingly projected onto the material and immaterial worlds — nature recognizes only strength and endurance: you must endure what you are not strong enough to stop. Further, suffering tests the character as surely as flame the blade. Who am I? Who do I wish to become? After all, who would the great hero have been without his labors? Not Herakles but Eurystheus! At which point I've usually managed to pull myself back from the ledge of despair and resolve to face my adversity with courage and fortitude.

That's not to say that I don't have moments of weakness and doubt. I do, absolutely. And instead of beating myself up for them I let myself go through them, feel and learn what I need to from them, and just keep going. As surely as we suffer, nothing in this world is permanent or immutable. All is flux. Which means that this, too, will pass. Further, I use this as an opportunity to remind myself that feelings are something I *have*, not something that defines me. I am the choices I make and adhere to, not an aggregate of ephemeral emotion. So when I feel like shouting "Fuck you!" to the heavens and throwing in the towel I indulge that momentarily (it's easier to let it out than repress it) then make appropriate apologies and get back to the long, hard and unglamorous work of maintaining a devotional relationship with my Gods and Spirits. Not only has this approach minimized the intensity of such outbursts but it's also diminished their frequency. At this point I hardly feel the need to rail when things go to shit. Mostly I laugh, wipe off my hands, and ask, "Alright. Where do we go from here?"

It also helps that I think of my life in terms of Story — if nothing ever went wrong and there was never anything to overcome, well, that would be a pretty damn boring story, now wouldn't it?

In one of the more curious anecdotes from Eunapius' *Lives of the Philosophers and Sophists*, a group of gullible students were attending a theurgic séance wherein an Egyptian priest conjured a visible apparition of what purported to be the God Apollon, but when the Neoplatonic holy man Iamblichos inspected it he laughed and (I'm paraphrasing here) proclaimed, "Why are you falling to your knees filled with reverent terror — this is just the ghost of a humble gladiator!"

Iamblichos was hardly a hidebound skeptic; in fact he engaged in a protracted dispute with his elder colleague (and former teacher) Porphyry over the efficacy and appropriateness of magic, divination, demonolatry and related topics, most famously — and adroitly — defending these noble practices in his treatise *De Mysteriis Aegyptiorum*. It was primarily because he took such matters so seriously that he advocated the application of reasoned inquiry or what the Christian mystics came to call "spiritual discernment" when encountering paranormal phenomena. The consequences are simply too high not to.

Man may well be the measure of all things, as Protagoras averred, but we're not very high up on the food chain when one considers the profuse array of divine and spiritual entities who inhabit this world alongside us. Not only do they vastly outstrip us in knowledge, power and access to other planes of existence, but they are not constrained by any kind of universal moral code. There are dangerous and deceptive forces out there who want nothing more than to see the human race wiped from this planet — and they aren't even necessarily what one would consider "evil" beings. Those exist too, in their plenitude, as well as things that are hurt, confused, scared, lonely or trapped.

Indeed, much of the work that the ancient Bacchic Orphics did involved seeking deliverance for these beings, be they mortal or otherwise, as we see in both Plato:

> But the most astounding of all these arguments concerns what they have to say about the Gods and virtue. They say that the Gods, too, assign misfortune and a bad life to many good people, and the opposite fate to their opposites. Begging priests and prophets frequent the doors of the rich and persuade them that they possess a God-given power founded on sacrifices and incantations. If the rich person or any of his ancestors has committed an injustice, they can fix it with pleasant things and feasts. Moreover, if he wishes to injure some enemy, then, at little

expense, he'll be able to harm just and unjust alike, for by means of spells and enchantments they can persuade the Gods to serve them. And they present a hubbub of books by Musaeus and Orpheus, offspring as they say of Selene and the Muses, according to which they arrange their rites, convincing not only individuals but also cities that liberation and purification from injustice is possible, both during life and after death, by means of sacrifices and enjoyable games to the deceased which free us from the evils of the beyond, whereas something horrible awaits those who have not celebrated sacrifices. (*Republic* 2.364a–365b)

and the Derveni Papyrus:

… prayers and sacrifices appease the souls, and the enchanting song of the magician is able to remove the daimones when they impede. Impeding daimones are revenging souls. This is why the magicians perform the sacrifice as if they were paying a penalty. On the offerings they pour water and milk, from which they make the libations, too. They sacrifice innumerable and many-knobbed cakes, because the souls, too, are innumerable. (col. 6.1-11)

In these quotes we also see what sets our religious specialist apart from the masses, permitting them to command respectable fees for their service: they possess superior knowledge. This ἐπιστήμη allowed them to better navigate strange terrain and be on a more elevated footing with the para-human entities whom they engaged with on behalf of their clients.

What did this knowledge consist of?

o   The ability to recognize who they were encountering through certain signs or other means of communication.
o   Diagnoses of psychospiritual ailments.
o   The knowledge of appropriate songs, stories, ceremonies, offerings, cures, taboos and other magicoreligious pre-scriptions.
o   How to bind, loosen and trace the threads.
o   Methods of adapting all of the above to the particular situation of the client.

This was a massively competitive and high stakes profession — slip-ups could result in damage to a client's physical or mental health which in turn would bring shame and ill-repute upon the Orpheotelest, *mantis* or *goes*. When one's livelihood depends entirely on word of mouth having a tarnished reputation can be disastrous, so they made damn sure they knew what they were talking about before recommending a particular course of action.

How do we know any of the things that we think we know?

- o   Inference.
- o   Other people's testimony.
- o   The direct experience of our senses.

It's been a couple decades since I took an introduction to epistemology class in college so I could be missing a couple, but that trio are the really important ones.

Not a one of them is 100% reliable, however. Hell, philosophers are still trying to convince one another that they really do exist really, truly — and without much success. I'm a Jamesian pragmatist, so I don't concern myself with trifles of that sort — but I'm also aware that I am making such an existential assumption, and that is key.

In life — and especially the life of a religious specialist — you want to make as few assumptions as possible, and when you do you need to factor that into the decisions you make. Assuming isn't just sloppy, it creates vulnerability and confusion and can set off a whole chain of unintended and undesirable consequences.

To guard against assumptive thinking, memorize the following questions and apply them promiscuously:

- o   What is it you know?
- o   How do you know it?
- o   Why is that a reliable source of information?
- o   Are there other ways to arrive at the same conclusion?
- o   Is everyone operating with the same understanding of the relevant terms? If not why, and how is that affecting their decision-making process?
- o   What difference does it make if one or another piece of information, despite appearances to the contrary, is wrong? What if everything is wrong?

Obviously, there are situations where we cannot know the answers to these questions, or we don't have the luxury of being able to conduct such an extensive audit because a snap decision must be made and sometimes this information just isn't terribly helpful.

In which case you either perform divination or trust your gut.

As an intellectual and an artist and an avid explorer of the further reaches of the human experience I tend to be of the opinion that individual, rational consciousness is a pretty nifty thing. But as an evolutionary strategy it's not very popular among the myriad lifeforms that inhabit this planet along with (and inside) us, particularly the more successful ones.

Even among hominids it's a relatively recent experiment and the jury's still out on its respective merits. (If you haven't already read it, I highly recommend Julian Jayne's *The Origin of Consciousness in the Breakdown of the Bicameral Mind*; that shit'll have you doing your best Keanu Reeves impression.) Which means that we have all kinds of ways of navigating through this world of ours that we never or rarely access because we've been conditioned to favor that individual, rational consciousness, complete with all of its biases and limitations.

But then there's that mix of intuition, instinct and hypersensitivity we call "the gut." (Or the heart, the spleen, the nose, etc. Different cultures have different idiomatic organs of perception, most of which are biologically indeterminate.) Whatever it is, or how it works, you can use it to help bring clarity to uncertain situations. No method should be relied on exclusively, not even divination; we need all of them working in concert to be at our best. And as with most abilities, disuse degrades them. It's something you need to develop and maintain through rigorous application and experimentation.

Thus far we haven't so much been discussing spiritual discernment as cognition, critical thinking skills and tools for decision making, but before we move on to our intended topic I would like to share another valuable technique, particularly when one encounters a logistical error, paradox, obstacle or dead end and that's the Thread of Ariadne.

It was commonplace in Plato's time to compare the quest for truth to the beguilingly circuitous paths of the Labyrinth, as we see in the *Euthydemos*:

> Then it seemed like falling into a Labyrinth: we thought we were at the finish, but our way bent round and we found ourselves as it were back at the beginning, and just as far from that which we were seeking at first.

As Carl Kerényi archly observed in his commentary on this passage:

> Thus the present-day notion of a Labyrinth as a place where one can lose his way must be set aside. It is a confusing path, hard to follow without a thread, but, provided the traverser is not devoured at the midpoint, it leads surely, despite twists and turns, back to the beginning. (*Dionysos: Archetypal Image of Indestructible Life* pg 92)

Wikipedia explains the application of this infallible guide as follows:

> The key element to applying Ariadne's thread to a problem is the creation and maintenance of a record — physical or otherwise — of

the problem's available and exhausted options at all times. This record is referred to as the "thread," regardless of its actual medium. The purpose the record serves is to permit backtracking — that is, reversing earlier decisions and trying alternatives. Given the record, applying the algorithm is straightforward: at any moment that there is a choice to be made, make one arbitrarily from those not already marked as failures, and follow it logically as far as possible. If a contradiction results, back up to the last decision made, mark it as a failure, and try another decision at the same point. If no other options exist there, back up to the last place in the record that does, mark the failure at that level, and proceed onward. This algorithm will terminate upon either finding a solution or marking all initial choices as failures; in the latter case, there is no solution. If a thorough examination is desired even though a solution has been found, one can revert to the previous decision, mark the success, and continue on as if a solution were never found; the algorithm will exhaust all decisions and find all solutions.

The terms "Ariadne's thread" and "trial-and-error" are often used interchangeably, which is not necessarily correct. They have two distinctive differences. Trial-and-error implies that each trial yields some particular value to be studied and improved upon, removing errors from each iteration to enhance the quality of future trials. Ariadne's thread has no such mechanic, making all decisions arbitrarily. For example, the scientific method is trial and error; puzzle-solving is Ariadne's thread. Trial-and-error approaches are rarely concerned with how many solutions may exist to a problem, and indeed often assume only one correct solution exists. Ariadne's thread makes no such assumption, and is capable of locating all possible solutions to a purely logical problem. In short, trial and error approaches a desired solution; Ariadne's thread blindly exhausts the search space completely, finding any and all solutions. Each has its appropriate distinct uses, and they can be employed in tandem.

This is a particularly effective method for when you're stumbling around in metaphorical darkness and divination has proven inconclusive. It can also be useful when you are trying to diagnose an ailment by tracing it back to its root cause, which may be a past trauma or guilt either directly experienced or inherited from one's ancestors — a topic we shall loop back upon later.

Now we're ready to get to some Discernin' With Spirits.

So, you're confronted with a perplexing situation or an entity which seeks to communicate something to you. Where do you go from there?

The first thing we need to establish is whether the source of this information is something happening directly to you or if it's a message coming through an intermediary such as a diviner, a medium or oracle or some random homeless person that's approached you on the street, because the process of evaluation differs accordingly. In fact, spiritual encounters in a group setting bring in a whole gaggle of issues so I'm going to limit myself here to just private ones.

If it is just you and the entity then you need to perform an exhaustive self-inventory to minimize the potential for human error.

What has been communicated to you? At this stage, keep it just to the facts. Don't fill in the gaps, make inferences, analyze what the message personally means to you or any of the other interpretive methods we regularly employ. You want the message to be as clear and concise as possible. You can do the rest of that later.

How has this been communicated to you? Did the encounter happen face to face or through indirect means such as divination? Was it the result of a dream, vision, or out-of-body experience? Was it something you observed, something you heard, something you intuited or arrived at through other means? Did it involve external perception or was the communication internalized? How much trust do you place on it depending on whether it's the one or the other?

How reliable is your perception at the moment? What is your current mental, emotional and physical status and how might this be influencing what you receive? Is there a lot of internal chatter or stress that could be compromising your signal clarity? Are you suffering a depressive, hypermanic or delusional episode? How is your sleep routine and nutrition? Are you on any medications or recreational drugs? Note that none of these are sufficient to rule out a message received, but all of them can and will influence your perception.

How do you feel about the message being communicated? Is it challenging or upsetting, completely novel or exactly what you expect, what sorts of other emotional responses does it stir in you and so forth. None of these speak to the accuracy of the message, but it's definitely something you'll want to be aware of lest you fall into a series of errors one need only survey the majority of polytheist and neopagan communities to find amply on display.

Now let us move on to the communicator.

If you have prior experience with the entity, use that, along with the known lore concerning them and the accounts of contemporaneous devotees, as your basis for evaluation.

Is the entity behaving in a manner that is consistent with the above?

Do they "feel" like they normally do? Are they employing recognizable speech patterns? Are the appropriate signs and symptoms present?

By signs and symptoms I mean the type of phenomena described in Proklos' *On the Signs of Divine Possession* (as quoted in Psellus' *Accusation against Michael Cerularius before the Synod*):

He speaks first about the differences which separate the so-called Divine Powers, how some are more material and others more immaterial, some joyous (*hilarai*) and others solemn (*embritheis*), some arrive along with daemons and others arrive pure. Straight afterwards he goes on to the proper conditions for invocation: the places in which it occurs, about those men and women who see the Divine Light, and about the divine gestures (*schêmatôn*) and signs (*sunthêmatôn*) they display. In this way he gets around to the Theagogies of divine inspiration (*tas entheastikas theagôgias*)[a *theagôgia* is a drawing in or drawing down of the divine]. "Of which," he says, "some act on inanimate objects and others on animate beings: some on those which are rational, others on the irrational ones. Inanimate objects," he continues, "are often filled with Divine Light, like the statues which give oracles under the inspiration (*epipnoias*) of one of the Gods or Good Daemons. So too, there are men who are possessed and who receive a Divine Spirit (*pneuma theion*). Some receive it spontaneously, like those who are said to be 'seized by God' (*theolêptoi*), either at particular times, or intermittently and on occasion. There are others who work themselves up into a state of inspiration (*entheasmôn*) by deliberate actions, like the prophetess at Delphi when she sits over the chasm, and others who drink from divinatory water." Next, after having said what they have to do [i.e. to gain divine inspiration], he continues "When these things occur, then in order for a Theagogy and an inspiration (*epipnoian*) to take effect, they must be accompanied by a change in consciousness (*parallaxia tês dianoias*). When divine inspiration (*entheasmôn*) comes there are some cases where the possessed (*tôn katochôn*) become completely besides themselves and unconscious of themselves (*existamenôn...kai oudamôs heautois parakolouthountôn*). But there are others where, in some remarkable manner, they maintain consciousness. In these cases it is possible for the subject to work the Theagogy on himself, and when he receives the inspiration (*epipnoian*), is aware of what it [i.e. the Divine Power] does and what it says, and what he has to do release the mechanism [of possession](*pothen dei apoluein to kinoun*). However, when the loss of consciousness (*ekstaseôs*) is total, it is essential that someone in full command of his faculties assists the possessed." Then, after many details about the different kinds of Theagogy, he finally concludes: "It is necessary to begin by removing all the obstacles blocking the arrival of the Gods and to impose an absolute calm around ourselves in order that the manifestation of the Spirits (*pneumata*) we invoke takes place without tumult and in peace (*atarachos kai meta galênês*)." He adds further, "The manifestations of the Gods are often accompanied by material Spirits which arrive and move with a certain degree of violence, and which the weaker mediums cannot withstand."

If all that does not jive, what is different and how might this be accounted for?

After all, Gods and Spirits often have a plurality of forms and the situation might require them to be more or less formal than they ordinarily would be.

But sometimes you can tell that something is off and what you're encountering is just a bad drag routine.

At which point, ask for confirmation. I have set up codewords with all of the core Gods and Spirits that I work with, and if the being cannot provide them it's a dead giveaway that they are not who they seem to be. (This is also an excellent means of verification when a third party comes forward claiming to have messages for you. If the God or Spirit doesn't provide authentication it either means the message is not of utmost urgency or the person is not as perceptive as they are presenting themselves to be.)

Another method is to make reference to past encounters with the entity but include false information; if you are not corrected, that can be a red flag.

Thirdly, and finally, you may intone their epithets and project a sigil or charged mental representation of the God or Spirit which will either empower or pass straight through them if they are that being (or very closely aligned to them) but will cause distortion and disruption if it is something merely pretending.

Some Things You Can Do When It Gets Intense

Establish your personal limits.

One of the things that Dionysos is really big on is consent and respecting boundaries. But he takes you at your word, meaning the God and his Spirits are going to push and push and push until you say stop — and then they will. No explanation required, no judgment, just respect for you recognizing and asserting your personal limits. But it won't let up one second before you do that and he'll also let you take it far past what's safe or healthy, if only to teach you the necessity of knowing yourself and determining your personal boundaries. I've seen folks get hurt real bad as a result of that, and I don't want to see it happen to you. This is about self-discovery not dick measuring. The only one you're in competition with is yourself. (Besides, I have the biggest dick of all!)

Meaning that if things start getting really, really bad, stop your work and seek whatever kind of treatment you need. You might be cracking under the pressure or this may have exacerbated a mental condition (or even revealed one previously undiagnosed). I can't give you the proper care or supervision that should normally accompany work of this nature. That means you've got to look after yourself. Don't make any rash decisions, especially if you're having suicidal ideation, and if you're confused or considering something that's really out of character for you, talk to somebody whose opinion you trust and see what their take on the situation is. They may be right, they may be wrong, but at least you'll have another outside perspective to consider.

And remember, if you're ever in doubt about whether something is coming from the Gods and Spirits or your own craziness, there's always divination. If you're under major stress or don't feel you can trust your signal clarity, consult a competent diviner rather than doing the reading yourself — especially one who is completely outside the situation and has little to no knowledge of what's going on with you.

However, none of this abdicates your personal responsibility to make proper choices for yourself. Just because a friend, a diviner, or even a God or Spirit is telling you to do something that doesn't mean you actually have to. You can argue with them, renegotiate terms and arrive at a mutually satisfactory compromise, or even flat out tell them no. You don't just have the right, you have an obligation to decide things for yourself — and of course part of that involves accepting the consequences that come of such a decision. Every choice we make opens up certain options for us and closes off certain others. If a person (or Person) is asking you to do something and you refuse, yeah, that could remove opportunities for you or even end your relationship with them, and that would suck — but it would suck more doing something you knew was wrong for you simply as a way of seeking external validation. (And compromising your personal integrity can have far worse, long lasting consequences so really, *don't do that shit.*)

Take care of yourself.

There's a reason we refer to this kind of intense engagement with Spirits as "work" — and that's because it can be tremendously taxing. Physically, spiritually, psychologically and interpersonally. Even if you have supportive friends and family, this is something you're going to need to take personal responsibility for because if your needs aren't getting met you're not the only one who's going to suffer. Shit runs downhill, so don't leave messes for your descendants to clean up. That involves obvious things like making sure that you are properly hydrated and fed, that you get sufficient rest, regularly performing a personal inventory of your emotional state, and so forth — but also make sure that you're giving yourself enough time to transition and recover. If you're having to go from an intense and transformative spiritual encounter right into stressful and noisy social situations, that can be really jarring, disorienting and damaging to the psyche, as well as compromising to the work you're doing.

A lot of my practice involves altered states of consciousness so this is something that's particularly important to me and thus I take a lot of time preparing for ritual. Often more than the actual ritual itself. For instance, about an hour before I intend to do something I'll light candles and make offerings at my shrine, play appropriate music, put on ritual jewelry and clothing as a mental cue that I'm going into work-mode, do any purifications (of the space or myself) I feel are required, read material that helps put me in the right mindset, still and focus my thoughts on the Gods and Spirits through meditation, smoke weed and drink some alcohol as well as dance, chant, pray and adopt sacred postures and movement. This can be more or less formal as the situation requires, but I try to create this bubble of the sacred around myself meaning that if I'm talking with someone I avoid chit chat, mundane or upsetting topics, I make sure the television or radio aren't blaring in the background, I don't check my e-mail or fart around on the internet, I try not to think about bills, or upcoming appointments or the dumb and annoying shit someone on Tumblr may have said earlier that day. Among the offerings I give to my Gods and Spirits is space in my mind and I want that space to be worthy of and able to receive them, so all of this prep is nearly as important as the eventual worship itself.

Likewise, you should put thought and care into what you do to bring yourself back after you've finished the work. Spend time collecting and reorienting yourself. Listen to music that'll put you in the proper mood or watch a movie with relevant themes. Eat, even if it's something simple, as the act of taking in nourishment can really help ground you in your body, and drink something that's non-alcoholic, especially water or tea. Do some light reading, write in your journal, or make a piece of art. When you finally stumble forth and rejoin humanity, explain that you're in a vulnerable state and ask them to take that into consideration when talking with you (i.e., save the heavy and emotionally wrought conversations for later, don't get upset if it takes me awhile to respond or I find it difficult to follow thought trains or otherwise act a little oddly, etc.). If possible, take a nap even if it's just a 10 or 20 minute quickie. (Sleep can be rejuvenating, act as a buffer between different mental states and gives the Gods and Spirits a further opportunity to continue the conversation through dream.) Another thing that can help is taking a shower or bath, especially if you put herbs and other smelly stuff with cleansing and grounding properties in the water.

Be present and mindful.

Stop. Breathe. Focus. Whatever's happening is probably not going to kill you. It may hurt, it may really, really suck, but you're going to get through this. Chances are, you've probably been through much worse before. Everything changes; it's the only constant in this world. So the situation you're facing, it's just temporary. It could get better, it could get worse, but it's definitely not going to be like this forever. So let it pass, let it wash over you and continue on its way, just as you will.

This is especially important to keep in mind when the work triggers past traumas or dredges up shit long forgotten. That was then, this is now. Everything is different. No matter how scary and painful it is, how vividly it's presenting itself to you, you're safe, in another place and time, and you're not the person you were then. Go through a personal physical inventory: "These are my fingers, this is my arm, this is my shoulder, this is my head, this is my nose, etc.," which will help override the fear response as well as ground you in your body. If you can't stop the badness, try to ride it out. For instance, tell yourself no matter how horrible this is I can endure it for a minute. It's just sixty seconds of sensation. When you've gotten through that, do it for another minute, and another until it's done.

Once you have removed yourself from the situation and gotten your mind and emotions stabilized, you may want to try analyzing what happened and your responses to it. Pain, fear and the like are messengers and teachers. If we fight or run from them we just make things worse and deprive ourselves of the understanding they offer. What's causing this, why am I responding in this way, how does this new information change the way I think about things, does it have to only change them in that way or can it mean this other thing altogether? One way to process this is to write stream-of-consciousness style in your journal. Give yourself permission to put it all out there on the page, without editing or censoring or worrying about what others will think. Once you're done let it sit for awhile and then read through it and do the same thing with whatever that stirs up in you, until you've reached a point where you're okay with things, or at least okay enough to share what's going on with someone you trust — and even then you can just share with them what you want or need to, without ever letting anyone glimpse your messy process. If it's really sensitive and you don't want to keep it around — either because someone might discover it or because you don't want to be reminded of it — feel free to destroy that material. Hell, consigning the pages to the flames could be a powerful cathartic act in and of itself.

Recite a mantra.

Especially if your thoughts are agitated or stuck on an endless loop, having a special phrase to repeat over and over again can really help break that. There is power in words, but even on a psychological level it distracts your conscious brain and gives it something else to focus on. Find something that's personally meaningful to you, even if it's just a string of Dionysian epithets or a line from a poem.

Within the Starry Bull tradition we have a mantra that's effective not only for this kind of mental jamming, but also works really well for cleansing, consecration and healing. Hell, it's pretty much my go-to any time I need to say something meaningful in ritual. It's taken from the *Orations* of Aelius Aristides and runs:

> Nothing can be so firmly bound
> by illness, by wrath or by fortune
> that cannot be released by the Lord Dionysos.

Although merely repeating the words can bring about the desired release, it really helps if you think deeply about what you're saying and how Dionysos has acted in this capacity — in your previous experience of him, in the lives of those you know, as well as in myth. What does it mean to unbind and release? What are some of the ways that he could do that with regard to the ordeal you are presently going through?

Cool your head.

Take a white linen cloth and soak it in *chernips*, then lay down and place the cloth over your eyes and forehead or entire face. This bit of Starry Bull ritual tech is useful in a number of situations: when your thoughts are racing or your emotions are out of whack, when you're having a bad trip or spiritual encounter (particularly if it just keeps repeating), when you're coming down from altered states or are physically exhausted from dancing, when you're reeling from the effects of contact with miasma, etc.

The color white has a wealth of associations within our tradition but chief among them are purity, healing and things pertaining to the ancestors, as does linen which tended to be favored by Bacchic Orphic initiates over woolen objects because of the strong taboos attached to the latter. *Chernips* is made within the Starry Bull tradition by extinguishing a flaming branch or leaf in a basin of water, with or without some talky bits to give it extra oomph. (I usually use the mantra discussed above.)

There's a lot of complicated woo stuff I could get into with regard to this practice but instead I'll point out its obvious positive practical application: doing this forces you to just lay there focusing on the damp cloth that's sending droplets down your neck, instead of the roiling mess that is the inside of your head. Breathe. Relax. Do some of the mindfulness exercises described above or recite the mantra. Visualize the badness being absorbed by the cloth and leaving you. Keep it on for as long as you feel it's necessary, though I'd give it at least a good 5 to 10 minutes to do its thing.

Once you're finished, submerge the cloth in the bowl of *chernips* to neutralize any miasma it may have picked up and let it sit overnight. Then wash and dry it (I prefer air-drying it but that's a personal thing) then cover the cloth with some sea salt or natron and let it sit like that another night. That should clear it of any lingering gunk, at which point you can stash it with the rest of your ritual gear until your next freak out.

Egg cleanse.

Most cultures have some form of healing, cleansing or divination involving eggs and unsurprisingly considering their cosmology and the frequency with which eggs were offered to Dionysos Chthonios, this was a thing among the ancient Bacchic Orphics too. Within the Starry Bull tradition we have a number of different but related practices involving eggs, so I'm just going to give you a very basic, watered down version.

When you're feeling sick, emotionally frazzled or blocked by psychic gunk, take a raw egg (or better yet have someone else do it) and, holding it about an inch above you, run it over the length of your body starting and ending at the top of your head. As this is done, open yourself up and allow all of the badness to be sucked from you up into the egg. You can do this in silence, while chanting appropriate Dionysian epithets or vibrating the Greek vowels or even while reciting the aforementioned mantra. This practice is more effective if you have some background in energy work, but that's by no means a prerequisite. Just try to visualize or feel the grossness leaving your body and going into the egg.

When you're done, either crush the egg in your hand (especially if you need to feel as if you vanquished whatever you're trying to get rid of) or throw it as far as you can, releasing that shit into the world. Not only is this magically and psychologically effective but it's a hell of a lot of fun. Word of warning, though: don't do this indoors, because egg is a bitch to get off the walls.

More on Spiritual Discernment

Serving as a *mantis* or other kind of religious specialist, you're going to encounter a lot of folks at their worst. That's why it's important to understand how to practice διακρίσεις (or discernment) when one is suffering an episode of mental or emotional instability, both for yourself and your clients.

Step One: Self-evaluate. What's going on, how bad is the episode, does it respond to the treatments I've advised elsewhere, how is it impairing your mental and other faculties, can you talk it through with a friend, colleague or trusted elder or do you need the kind of assistance that only a competent professional can provide, etc. Along with self-evaluation should come self-care. It's okay to put things aside until you're able to deal with them again later. That doesn't always work — sometimes shit just keeps happening, whether we want it to or are capable of handling it — but know it's at least something you can try, and that doesn't make you less of a devotee, spirit-worker, etc. It takes more time and more effort to come back from a break, so don't be irresponsible and bootstrap it when you know you shouldn't.

Step Two: If this situation is not at a crisis level but is still affecting your perception and ability to function, begin by writing everything down. Just because you're having an episode does not mean that everything you're experiencing is automatically the product of delusion. On the other hand, you can't be certain that it isn't, either. So don't make any rash decisions or take immediate action based on what you've received. Instead, come back and analyze the material once you feel more stable. Does it still make sense or does it read like the ravings of a lunatic? More importantly, of what use is this information? If it has the potential to alter your understanding of the Gods and Spirits and how you relate to and worship them or is deeply personal, then keep pursuing your line of inquiry; if not then either discard it or file it away for future reference, as it may end up making more sense down the line.

Step Three: At this point, you have several options open to you. You may choose as many as are helpful and execute them in whatever order suits you, or not.

    o   Pray for guidance, instruction, discernment and any other spiritual gifts that will help you navigate this uncertain terrain. While you may get a direct response from them it is best merely to ask for assistance and confirmation going forward, as your signal clarity could have become compromised. Besides, when asking for help you should listen more than you talk.

o   Hit the books. See if you can find corroboration in the lore, academic literature or the writings of contemporary practitioners. Some of the most bizarre stuff I've encountered while working with altered states or while suffering from a manic episode has turned out to be a strain of tradition I simply had not been aware of previously. A lot of information can be found online, but tread carefully as most of it is utter crap. Now, just because something appears in a book or on a website does not make it true; likewise, plenty of true things have never been written down. All that this material can do is provide you a glimpse into other people's experiences and insights. Sometimes there's convergence; plenty of times there is not. Also keep in mind that experiences with Gods and Spirits are always idiosyncratic; two people may go through the same thing but describe it very differently.

o   Talk with friends, other people who are doing similar work, or a religious specialist whose opinion you trust. See if they have had similar experiences, if they have suggestions for further research, if they can recommend other people you can talk to and if they have any thoughts on what's happening or how you should proceed. Now, depending on your relationship with and level of trust and respect for this person you will know how much weight to give their suggestions. That's all this should be — it still falls to you to decide whether you accept what happened or not, and to act upon it. If everyone is telling you it sounds like bullshit, that's definitely something to pay attention to — but on the other hand they may not have the first clue what they're talking about. All this and the previous line of inquiry can do is suggest; you still must decide for yourself.

o   Divine, divine, divine. Because of your closeness to the situation, you may want to have a trusted diviner read for you in addition to whatever divination you perform. Different traditions have different protocols on this, but I tend to hire three diviners and then compare the results from each reading. No matter how bizarre your experience, if all three come back positive it's a pretty good indication that this is a legit thing. Keep in mind that this is very different from shopping around your questions until you get an answer you want and I strongly advise you to only provide the absolutely necessary information and keep back some significant piece as a means of verification. Of course, just because that piece doesn't come up in the reading does not necessarily render it invalid: often the Gods and Spirits will only provide answers about what you asked (and how you asked it) which is why you must choose your words carefully — but if those details show up it's a pretty solid indicator of who's on the other end of the line.

o   Ask for a sign. Something specific enough that you can be relatively certain when you see it, but also open enough that you do not strain their ability to act. For instance, you may ask for a clear message or *kledone*, or that a certain symbol appear three times. Set a reasonable timeframe, and then pay attention because signs often come to us in unexpected ways and unconventional forms. If you receive your sign make a generous offering to the God or Spirit since they've gone out of their way to assuage your doubt. If no sign appears then that means no sign appeared. It probably also means that you were wrong but that cannot be inferred just from this. Sometimes a sign doesn't appear because you need to do this without knowing, trusting in their guidance.

Next let's consider what to do when one is reasonably certain about a divinity's identity but what you're receiving doesn't really line up with what others get.

You should add that to the list of evidence you're compiling and then move on with your inquiry. All by itself the fact that your experience does not line up with the experiences of others is of limited significance. Worth noting, to be sure, but there are plenty of perfectly valid explanations for why this might be:

o   You are encountering a distinct, localized expression of the divinity.

o   Either your encounter with the divinity was not as deep as theirs or it was much deeper. The divinity may be showing you a different side of itself because each person will have different needs, degrees of intimacy or roles to perform.

o   Either you or they may be encountering an entity which is masquerading as the divinity. This can either be because that entity is part of the divinity's train or retinue and thus partakes of their nature, because it is malign and trying to deceive you, or because the divinity and the entity have made a prior arrangement and there's some reason why it must engage with you in this form. Or your brain is just reading them as X because of their closeness to the divinity and no deception was intended on their part.

o   Others may be wrong, delusional or lying. Conversely, this may be true of you whether you realize it or not.

It is especially worth paying attention to if your experience not only doesn't conform to the experiences of the majority of the divinity's devotees, but also does not reflect what is commonly known of this divinity's personality, attributes, powers and domains, as well as conflicts with what may be found in the lore and academic literature on them. All of these, individually, may not hold much weight but taken together they provide a pretty solid argument that what you're encountering may not be what it seems. Now, again, you may just be dealing with a different form of them, but it should give you cause for reflection, to say nothing of prompting one to seek divination and other external methods of corroboration.

If everything points to them really being them, and they seem okay with it, then just start dealing with them in this particular form. Figure out what their preferences are, if there are specific rites that need to be performed or taboos observed and go about building up a devotional relationship with them as you would any new divinity you happened to meet. You may or may not maintain separate cultus for this divinity under their more conventional form.

One of the things you'll need to decide is how much you share with others, particularly when they deal with a radically different form of the divinity. Specifically, what do you get out of sharing; how does the other party benefit from the sharing, and is it something they can actually do something with or will it be purely theoretical for them; how likely are they to respond negatively to this information; what can you lose by sharing it; is it the proper time and space to share such information; how does the divinity feel about you sharing what is likely very personal and intimate; and are there specific protocols associated with its sharing?

Which brings us to the final point I'd like to discuss: how we can avoid letting preconceptions about a divinity limit our interactions with them.

The simple answer is to seek them in their fullness, without distinction or judgment. But simple is not always easy, especially when you don't know how to do the thing in the first place.

So begin by asking yourself:

o   What preconceptions do I have?
o   How did I arrive at them?
o   Is there any basis in reality or are they shaped entirely of supposition, fear and uncertainty?
o   Why do I hold onto them?
o   In what ways do they influence me, even if on an unconscious

level?
- o What would it mean to lay them aside?
- o Specifically, how would laying them aside change how I under-stand and interact with this entity?
- o What would laying them aside even look like?
- o What would I replace them with?

Sit with these questions for as long as you need to. Spend time actively reflecting on them as well as letting your brain mull them over while you go about your day and its normal activity. (Do you know how many epiphanies I've had while washing dishes or on the toilet? A lot.) If it helps, try writing out your answers stream-of-consciousness style in addition to taking notes.

Once you have answers, go back through and feel out what it would be like if your answers were completely different.

Then actually try doing it.

It's going to feel weird, artificial, and awkward at first.

How can you consciously change your thoughts or alter your emotions? If you are determined enough you can do anything.

In the early stages you may want to tie a string around your finger or wrist as a mnemonic aid, and when you notice it reinforce your change of mind and behavior through affirmations. (Remember — the brain doesn't hear "no," so frame it as a positive.)

You may find yourself falling back into old patterns of thought or encountering mental blocks you had dissolved already.

Keep going.

With time and practice, it'll feel more natural to you and you may only need to do it long enough to facilitate some kind of personal breakthrough in your relationship with the divinity.

Alternately you may want to ritualize the process by tearing up, cleansing or burning cards representing your preconceptions so that they will no longer have any power over you.

The Ethics of Mantike

One of the most important lessons I've learned as a *mantis* or diviner is a bit of wisdom that was inscribed at the temple of Apollon at Delphi, one of the holiest and most important oracular sites in the ancient world. Thales is generally credited with first giving this sage advice, though it was also attributed to Chilon, Bias, Cleoboulos, Periander, Pittacus and a variety of other ancient wise men. (And at least one wise woman as well, the poet Phemonoe!) All of these people had a strong connection to the God Apollon, so you wouldn't be far off the mark if you were to claim divine inspiration for the words. They are, after all, essential for anyone who seeks to live a wise, pious and successful life. I mean, of course, the famous admonition γνῶθι σεαυτόν (*gnothi seauton*) which can be rendered into English as "Know Thyself."

Historically there have been two primary ways to interpret the injunction, both of which are relevant to those seeking to take up this divine craft. (There are, as I'm sure you're aware, many other equally valid ways to interpret the phrase, but one would need to devote a whole essay — at the least! — to exploring all of them. There's a reason why Apollon was granted the *epiklesis* Loxias.) The most familiar of the two, thanks to the Socratics, is as an encouragement towards introspection and authentic self-discovery and expression. The founder of that school so aptly observed that the unexamined life was not worth living and through the process of dialectic he challenged people to critically examine their basic assumptions about who they were, how the world worked and what concepts such as love, truth, wisdom, piety, beauty, courage, etc. actually meant to them as opposed to the definition insisted upon by unthinking society or convention.

The second interpretation — which is probably more in line with the original intent of its author, even if it isn't as well known — is that we should know ourselves in the sense of knowing our proper place in the world, observing respectable boundaries of thought and deed, avoiding overreaching pride, arrogance and impious aspiration. Similar Delphic maxims include "nothing too much," "observe the limit," "think mortal thoughts," and so forth.

Both ways of reading this admonition have relevance for those who would pass on the sage counsel of the Gods to their communities, regardless of the tradition within which they work.

To begin with, the *mantis* must have a proper understanding of exactly what it is they are doing. They must know where the information is coming from, be able to carefully distinguish the messages of the Gods from their own thoughts and emotional responses to the issue, and must accurately report everything that comes through and limit what they say only to what was communicated without subtraction, embellishment or unasked-for interpretation and commentary. After the message has been given, the querent may ask the *mantis* for their opinion or further clarification on an obscure point of the message, but in doing so the *mantis* should make it perfectly transparent what came from the Gods and what is their own private interpretation. They should be especially careful not to force their opinion on the querent since it is often part of the process for the person to figure out what the oracle means to them personally and one should also avoid idle conjecture or in other words, if you have no idea what an oracle means don't guess or you're liable to be wrong and unhelpful.

Now to offer further clarification on some of these points.

I am a trained *mantis* with over two decades worth of experience under my belt. That does not, however, mean that I am a therapist or possess the necessary knowledge, training or certification to diagnose mental problems or offer practical, emotional or spiritual counseling. Anyone who comes to me seeking that sort of thing gets redirected to qualified personnel — in fact, I'm reluctant even to offer friendly advice because, to put it mildly, I'm shitty at handling my own problems and I'd undoubtedly be much worse at sifting through other people's crap.

Unfortunately a lot of folks in this line of work don't share my misgivings and I've seen them royally fuck people over as a result. They didn't mean to, of course — they went about their advice-giving with the best of intentions. But when it came down to it they just didn't know enough about the situation or the workings of the human psyche to be truly helpful. Even if their advice was excellent and exactly what the person needed to hear at that precise moment, it can be extremely difficult to remove one's ego from the equation. A lot of people just aren't prepared to be ignored or misunderstood, which happens the majority of the time that advice is given. You may see with perfect clarity that your friend is in a dysfunctional and abusive relationship and needs to drop that bitch and start his life fresh as far away from there as possible — but your friend may not be ready to do that just yet, even if he'd agree 100% with you. He may be worried about the economic consequences of leaving his wife, he may still be making all sorts of excuses about why it happens (she didn't really mean it, she only does it when she's had too much to drink, I brought it on myself by provoking her) or he may be in denial or ashamed to admit that things have actually gotten that bad and so on and so forth. The only thing you can be certain of in a situation like that is that the person won't leave or seek the necessary help until they are good and ready to — and even then it may require several frustrating abortive attempts before it finally sticks.

It can be maddening to watch the cycle of abuse play itself out over and over again, but you can't force a person to change against their will. Often their impotent rage will become directed at you if you try and push them since you are a safe target for their venting or else they might perceive you as a threat to the status quo. Your actions may inadvertently heighten their sense of shame and isolation, which only serves to ensconce them deeper in the dysfunctional situation. You, yourself, may become frustrated that they aren't listening to your wise advice or are hell-bent on a path of despair and self-destruction. You may, in turn, lose all respect for them or no longer wish to associate with them lest you become culpable in their abuse by knowing about it and not being able to stop it.

This is, of course, a fairly radical situation but I've seen plenty of friendships destroyed over things of far less consequence as a result of indiscriminate advice-giving. I feel it best to avoid this altogether — or at least not to proffer advice until asked for — but if you feel that you absolutely *must* give your opinion, make sure that you do so devoid of any expectation. Once your words have been spoken, leave it at that, granting them the freedom to act on it or not as they see fit. You should be willing to stand by your friend regardless of how they choose to put your advice into action, and if you cannot withhold judgment either keep your feelings to yourself or end the friendship without making a huge deal of it. You do not want to get embroiled in unnecessary drama and transform the person you once considered a bosom companion into a mortal enemy.

There are many ways, in fact, that we need to keep ego in check when it comes to serving as a *mantis*. Related to the above principle, it is incumbent upon you to remove any personal investment or consideration from your oracles. Your job is to transmit a message from the Gods or Spirits to the querent. Once you have successfully done that your obligation ceases. How the person accepts it and what they do with that information is entirely up to them. It should be no concern of yours whether they misinterpret the message, incompletely or incorrectly implement what was asked of them or ignore it outright. Honestly this can be one of the hardest parts of the job, especially when the oracle comes through unambiguously or you see the person still struggling or complaining about a situation months or years later, all of which could have been swiftly and satisfactorily resolved had they only done what they were told. It's even more frustrating when the person comes back to you later on with the same question, seemingly hoping for a different answer. You come to feel annoyed, ignored, disrespected — and this can have unpleasant consequences for your friendship if you're not careful.

The best thing that you can do is to know your place. Your place is to give the oracle not to lead the person's life for them. That is their responsibility and they will suffer the consequences of their insolence, indolence and ignorance. You also need to understand that everyone responds to situations differently. Maybe it's going to take this person longer to overcome an obstacle than it would have for you. Maybe they have important lessons to be learned which can only come about through repeated failures. Maybe the God never intended for them to do what the oracle said but rather was subtly urging them onto a different path which they could only discover through attempting something and then realizing that it wasn't right for them. And maybe what you see so clearly in the oracle isn't what the God wished to communicate to them, so even though they may be interpreting it "wrong" from your perspective, they are actually doing what is pleasing in the eyes of the God. Regardless, even if you are right and they aren't it's their oracle to do with as they please, even if that's nothing.

Another reason not to take it personally is because if you're doing your job as a *mantis* properly then the message was never yours to begin with. It originates from the God and you are nothing more than a messenger passing it on to its intended recipient. And at that point the matter rests entirely between them and their God. Or to think of it in another way: you are just a vessel into which the Gods pour their blessings. A cup has no feelings and no purpose other than to be a receptacle for fluids. It has no say and indeed it hardly matters whether wine or water or milk or anything else is dumped into it. It doesn't matter whether the person drains the cup in a single draught, takes only a tiny sip and then walks away never to taste it again, or even if they dump it out or just let it sit there growing mold. The cup's sole purpose is to hold what's poured into it without leaking, to serve the needs of the one pouring something into it and the one that is going to drink out of it. Thus, like the cup the sole desire of the *mantis* ought to be for utility without any concern for how they are being used and what follows after. In keeping with this I feel that it is the supreme obligation of the *mantis* to get themselves out of the way as much as possible. You are facilitating communication between the Gods and their people and your job is to transmit those messages as clearly and carefully as you possibly can. Always remember your place and stay mindful of its humble position in the grand scheme of things.

The people are not coming to you to hear your wisdom or gain your valuable opinion on important matters. If you want to send your own message out into the world then take up the noble craft of the writer or become an orator, a therapist, a teacher, a philosopher, some crazy drunken dude on the street corner or something else along those lines. But when you take up the calling of the *mantis* then you must always be conscious that you are a servant of the Gods and faithfully report exactly what they tell or show you. Nothing more and nothing less than that should ever pass your lips or fingertips when you are engaged in this sacred vocation.

Long before the aspirant *mantis* begins offering their services to the public they must cultivate the spiritual faculty of discernment, the ability to listen for the voice of the Gods (however that is expressed to them, and this can indeed come through in many different ways depending on the Gods and the person involved) the ability to identify who and where it's coming from (since there are so many Gods, Spirits and assorted divine beings out there) as well as being able to recognize how this differs from one's own thoughts, feelings, personal convictions and the detritus floating about in one's brain. This can be incredibly challenging especially when one is first starting off on the path or when the issue is one that directly involves the *mantis* or those close to them.

It's even trickier when you do the sort of direct trance-possession oracles that I've been specializing in with Dionysos for a number of years now. After all, if you're employing some form of external, mechanical divination such as Tarot, Runes, I Ching, augury or the like there's a measure of control and corroboration that you can rely on. This is what the tools turned up, this is the traditional meaning and here's how I interpret the symbolism. Even if that is just the starting point and you rely on inspiration and free association there's still a degree of concreteness to the process that's generally lacking when you are shown visions, hear the words of a God or some other form of intimate, often internal com-munication takes place. You have to be constantly on guard that the message is coming through clearly, that it isn't getting distorted by errant thoughts and astral junk, or that you accidentally and perhaps even without being aware of it are twisting things to conform to your own biased expectations. This is not a perfect science no matter how diligent and disciplined we are or what added precautions we take. Furthermore we are faulty human beings. The Gods and Spirits exist on a level far beyond us with an understanding of the world and the things in it which is radically different from and dwarfs our own. The act of transmitting this through an imperfect human vessel, translating transcendent under-standing into finite human speech and thought is a process fraught with peril. It's like representing a multidimensional construct using only length and width. Much, inevitably, is going to be lost in the process. But it's your job to ensure that things run as smoothly as possible, that the wires don't get crossed, the information corrupted and contaminated as little as possible and that you don't interject your own take on things, unless asked for by either party.

One of the most important elements of this is communicating the message as it was given, regardless of what you personally feel about the issue. Many times over the years I've received messages that didn't make much sense to me or quite frankly were a complete one-eighty from what I would have told the person had they come to me seeking advice. Sometimes the message is uncomfortably direct and harsh. In those instances you've really got to struggle against the tendency to impose order on it, make it more sensible and directly relevant, or to sugarcoat it. You have to trust that the Gods and Spirits are far wiser than you, that they are seeing a fuller picture or referencing something that will be intelligible to the person receiving it either now or later, even if it's incomprehensible to you, that if it means nothing to the person now it may in time when more of the puzzle pieces have fallen into place and that the Gods or Spirits have a reason for saying what they do and in the manner that they have chosen regardless of how you feel about all of it. Even if they aren't as polite as you would like, you have to consider that that brusqueness may be there because that is exactly what the person needs to hear in order for the message to get through their defenses. And if they take it out on you, suggest the message came from you and accuse you of being too harsh and judgmental, well, that's the risk you've got to take if you want to be a messenger of the Gods. You're not in this to win friends and accolades, and it's not your business to adulterate the words of the Gods or soften their blow — only to deliver it. Conversely there have been times when I was expecting a forceful reply and the oracle came across gentle and somewhat coddling to my complete surprise. Clearly that's what the person needed to hear in that instance and the Gods recognized that bashing them over the head with it wouldn't have done any good. The more you encounter oracles like these the more you come to realize how little a role you play in all of it and how clearly they originate from somewhere outside of yourself.

For these and many other reasons I try to go into an oracular session knowing as little about the circumstances of the question as humanly possible. I do not ask for background details or clarification unless it's absolutely necessary, I only skim the requests when I receive them to determine if there are other matters that need to be addressed, I keep the requests in a folder and transcribe them early in the evening hours before I start my preparation, I try to avoid thinking about the question or discussing it with the person beforehand and I go through an elaborate series of preliminary ritual actions which are not only highly devotional in nature but also help to clear my mind and focus my attention on the sacred work before me so that I won't have any room for mundane concerns or dwelling on the details of the request. And on the rare occasions when none of that works because I'm too involved or close to the situation and person I've straight-up told them that I couldn't do it and they should seek assistance from a different source. I've only had to do this a handful of times over the years but I feel that it is a necessary step to take to preserve the integrity of my calling and ensure that I am providing the best possible oracular service that I can.

Likewise when an oracle that I receive is too jumbled and income-prehensible and all further attempts to gain clarity prove fruitless, or I just can't get into the proper oracular state I admit as much to the person and either offer to try a different divination method or advise them to seek an answer elsewhere or accept that this is not something that they are going to gain insight on at this time. Some may find it uncomfortable to admit fallibility but I'd rather the person think me a failure than to know myself to be a fraud, manufacturing messages when none are forthcoming or twisting the details so that they appear more sensible. To distort things in that way is a violation of the sacred trust that both the Gods and my community have placed in me. This work is difficult and demanding and it requires integrity, courage, dedication, discipline and all of the other virtues upon which character is based. If I compromise even a little, give less than my absolute best — even if no one else is aware or likely to ever find out about it — it is ultimately going to undermine my confidence in myself and cause me to doubt my ability to hear what the Gods are saying and communicate that to others. So even setting aside the considerable moral obligation I have to those that approach me with their questions, it is in my own best interest if I intend to continue in this vocation to be as honest and uncompromising as possible. I've got to live with myself and look myself in the mirror — how could I possibly do that knowing that I had deceived and cheated someone in the name of my God?

As an extension of that I feel that a *mantis* should always be conscious of what their office means to those who seek their assistance, the importance and dignity and sacredness of it. We help bridge the gap between the mortal and divine realms. People come to us to learn about the Gods and to hear their messages. While I agree with the general principle that no one needs an intermediary between themselves and the Gods, that the Gods can hear our prayers, accept our offerings and make their will known to us in a multitude of ways — practically speaking there are often circumstances that make things much more complicated than that. Perhaps the person is full of doubt or too close to the situation to gain any kind of useful clarity. Perhaps they are in a state of impurity, do not know the proper methods of communicating with the divine or how to recognize such communication in the first place. Perhaps they are new to all of this, lack proficiency in divination, are spiritually blocked or deaf and blind to the invisible world. Maybe they're in over their heads, facing a situation they could never have conceived of before or are just looking for an outside perspective or confirmation of things they have already intuited. There are a thousand and more reasons why a person might consult a *mantis* and it is our job to be there to lend our assistance where and in whatever way we can.

This is both an immense honor and an incredible responsibility because when we take up this office we become the representative of our Gods here on earth. Everything that we say and do — whether in our capacity as a *mantis* or outside of it — reflects back on the Gods we serve. We must be diligent in our execution of our religious duties, must conduct ourselves with integrity, character and proper decorum and never do anything that would cast aspersions on our holy office or cause others to doubt the existence, wisdom and benevolence of the Gods. And note that morality is relative and in this context largely determined by the Gods or Spirits whom you are working for. The qualities favored by a God like Dionysos or Hermes are very different from the standards insisted upon by Apollon or Athene, to the point where I'm strongly hesitant to have anything to do with the latter pair beyond what is required within the Starry Bull tradition.

When people see someone who claims to be a mouthpiece for the Gods acting in a haughty, shameful, cruel or unnecessarily contentious fashion it is natural for them to wonder how such a person could have an intimate communion with the Gods or if it's all just empty hokum and vain posturing. Doubt that begins with the person spreads to the Gods: how wise and moral could they possibly be if they would entrust their message to such an undeserving person?

We may feel that this is unfair since we are all fallible human beings and virtue is not an easy path as evidenced by how few truly good men there are in the world. Further, spiritual aptitude is not always dependent on or even consistent with conventional morality as evidenced by the deplorable lives led by many visionaries, religious figures and artists down through the centuries. Regardless this is still the common perception and fair or not we are held to this standard with grave consequences for those who fail to measure up. The thought that one's careless actions might drive people away from the Gods ought to fill any *mantis* worthy of the title with abject horror.

And finally, I'd like to include a word on asking and receiving. Remember, always, that *a God is talking to you*. It's not the same as checking your horoscope in the paper or seeing what weird shapes your coffee grounds have formed. (Though these, too, can convey the will of the Gods to those who are properly paying attention.) Ask questions that suit the dignity of the occasion, not something you can figure out on your own with a little critical thinking. Don't do it as a lark, because you're bored or to try and test the Gods. And above all else, show respect by taking the answer you get seriously. That means spend some time really thinking about it and how it applies to your life. Don't jump to the most obvious conclusion, especially when the oracle has been phrased enigmatically. History is littered with those who failed to see clearly what the Gods had indicated and brought untold suffering on themselves and their communities as a result. The Gods gave us rational faculties with the intent that we'd use them. That may require you to do a bit of digging and meditation before the ultimate meaning reveals itself to you, but as with all things in life you get out of stuff what you put into it.

Likewise, when an answer is clearly and unequivocally presented to you, you should strongly consider doing what it says. Why ask the advice of the Gods or Spirits in the first place if you're just going to ignore what they've got to say? Now, obviously, choice comes into play here. You're not a robot and you can very well disagree with what a God or Spirit is telling you to do. Maybe the sort of life you want for yourself isn't what they've got in mind for you, or maybe the risks and consequences just don't add up. I tend to think the Gods and Spirits are wiser than us, more aware of the things that lurk beneath the surface or the chains of reaction that simple acts can set into motion — but hey, it's your life, so do as you please. But on the other hand, don't keep asking the same question over and over again hoping for a different result and don't expect your situation to change if you're not willing to act in a manner which they indicated will have a favorable outcome. Sometimes, a lot of the time actually, you've got to put in the work first before things will make sense to you. This is where trust comes into play. Don't demand understanding and desirable results before you've done your part. If you've done everything asked of you and there's still been no change, then perhaps you're justified in getting upset and demanding an answer. But be careful about deluding yourself. Often we may think we've done everything in our power when we've really just skimmed the surface.

We've all encountered people in the community who get divination results or channeled oracles that perfectly line up with the views they already regularly express; here are some possible explanations for why that might happen.

1) The closer we get to a divinity the more our values and choices come to reflect theirs, often on an unconscious level. Thus, without even necessarily thinking about it we may find ourselves parroting our Gods and Spirits.

2) Like calls to like. Thus devotees are naturally drawn to divinities who possess similar character traits and values as their own.

3) The divinity may be communicating with their devotee outside divinatory or oracular channels and so the person already knows what the divinity wants before the question is formally posed.

4) Divinities may communicate different things to different devotees, either because their agendas are large and complicated enough to encompass both positions, because they have specific tasks for each party, because they feel that devotee A is not emotionally capable of handling what is communicated to devotee B, because the divinity is playing both sides against each other, and so forth.

5) People see only what they want to. Meaning, that message may be there but is just an isolated scene in a larger tapestry and they're not able or willing to take in the whole or they may extrapolate beyond what was said. For instance a divinity might advise one simply to "care for the suffering" which is then interpreted as promoting a specific political ideology or movement.

6) The devotee is willfully twisting the message to suit their ideology and agenda, or the fault lies with the oracle or diviner, who may be confused, biased or deceitful. Not all who present themselves as mouthpieces of the Gods are as competent or ethical as they should be.

7) As an extension of the above, the person may be in contact with something that isn't what it's presenting itself as — either a mental sock puppet, or a deceitful and possibly malign Spirit or God that's masquerading as someone else. Spiritual discernment is decidedly rare in our communities.

8) People lie. To themselves and to others. It happens all the time, and religious communities are certainly not immune to this, especially not those on the pagan/polytheist spectrum.

9) Mental illness is also prevalent in our communities. While madness has many blessings it can also make "reality" a little fuzzy.

Over the years I've received and given to others what I've come to think of as "problematic" oracles. Basically, these are messages that don't conform to the reality of a given situation. They are, in other words, false.

Now, sometimes we're a little premature in judging them as such. I can't tell you the number of times I've had someone say that an oracle didn't apply to their situation or made no sense to them whatsoever, only to hear back from them in a couple months or a year that everything ended up exactly as predicted. Other times we think it's pretty clear what a message means, and really how could it mean anything else? Only to discover later on that it had actually been talking about something else entirely. And, sometimes, as much as I hate to admit it and try my best to ensure that it doesn't happen, an oracle can come out garbled. I put too much emphasis on one part while ignoring the truly relevant material; I mishear something; I put it in such a way that it confuses the person; or maybe wires get crossed and I just have a bad night. It happens to everyone in this business at one time or another, no matter how careful we try to be.

But what about when none of this applies and the oracle is still wrong?

Can the Gods ever be mistaken?

Can they lie?

Plenty of folks with philosophical inclinations will tell you straight up, "No. Never. It's just not possible. The Gods are all wise and all powerful and more to the point they are perfect and good and entirely different from us foolish, frail mortals."

The only one of these I really agree with is the last point. The Gods are, indeed, very different from us but all the rest is just wishful thinking on our part. Just because the human mind can conceive of something like a perfect, omnipotent and omnibenevolent deity doesn't mean that you'll ever find such a thing in reality. Just look at nature, which the philosophers will often tell you is supposed to be a reflection of divinity or a God in its own right. Can anything be more harsh, indifferent and prone to making horrible mistakes? Why does the tortoise lay a hundred eggs when only a couple will live long enough to reach maturity? Why are most planets incapable of sustaining life? Why does the platypus or Tom Cruise exist? Anyone who has pondered such questions for long must eventually come to the conclusion that philosophers aren't half as wise as they think themselves.

I find the theories of the ancient myth-tellers to be far more reasonable. There we find a multitude of Gods and Spirits with different interests, powers and opinions. Not only can they disagree with each other, but they often quarrel and oppose the efforts of their fellows. Further, none of them is all-knowing or all-powerful. Wiser and stronger than us, certainly. Wiser and stronger even than some of the other Gods and Spirits that, too, makes sense. But when you start making them omni- this and omni- that you run into patently absurd paradoxes, especially if you maintain any pretense of morality among them.

So, what has this to do with oracles? Well, I think it offers a couple valuable solutions for the problematic ones.

For instance, a God can simply be wrong. Perhaps they did not see far enough. Perhaps the situation changed after they made their proclamation. This, alone, could take multiple courses of action. Another God may have intervened on behalf of the person, thwarting what the other had willed or seen; alternately, the oracle could have been about the likeliest course of action until the person made certain choices which opened up other avenues of possibility.

Although I believe in Fate I reject the notion of predestination. First, I think it renders our lives meaningless, reducing us to the status of mindless automata. So, even if it's true — and if it's true then it makes no difference what I believe — I reject predestination because such a notion is incompatible with truly lived virtue and goodness.

Secondly, it just doesn't appear to be the way things work. Fate is like a busy one-way street. Once you turn onto it you're pretty much going to end up following along until you reach your destination or turn off somewhere else. Of course, there's nothing stopping you from opting not to follow that path. You can abruptly stop your car and refuse to budge. You can turn around and go against the flow of traffic, weaving in and out of oncoming vehicles until one of them smashes into you. Or you can get out of the car and run screaming into the woods by the side of the highway. Granted, all of these are difficult, dangerous and undesirable choices — but it's still within your power to make them. So, all of these could account for problematic oracles. And if predestination is true, what's the point in getting an oracle at all? That makes it a cruel joke, a God going "Neener neener boo boo. Here's what's gonna happen and you can't do nothing about it."

But there's also another option, namely that Gods can lie. They do it amongst themselves all the time in myth, and they've done it to us plenty of times before. My favorite instance of this — which is quite relevant to our discussion — took place before the start of the Persian War. At the time Persia had been making some aggressive noise. They'd annexed a number of the Greek cities in Asia Minor. They'd been instigating inter-communal conflicts among the *poleis* in the Greek mainland. They'd sent ambassadors with their demands. And they'd done a pretty good job of swallowing up the rest of the ancient world. But even with their intent made so clear, the Greeks — and especially the Athenians — were uncertain of how to proceed. Some thought they'd never reach this far and posed no serious threat anyway, being a bunch of skirt-wearing, mother-loving barbarian wussies. Others thought they could be bought off or alliances could be made with them, which would help eliminate their more annoying neighbors. There were as many opinions as there were people in the *agora* and as the matter continued to be hotly debated the Persians made their slow progress through Asia.

Eventually someone got it into their head to ask the Gods what they should do, so they sent some representatives to consult the Pythia at Delphi. Horrified, the representatives returned to Athens saying, "Woe to the sons of Athens, all is lost! You shall be utterly defeated, the land of your ancestors taken from you and the holy temples of the Gods burned to the ground! Run! Flee like the weaklings you are. Your only hope is to get as far away from here as possible, as fast as you can. Don't even look back; the sight will haunt you the rest of your days."

I'm paraphrasing, as anyone who has read their Herodotos knows, of course, but that was the gist of Apollon's message to the Athenians. And it *completely* pissed them off. "The God thinks so little of us? Well fuck him, safe up there on Parnassos! If we're destined to die, we'll go down on our feet, fighting to the last, taking as many of the rag-heads with us as possible."

And, well, that's pretty much what they did. The Athenians put aside their long-standing hatred of the Spartans and presented a unified front with the other Greeks against the barbarian hordes. They fought them by land and by sea in a long and bitter war, countless score perishing as a result. At one point the Persians even managed to push through and put the Athenian Acropolis to the torch, burning many of the city's oldest and most important temples. But the Greeks fought back and eventually drove the invader out of the land. Then they rebuilt, making the temples — the Parthenon in particular — bigger and better than they had been pre-viously. They had been tested in the crucible and emerged from the flames strong and pure and wise. This was the time of Athens' Golden Age, when she excelled in the arts and sciences and wielded great power and wealth. All because Apollon lied to the Athenians.

Imagine if the representatives had come back with a different message from the Pythia. "The God says everything's gonna be quincelike. The Persians aren't going to set up residence here. In fact we're about to see a time of great prosperity and success. Yay us!" How do you think they would have responded to the threat then? Apollon had to deceive them in order to goad them into action, show them the thing they feared and despised most so that they would fight all the harder to ensure it didn't happen.

So I don't have a problem with the fact that the Gods can lie to us, even when it's motivated by less benign intentions than those of kind-hearted Apollon. There are Gods and Spirits out there who really don't have our best interests in mind. Of course, Dionysos isn't one of them, but I wouldn't put it past him to lie if he felt it was necessary. He's also pretty good at speaking the truth in a way that's easily misunderstood, as Euripides made abundantly clear in *The Bakchai.* This is where our rationality must come into play.

We should never just accept the words of an oracle at face-value. The oracle is but a first step, an outline, an invitation, a challenge. Of course, we shouldn't overthink the oracle, either. I've known folks who initially understood it but weren't happy with the results and so kept twisting it to make it say what they wanted to or kept looking for a deeper meaning for so long that it just became a string of empty syllables. When they came back, wanting more, the God was reluctant to give it to them, and I certainly don't blame him.

What are you going to actually *do* with the information that's been given to you? That's the important question. That's what it always comes back to.

How To Worship the Starry Bull Way

Start by figuring out how you want to honor the Gods and Spirits of the Starry Bull pantheon. Do you feel called to do shrine work? Then set up a shrine for them. Do you feel called to do spontaneous ecstatic ritual with them outdoors? Then do that. Do you want to get to know them first through study, reflection, art and simple acts of devotion then see where it goes from there? Perfect! There really is no wrong answer here, except sitting on your ass and doing nothing at all. However, that advice is not terribly helpful for the complete novice so I'm going to break it down even more for you.

What I'd recommend is to begin with the basics. Go through the pantheon and see if any of them stand out for you. Some may be familiar, some may be completely new, and don't just go with the ones you immediately like. Some of the deepest and most important divine relationships I've formed started out with aversion and resistance.

Once you've got a manageable group (and don't try to juggle more than you can reasonably handle; there's plenty of time to get to know the pantheon better) start learning what you can about them. Not just in a vague, abstract and generalized Bullfinchean sense but specifically how they are understood and interacted with in the context of the Starry Bull tradition, which is strongly rooted in Southern Italy and Bacchic Orphism. That doesn't just mean that we favor the forms of the divinities and the different, localized stories known to the people of that region, though this is certainly part of it; our vision is informed by their worldview. It is a worldview that emphasizes the bizarre, the monstrous and the tragic; a worldview that is dark, sensual, earthy and mad; a worldview dominated by the Labyrinth, that place of mysterious intersection between death, dream and desire. Our pantheon is shaped not just by who is in it but by how they are seen in it. We find the light in the dark and the dark in the light. Everything is broken; everything is beautiful. That's the lens through which we perceive the myths and the figures behind the myths that make up the Starry Bull tradition. And as you immerse yourself in it, you will come to do so as well.

While this process is going on, begin engaging with the Gods and Spirits you've chosen through cultus. Don't worry about setting up an elaborate shrine right off the bat (they're best if they develop gradually and organically anyway) and don't let your lack of knowledge about them or their preferred method of veneration hold you back. You'll learn this with time and practice and no doubt by making a couple serious blunders. You've got to get things wrong in order to figure out what it means to get things right, so don't be afraid to experiment. Besides, we place a strong emphasis on forging a personal relationship with the Gods and Spirits of our pantheon and they often ask different things of different people, which is why plenty of room is left for folks to individually tailor Starry Bull practices and observances.

A good way to get your toes wet is by making regular offerings to a God or Spirit. This can be really simple: lighting a candle, pouring out a libation, reading a poem or praying to them with one's own words, spending some quiet time communing with them or just focusing your thoughts on them and then thanking them. Once you start getting a feel for who they are and the sorts of things they like you can begin introducing more specific offerings and devotional activities. If you aren't particularly sensitive you can ask others for suggestions, consult the Gods and Spirits directly through divination or ask a competent diviner if they can acquire that information for you. Once you feel as if you've reached a comfortable level of engagement with them you can move on to the next name on the list, either carrying forward the previous divinity's cultus or starting completely fresh with the next God or Spirit. You may also come up with your own religious routine or adopt the system of devotional days and festivals that we've implemented.

Now at this level you don't really have to worry too much about purity and related issues, but if you begin engaging more deeply with our Gods and Spirits you may feel drawn to create a shrine or other dedicated holy space for them and that's usually when the need for more conscious ritual etiquette kicks in. You may find it difficult to approach their shrine while in a state of miasma, or undesirable consequences may result when you do so; alternately, because of the nature of the beings we engage with and the types of activities we carry out for them, the problem may not be when you come to them but when you go to others afterwards. Unless you get a strong sense that impurity is a prerequisite of the work you're being called to do you should probably err on the side of caution and perform cleansings before any engagement with their shrines and after any particularly intense encounter, especially if blood, sex, death or madness are involved. While access is certainly important, there are other considerations — miasma can affect our physical and spiritual well-being and make us vulnerable to malign influences. More to the point it's contagious — something we should always keep in mind when dealing with others.

In order to maintain right relations with the Gods and Spirits of our pantheon, you may have to do more than sprinkle *chernips* on yourself and fumigate with burnt laurel leaves — and I don't just mean beefing up your purifying rituals. The Gods and Spirits of our pantheon are not fond of boundaries, especially the arbitrary ones we try to draw between our religious and mundane lives. As your relationship with them grows, you may find it intruding into everyday activities like what you wear or what you eat or what kind of media you consume and a whole host of seemingly unrelated things. Through these choices we shape who we are and what our life consists of which determines what is drawn into our sphere or repulsed by it. This is especially so with Gods and Spirits — each of whom operate at different "frequencies" (to use a metaphor I don't at all care for) thus requiring different things of us in order to be attuned to them. However, just as we should not infer from the wants of one divinity the desires of the rest, we must not make the error of assuming that one divinity will necessarily want the same things of all people. Just because a fellow member of the tradition has specific prescriptions and prohibitions does not mean that you will be saddled with them too or that you are somehow better or worse than them for it. Are you doing what the Gods and Spirits want of you? That is all that matters.

And how you can tell is by paying attention. How do you feel while doing a particular act, especially within a ritual context? How do you feel afterwards? Do certain things regularly occur as a result of it? How does this impact your feeling of closeness or distance to the God or Spirit? Do your thoughts consistently, perhaps even obsessively, turn to certain things? Do you have a positive or negative emotional response to such thoughts? How you answer can give you a pretty good sense of where you're at with regard to purity requirements, though it's usually a good idea to get confirmation through divination before codifying something as part of your practice.

However, a word of warning: there is a huge gulf between suspecting something and having it come up through divination. Don't ask unless you are prepared to act accordingly. You may or may not be held accountable if you're just fumbling around in the dark — but intentionally breaking a known taboo can bring with it some pretty serious and unpleasant consequences.

Once you have a sense of who you want to focus on in the Starry Bull pantheon (and it's fine if you don't feel a strong attraction to any single member or are just equally drawn to all of them) and have worked out the parameters of your relationships (or as much as you can at that point) it's just a matter of honoring them regularly and refining your technique. Each divinity has many paths of devotion and all can take you to fabulous places with them so keep exploring and experimenting and trying to do it better, whatever it is. In particular strive to make your worship a thing of beauty and artistry — our Gods and Spirits are aesthetes and appreciate that extra effort. Mind you, they are also ferocious and chthonic so their standards may be a bit skewed, but that doesn't mean they don't have them!

A Starry Bull Offering Rite

Cleanse with *chernips*.
Apply *titanos*.
Ring a bell seven times.
Light a candle.
Inscribe or trace a Labyrinth.
Offer incense.
Make a triple libation of:
– wine
– milk
– water.
Offer grain.
Offer fruit or flowers.
Offer honey.
Offer an egg.
Recite a hymn.
Ask blessings for your community.
Thank the God or Spirit.
Thank the predecessors and preservers of the tradition.
Spend some time in personal prayer, meditation and communion with the Gods and Spirits.
Perform divination.
Close the rite by ringing a bell three times.

Notes

Chernips is created by extinguishing a burning branch or leaf of laurel or some other sacred plant in a basin of water. The water is then used to purify and consecrate the space, objects and one's self through sprinkling with a branch.

The *titanos* is made by burning previous sacrifices, aromatic or sacred herbs and sheets of paper on which prayers, hymns and blessings have been written and mixing this ash with wine or *chernips* to form a paste. One may also use other white, powdery substances in place of the ash. One may cover their face with it or inscribe sacred characters such as a spiral, bull's horns, an eight-pointed star, the letters delta or omega, a lightning bolt, a snake or the Orphic egg. One does this for purification, protection, empowerment and intensification of focus.

Ring a bell seven times to signify that you are ready to begin.

The light and warmth of the candle draws them.

One may inscribe the Labyrinth on a sheet of paper or the surface of the shrine's altar or on an object; alternately if one has a permanent representation of the Labyrinth on their shrine one may trace its pattern with their finger. This opens the door to the realm of the Starry Bull Gods and Spirits; one's offerings should be placed on or near the Labyrinth so that they will be received by them.

Each of the offerings are deeply symbolic; one should contemplate their associations as they are being made. One may come up with set phrases or chants, speak *ex tempore* or make the offerings in reverent silence as suits one's ritual preferences and style.

One may recite an ancient hymn, such as those by Orpheus, Homer, Proklos, Julian etc.; one may recite the appropriate Starry Bull communal hymn or hymn from *Thunderstruck With Wine* for the day; or one may recite a piece of one's own composition or a favorite poem that reminds one of the God or Spirit being honored. One should reflect deeply on what one is reciting and how the words feel as they leave one's mouth. Experiment with tone and cadence and breathing; try chanting or singing as this powerfully enhances the recitation. One should sit quietly for several moments after finishing, opening one's self up to the presence of the Gods and Spirits, reflecting on their nature and powers and stories, as well as one's previous experiences with them.

One rings the bell three times to send one's worship above, below and through the Labyrinth and to open doors so that the blessings of the Gods and Spirits may flow back from these directions into one's life.

Though not included in the outline of this rite, one may give their blood while making the other offerings in order to strengthen their bond with the God or Spirit. However one should confirm through divination that this blood sacrifice is actually desired before one does so.

Feel free to adapt this rite to suit your needs.

Keep all of your ritual tools in a *kiste* (wicker basket) when not in use.

Fill a bowl with water and plunge a burning laurel leaf into it to create *chernips*.

Wash your hands, forearms and face.

Apply *titanos* or sacred ash to your forehead and cheeks.

Go around the ritual area using a leafy branch to sprinkle it thoroughly with *chernips*.

Then go back over everything using a *tympanon* (hand-drum) to drive off any remaining impurities.

Lay the three cloths down in the order of red, white, then black, and put the cauldron in the center.

To either side of the cauldron place beeswax candles and in front of each of them set a plate and two offering bowls. Before the cauldron put the *rhyton* (drinking horn) and the *thymiaterion* (incense-burner.)

Take out the *agalma* (which may be a pillar, a stone, a piece of wood, a phallos or large pinecone) and remove its linen veil. Place it in the cauldron, anointing it with sacred oil.

Sit facing the *agalma* with your eyes closed for the span of nine breaths, quieting your mind and preparing yourself. Open your eyes and hold your arms up like the horns of a bull, palms turned out towards the *agalma*. Hold this posture for another nine breaths. Make your left hand into a fist, pounding your chest over your heart three times, then bow your head and hail the God as loudly as you can.

Light the candles and the incense, using the leafy branch or your hands to feed the smoke to the *agalma*.

Hang red, black and white *tainia* (ribbons or braided cords) from the *agalma* and then crown it with a *stephanos* (wreath of ivy or flowers.) Sprinkle flower petals around the *agalma* in the cauldron.

Pour milk into one of the bowls on the right side. Dip your index and middle fingers in and feed some to the *agalma*.

Pour water into one of the bowls on the left side. Feed the *agalma*.

Pour mead into the other bowl on the right. Feed the *agalma*.

Pour pomegranate juice into the other bowl on the left. Feed the *agalma*.

You may keep a cloth handy to clean yourself between libations or go right from one to the next.

Offer cakes or a loaf of bread to the *agalma* and then place it on the plate to the right.

Offer fruit (especially grapes, apples, pomegranates and figs) to the *agalma* and then place them on the plate to the left.

Offer three eggs to the *agalma* and then place them on the plate to the right.

Offer honeycomb to the *agalma* and then place it on the plate to the left.

Fill the *rhyton* with wine and hail the God by his various names. With each round pour some into the cauldron and then take a sip yourself. Do this until all of the wine is gone, and then set the *rhyton* in front of the cauldron.

Take out *krotala* (castanets or rattle) and shake rhythmically as you pray to the God or ask for blessings.

Let the remainder of the ritual unfold as it will, though dancing and singing are strongly encouraged.

When you are finished, kiss the *agalma* and extinguish the candles.

Leave the offerings for as long as you are able, up to three days, and then dispose of them in your customary manner. Return the ritual tools to the *kiste* when you are done.

You may add whatever prayers and sacred formulae you wish or perform these actions in silence, except where directed to speak.

Perform this ritual completely at the new or full moon; a simplified version may suffice for weekly or daily observance.

If you need to make cleansing water (Greek *chernips*), but aren't able to light a laurel leaf on fire and dip it into the basin of water (for instance, because you're at an event that doesn't allow open flame, or your roommate is sensitive to smoke and other strong smells, or you're a teenager practicing Hellenismos on the down low, or you just want to do things a little differently) you may use the following simple recipe.

For this you will need:

- ○ Water
- ○ A bowl
- ○ An ivy leaf

This form of *chernips* uses ivy because it is the sacred plant of Dionysos; indeed the God was even called Kissos, "the ivy" for in many respects it is his double. Ivy is a plant that, like Dionysos, has two births. The first birth is when it sends out its shade-seeking shoots with their distinctive leaves. But after the dormant months of winter, when the God himself is rejuvenated it sends out another shoot, one that grows upright and towards the light, thus honoring the return of the vibrant God. When the fire of Zeus' lightning consumed Semele — with Dionysos still in her womb — it was the cool ivy that surrounded and protected him. When the Satyrs were first given wine they were driven mad by its effects. Dionysos placed ivy around them and the plant extinguished the heat of the wine, allowing them to regain their senses — though ivy itself produces a strong poison which has intoxicating properties. The ivy leaf was tattooed or branded on the bodies of Dionysian initiates, and still is. Dionysos and his Mainades are always pictured wearing crowns of ivy.

Hold the leaf in your palm high above your head, like a tendril seeking the sun, and then slowly bring it down, plunging it into the bowl of water, as when young Dionysos plunged into the sea and the waiting arms of Thetis.

As you are bringing the leaf down feel the power and vitality of the God flow into the receptive basin.

Then lift the bowl to the level of your heart and recite *Orphic Hymn 47* to Perikionios (who is twined around the pillar) as follows:

I call upon Bakchos Perikionios, giver of wine,
who enveloped all of Kadmos' house
and with his might checked and calmed the heaving earth
when the blazing thunderbolt and the raging gale stirred all the
   land.
Then everyone's bonds sprang loose.
Blessed reveler, come with joyous heart!

And then carry the bowl around your ritual space, using the leaf of ivy to sprinkle the soothing and protective water as you repeat the previously mentioned mantra taken from the *Orations* of Aelius Aristides:

Nothing can be so firmly bound
by illness, by wrath or by fortune
that cannot be released by the Lord Dionysos.

Envision the drops of water cleansing whatever they touch and neutralizing any harmful effects through the power of Dionysos and feel it spread out until the whole space is covered in green, throbbing vegetation.

Orpheus, for instance, brought from Egypt most of his mystic ceremonies, the orgiastic rites that accompanied his wanderings, and his fabulous account of his experiences in Hades. For the rite of Osiris is the same as that of Dionysos and that of Isis very similar to that of Demeter, the names alone having been interchanged; and the punishments in Hades of the unrighteous, the Fields of the Righteous, and the fantastic conceptions, current among the many, which are figments of the imagination — all these were introduced by Orpheus in imitation of the Egyptian funeral customs. (Diodoros Sikeliotes, *Library of History* 1.93)

1.2

Cleanse yourself with a purifying bath.

1.3

Dress yourself in proper clean attire, placing the garland-crown upon your head.

1.4

Prepare yourself mentally and spiritually.

2.1

Take up the vessel of holy water.

2.2

Walk the circuit of your ritual space, sprinkling everything you encounter with the holy water to purify it.

2.3

Recite the following as you make your circuit:

You are washed clean by the life-giving waters of the Nile! You are pure! No man has set foot on you, for you are the primordial mound rising from the broad depths of the Ocean at the First Time. You are pure!

Commentary

1.2

Egyptian temple complexes had pools built in so that the priests could bathe before they entered the sanctuary. (Serge Sauneron, *The Priests of Ancient Egypt* p. 36) Herodotos remarked that the Egyptian priests bathed three or four times a day (2.37), and the lowest rank of Egyptian priests was called *wabu*, "the pure/clean ones." Cleanliness — both internally and externally — was of paramount importance.

There is, however, another reason why it is important to bathe before performing ritual: the act of doing so puts us in the proper mindset and helps spiritually regenerate us. For the Greeks and Egyptians, water was the holiest of all of the elements. Every river, spring, lake, stream and well had its presiding Spirit, Deity or Nymph. Both Greeks and Egyptians agreed that water was the primordial element out of which all life emerged. (Plutarch, *On Isis and Osiris* 364 D) In Greece Okeanos and Tethys were the divine progenitors of the Gods themselves (*Iliad* 14.200-244), while in Egypt we find in the *Pyramid Texts* the belief that originally only the watery abyss of Nun existed, before Atum caused the first mound of earth to emerge, upon which the Gods could stand and life could flourish. The annual flood of the Nile made life possible in the rain-scarce lands that bordered the Egyptian desert. Without it, there would only be death and desolate destruction. As the river overflowed its banks, it deposited the rich black alluvial soil that the farmers needed to tend their crops so that they could feed their children and life could prosper. Neilos was a potent, generative force: barren women would drink from it to conceive; the sick would wash away their illness in it; during the Imperial period the water from the river was collected and sent to Isiac temples as far away as Rome, Spain, Germany, and England to be used for purification and renewal; and any who drowned in its depths was granted instant immortality and provided cultus as deified heroes.

Meditate on this as you bathe before your ritual. All rivers are connected; not only do they flow into each other many times, but there is only a finite number of water molecules in existence, which are constantly being recycled through evaporation and rainfall. No matter where you are, at least some of the water molecules that you are bathing in belonged at one point to the most holy Neilos! So as you submerge yourself in the watery depths, think about yourself bathing in the Nile, or going back to the primordial waters of creation, Okeanos and Nun. Feel yourself washed clean, all the grime and pollution that you encounter on a daily basis dissolving away from you, your frustrations and fears drowning in the depths so that you are focused, holy, and clean. Feel the healing, generative powers of the water flow into you, suffusing your spirit. Feel yourself come into contact with that primordial divine potency that grants life, abundance, beauty, and purity. And when you emerge from the waters, emerge as if you were just coming into being, as things did in the First Time, when the world was still new. You are a pure creature, reborn and refreshed. All of your faults, your doubts, the hardships you've had to bear are washed away; all that remains is your love and devotion to the Gods. You are now fit to stand before them, pure in the presence of the pure ones, as it says in the Bacchic Orphic gold leaf from Rome:

> A: I come pure from the pure, Queen of the Underworld, Eukles and Eubouleus, noble child of Zeus! I have this gift of Memory, prized by men!
> B: Caecilia Secundina, come, made divine by the Law!

If you don't have the chance to take a full bath before the ritual — say, if you're doing this in a public place or with a group of people — then use some of the holy water to purify yourself.

Especially wash your hands and face, and place some over your eyes, in your ears and mouth. Feel the water enter into you and cleanse your body.

1.3

Some people dress up in replicas of ancient garments or have special ritual attire which they reserve solely for their worship. This is a fine thing, especially if it helps put the individual in the proper state of mind. (The act of dressing up in strange clothing can send signals to the brain letting it know that one is not in a normal setting, and therefore to act accordingly, to delineate between the mundane and sacred sides of one's persona; these vestments, further, through their exclusive contact with the holy can become imbued with its properties, and can thus become powerful talismans of a sort.)

However, I would like to point out that this is not in any way necessary. There is nothing inherently sacred about ancient costumes; the Greco-Romans wore chitons and togas during their rituals because that's what they wore the rest of the time. If a modern-day person were to put on clean, nice clothing — perhaps a little dressier than jeans and a t-shirt but nothing as extravagant as a tuxedo — then they would be doing exactly as the ancients had done. So what you choose to wear is entirely up to you.

However, there are some considerations. First off, it's best to wear linen during ritual. Wool and leather were forbidden inside the Egyptian temples (as well as several Greek ones) because these came from unclean animals. (Herodotos 2.81) We also find numerous injunctions to wear white clothing, as white symbolized purity (Sauneron pp. 40-42) — although less frequently we find other colors suggested, such as black for

Isis (*Orphic Hymn* 42), saffron for Dionysos (Seneca, *Oedipus* 401) or Hekate (*Orphic Hymn* 1), and so forth. The magical papyri numerous times forbid anything red to be used (*PGM* LXII. 1-24), since this color was associated with Seth-Typhon and thus was proper only to him.

If you associate specific colors with a deity, you can wear these as a way to feel closer to them — but otherwise you should go with white or black, and try to avoid clothing with brand names or slogans on them, as that can be distracting. It's best if you have a set of clothing reserved solely for temple use — a robe or modern Arabic *thoub*, perhaps, or loose-fitting shirt and trousers, like those worn by Yoga practitioners. Another consideration is foot-wear. Generally speaking, the sneakers you wear to work and play aren't appropriate inside a holy space. Egyptian priests wore special palm-sandals or went barefoot (*Instruction for Merikare* 17), and you should too. If you are doing the ritual outside, however, exceptions can certainly be made.

The *stephanos* or garland-crown was an important feature in ancient Greek worship, and was also worn by Egyptian priests. They considered it essential for prayer, and donned them every time they entered a temple, took part in a festal banquet, or did something important such as speak in front of the council or claim their victory at the games. The crown signified joyousness and festivity: it drew a tangible divide between normal reality (when one didn't wear them) and being in the presence of the sacred (when one did). Placing the crown on one's head imbued the wearer with the properties of the crown. They received generally the abundance and life of the fresh green leaves of the plant, and different qualities depending on what the crown was made of: purity for Apollon's laurel, civilizing intelligence for Athene's olive, heated ecstasy for Dionysos' vine, cool for his ivy; beauty and love for the rose and violet of Aphrodite; chthonic fertility for the myrtle, and so forth. (See Athenaios' *Deipnosophistai* for a lengthy treatment of the symbolism of festal crowns.)

If you do not have the time or inclination to string flowers and leaves together into a temporary crown, you can make a permanent artificial one using strands of plastic vegetation found at most craft stores. These can be quite lovely and serve as decoration for your shrine when you're not wearing them.

1.4

At this time take a couple moments to get yourself ready internally. Clear your mind of all external concerns. Several temples had injunctions to maintain reverent silence once one entered the *temenos* and that all profane things were forbidden beyond that point (*IEdfou* 3.361.1). This held not just for unclean persons or taboo items — but also for errant thoughts, at least according to an inscription at Asklepios' temple at Epidauros.

Just as you have prepared yourself externally to enter the presence of the divine, you must do so internally as well, making your soul a worthy receptacle for the divine. You shouldn't be worrying about what your asshole co-workers said earlier in the day, how you need to balance your checkbook, what stupid celebrities are dating this month, or even concerns you might have about how successful the ritual will be. Close your eyes and take several deep breaths, calming yourself and filling your heart with love for the Gods.

Call up their image inside your mind: think about their epithets and attributes and all of the symbols and ideas associated with them. Feel yourself relaxing, slipping into a reverent mood. Let desire for the sacred take hold of you until you are trembling to be in their presence.

2.1

This holy water should be prepared beforehand, either before you take your bath or before things are set up if you're doing the ritual with others. There are a number of different methods for making it.

Option 1:

> Gather the water from a river, lake, or spring or set out a vessel to collect pure rain water. Because this water comes directly from the divinities, it is considered holy by nature and requires no further preparation. You should, however thank the Nymphai or Spirits of the water for their gift, and leave something in return for taking it.

Option 2:

> Fill a bowl with water, either bottled spring water or from the tap. Drop a couple granules of *natron* (salt and sodium bicarbonate or baking soda) into the water and let them dissolve. As you stir the mixture together, envision the *natron* mingling with the water and purifying it as if with a golden light like that of the pure rays of the Sun, transforming it into a salty substance like the tears that Isis wept over her beloved Osiris, which removed the grime and blood and made his body fit for burial. If you choose, recite words to that effect over the water, or simply visualize the whole process.

Option 3:

> Fill a bowl with water, either bottled spring water or from the tap or water you've collected from somewhere special. Take a branch (can be of laurel or pine or some other sacred tree) light it — with or without saying a blessing — and then dip the flaming branch into the water,

extinguishing it. The purity arises from the meeting of all the elements.

2.2

You can either use a branch or whisk for this, or simply use your own fingers. Dip it into the holy water and then sprinkle whatever you come across. Use this method to purify any participants in the ritual, as well as all of the ritual tools, the offerings, the altar, the image of the God, etc. The idea is to have the water touch everything — not necessarily to douse it, so be conservative in your sprinkling!

Only do this, however, if you have already undergone preliminary purification yourself. You don't want to put your dirty (from a religious perspective) finger in water you intend to cleanse the sacred space with after all.

2.3

Repeat this phrase as many times as necessary until you complete the circuit. As you speak the words think about the imagery associated with them: feel the sacred space becoming clean and renewed, full of the creative potential of life.

Dionysian Purity

What role should miasma and purification play in the devotional life of an average Dionysian?

Well, first off, I don't think that there is such a thing as an "average Dionysian." We are all unique, our experiences with him are unique and what he expects and requires of us is unique. That means that if you want to know what you should be doing for him the person you need to be going to about this isn't me but Dionysos himself. And if you don't have a strong enough connection to him that you can just ask and reasonably expect an accurate response (or if there's some other temporary reason why your signal clarity is bad) you can always resort to divination (that's why it's there!) or consult someone who is a diviner or doing oracular work whose results you respect and trust (that's why they are there!). Alternately you can ask him to show you through signs or just experiment and figure out what works and why through trial and error.

Another important option is to look back at what the ancient Dionysians did and build up your practices from that since it's fairly safe to assume that an approach that proved successful for them is still more or less going to meet with favor from the God, keeping in mind two caveats: (1) Gods, like anyone else, are capable of changing their minds over time (whether they actually have or not is an entirely separate matter, but to deny them such agency deprives them of personhood and that seems the height of impiety to me); as well as (2) context is everything.

Even if they had not reached our level of saturation, the Greeks were a highly literate people so we have an abundance of primary source material to draw upon — material that comes from and reflects all strata of their society. In fact, we have far more of this material than folks seeking to restore and breathe new life into the polytheistic traditions of the ancient Celtic, Slavic and Germanic peoples. And luckily enough for us, much of it has to do with the cult of Dionysos.

Therefore it is absolutely vital that one know how to evaluate this material within its proper context. Where does this text come from, what was going on at the time of its composition, what is the agenda of its author, how well does it reflect wider cultural norms, etc., are the type of questions that we should be asking ourselves any time that we read an ancient source. (And reading that source in translation should bring up all sorts of other questions.)

For instance, we may derive an understanding about certain aspects of domestic Dionysian cultus (a topic sadly under-discussed if you ask me) by reading accounts of Olympias or Pompeiia Agrippinilla or what was done during Anthesteria — but in the case of Anthesteria you've got a specific festival dealing with inversion, transgression and pollution; Pompeiia Agrippinilla was a wealthy noblewoman who led a private mystic cult association; and Olympias was fairly unconventional even by the standards of Hellenistic royalty, considering the degree of zealousness with which her piety manifested. (Many preferred to call her superstitious since her piety drew on primitive Thraco-Makedonian traditions and had a strong Orphic influence.) None of these will give you a proper indication of what a simple Dionysian on the streets of Athens might have done or believed.

Likewise a lot of information comes from private cult associations, whether those dedicated to enacting certain mysteries or groups consisting of nothing more than a bunch of guys who liked to get out of the house from time to time, get drunk, make business contacts, perform weird rituals that outsiders weren't privy to and have their funerals paid for and attended by members of the club — as we find, for instance, in the Athenian Iobacchoi, whose statutes read like something from the Masons or Oddfellows.

It is also important to remain mindful of the distinctions between private and civic cultus, as well as the special requirements to gain admittance to a temple. Most of the information we have, in fact, is concerned with these temples and reading through that material makes one thing abundantly clear. Each temple operated as an autonomous and localized body and a number of factors shaped what constituted an acceptable degree of purity for that temple. For instance we never find just a temple to Dionysos, even if it's referred to that way for the sake of convenience by later commentators or even contemporary sources. What you find is a temple to Dionysos en Limnaios or Dionysos Bakcheios or Dionysos Aisymnetes or Dionysos Psilax and so on and so forth. Each *epiklesis* refers to a different form of the God and each of those forms had specific functions and associations that distinguished it from the others. Therefore purity requirements were specially tailored to enable the individual to come into the presence of the God and align with him in this particular form. And while there were broad commonalities there were also instances of considerable divergence, which could result in conflicting requirements among the temples. This is why most temples had a long list of sacred regulations posted at the entrance so that visitors would know what had to be done for them to be in the proper state to proceed beyond that point and people didn't just assume, "Since Dionysos and I are buds I don't have to obey the rules!" or "This is how we did it back home, so by gum this is how I'm gonna do it here!"

That just isn't how ancient religion works.

I was first compelled to think seriously about these matters a number of years ago when I encountered a sacred law code from a Dionysion (temple of Dionysos) in Roman Asia Minor. At least, that's where I think the temple was located, but it's been a while and I unfortunately didn't bother to write the information down at the time, something I've been kicking myself over ever since. So they're going through the sorts of things you find in these codes — if you've eaten such and such food you are considered impure for so many days, you must abstain from sex with your wife for X number of days, Y for a free person and Z for a slave. (Interestingly, although this is a concern in the temples of most of the Greek Gods, a number of Dionysian temple codes leave out any mention of sex though they exhaustively cover other areas, suggesting that Dionysos might not have had the same concerns in this area that his fellows did. Except that there are also plenty of inscriptions that do mention it.) And then I read something that stopped me short: a woman who aborts her fetus is liable to the same degree of impurity as a murderer.

What made this so shocking is that you simply do not find that distinction made anywhere else. Not in other Dionysions, and as far as I'm aware, not in the temples of any of the other Greek Gods either. The translator of the text was just as surprised by it and remarked that unlike us the Greeks generally did not regard fetuses as independent living beings and it only became a child once it was acknowledged and accepted by the father. Even after birth, children were legally treated as the property of their parents (read: father) with infant exposure being a common practice, especially among the lower classes for whom resources were scarce. And yet at this temple, at least, all life was sacred and the mother had to undergo extensive purification before she was permitted to return.

The translator, unfortunately, did not include any details about the form of Dionysos honored at the temple, though it is interesting to note that the young (whether human or animal) are given a special place within the cult of Dionysos. Think about the Maenads nursing baby animals, the imagery and rites associated with Dionysos as Zagreus and Liknites, the way that children received their first tastes of wine on Choes, participated in grand civic processions at the Dionysia and Oschophoria and underwent rites of passage and new clothing representing their new status in the Italian Liberalia and similar festivals in Greece. But what *really* drives home the point is that the greatest punishment meted out by the God in myth was to drive a person insane so that they slew and usually cannibalized their children. Although this inscription is perhaps unique within the realm of Greek religion it isn't all that surprising that a temple of Dionysos would demonstrate such concern over young life.

Of course I bring this up to demonstrate the diversity that one finds within the cult of the God, *not* to suggest that Dionysos somehow hates women who have had abortions. It may have simply been that the form of Dionysos honored there was especially or primarily concerned with promoting fertility, and abortion — by definition — is the antithesis of fertility. Or that it was felt that women who terminated their pregnancies needed the psychological consolation that going through rites of passage and purification ceremonies confer and this wasn't being properly addressed within the society at large so they instituted these special rituals. Or something. The truth is we don't know anything more than that someone in charge of putting together this compilation of sacred law for this particular Dionysion felt the need to include such a clause. We don't even know how rigorously it was enforced.

And that is why I don't think it is particularly helpful to take a single written source and extrapolate about Dionysian worship in general from it. As a rough guideline, sure. But when things were clearly done differently depending on when and where you're at and there was often massive contradictions involved, a little more thought needs to be put in if you're going to do Dionysos worship properly.

In order to understand why it's necessary for miasma to be removed you need to understand what miasma is.

Miasma is not sin and for the most part it is a morally neutral condition. Obviously there are certain acts such as murder, blasphemy, sacrilege and attending marriages that are simply wrong as well as being miasmic, but the miasma produced by these acts is quite apart from their wrongness and most forms of miasma simply arise from our natural human condition. They're what happen when we brush up against the boundaries of mortality — birth, sex, illness, madness, and death all impart it, yet life would not be possible without them. So don't think of miasma as an inherently bad thing — it's just something that repels the divine like a pair of magnets turned back to back, or more accurately it clouds our perception so that we have difficulty discerning their presence around us.

If it helps you conceptualize it better, envision miasma as a spiritual substance, something analogous to a cloudy mist or dirty film that collects around us like soap scum or a black, sticky resin that's incredibly difficult to get off your fingers once it's there. It's like the afterbirth of creation, the sweat of mortality — and when left to accumulate it befuddles the senses, makes you dull and dense, dragging you down. Just as you'd want to be clean if you were meeting an honored guest (let alone a romantic partner!) so should you desire to come before your Gods and Spirits in a clean state.

The most effective way to remove miasma is by performing rituals of purification. These rituals always contain a physical component, because the Greeks understood physical and spiritual as part of a continuum, as Suda s.v. *Hêraïskos* makes clear:

> Hence his life also reached such a point that his soul always resided in hidden sanctuaries as he practiced not only his native rites in Egypt but also those of other nations, wherever there was something left of these. Heraiskos became a Bakchos, as a dream

designated him and he traveled widely, receiving many initiations. Heraiskos actually had a natural talent for distinguishing between religious statues that were animated and those that were not. For as soon as he looked at one his heart was struck by a sensation of the divine and he gave a start in his body and his soul, as though seized by the God. If he was not moved in such a fashion then the statue was soulless and had no share of divine inspiration. In this way he distinguished the secret statue of Aion which the Alexandrians worshiped as being possessed by the God, who was both Osiris and Adonis at the same time according to some mystical union. There was also something in Heraiskos' nature that rejected defilements of nature. For instance, if he heard any unclean woman speaking, no matter where or how, he immediately got a headache, and this was taken as a sign that she was menstruating.

You purify by manipulating natural and primordial elements. Look at what the Greeks purified with — fire and water and fragrance and plant matter and sound and movement and blood and mud and wool and oil and milk and wine and many other similar things, the more effective ones combining a variety of methods. There was always something *real* to it. You don't purify by thinking happy thoughts and reciting some pretty rhyming couplets. You gotta dislodge that shit! No reason you can't take a sacred bath and smudge and asperge yourself and the area with *chernips* and then again with wine while chanting the epithets of your God and dancing. No such thing as being "too pure," unless you happen to be on certain particular paths, I say.

I strongly recommend that folks experiment with different methods and combinations of methods in order to determine what works best for them and their divinities. Note how you feel while you're doing it, once you've moved on to the devotional or working portion of the ritual and also once everything has commenced. Sometimes it's only much later on that we realize, "Hey, my spirits have lifted, everything seems cleaner, fresher, less stagnant; I don't feel all closed in, my connection to the Gods has improved, and why even my luck is getting better!" Should you find yourself saying that, I think it safe to assume that you have properly conducted a purification. But if you're in doubt, you can always confirm it through divination.

Once you've hit on something that works you should stick with it so that that set of ritual actions will accumulate the power and weight of tradition through repetition. Don't worry if your practices seem piecemeal and unlike what the ancients did because there's no way to perfectly recreate what they did. You may have a proper replica oil lamp and incense-burner but do you have a black puppy you're willing to cut in half?

No? I didn't think so. Besides, innovation and cobbling stuff together is exactly what the ancients did!

There wasn't one all-purpose purification ritual that they used. People drew on a common body of practices and concepts, but with enough flexibility that they could adapt it to meet the needs of the situation. In fact it was the job of religious specialists to advise and direct people through this process or create something new if circumstances so required. It's interesting to watch the novel ways that these disparate elements were combined so that you find widely divergent groups doing roughly the same things. Therefore as long as you're drawing from the well of tradition and make an effort to understand what it is you're doing and why you're doing it and are careful not to bring together disharmonious elements I think you should be alright, regardless of what you end up doing. And if you aren't successful, do more and try different things.

You should also make an effort to avoid contamination as much as possible leading up to a big ritual. The attention that doing so requires will help you remain focused and mindful, making for a better ritual experience in general. Any time that such exposure is unavoidable — as it so often is, especially if you're leading a rich and deeply engaged life — then you should absolutely take the precaution of doing purification because even if you don't feel it that doesn't mean the miasma isn't there.

In fact miasma can result from internal conditions beyond our control as much as anything external, so unless you've got total mastery of your thoughts and emotions — and if we're honest, none of us can claim that — you're probably walking around in a low-grade state of miasma all the time.

Unless you have a prior arrangement with the divinity and are constantly doing devotions at their shrine, you should at least perform a minimal level of purification any time that you approach them, any time that you set foot in their territory. At the very least you are demonstrating right protocol and proper respect through your actions and it helps signify to yourself that you are leaving behind the concerns and bounds of mundane existence in order to engage in holy activity. It helps set your intent and focus and all of us, no matter how experienced and intimate we are with the Gods, require that. (If you got crystal clear voices in your head 24/7 you're either a saint or a fucking lunatic.) That's why when I'm doing anything beyond the most casual and spontaneous of devotions (and plenty of times even then) I start off with some form of purification, no matter how simple, especially if I'm doing something at a shrine or for a divinity outside of my very small personal pantheon.

Holiness and power emanate from a shrine that is enlivened by worship. Think of it as a benevolent radiation that spills out from the presence of a divinity, it's *charis* or grace. This is why we must be in a pure state to approach the shrine.

Consequently that means that whatever comes into contact with the shrine takes those qualities into itself. Thus something like a food offering, an *ex voto* or any of the material objects that constitute the shrine must thereafter be treated differently than you would ordinary objects. Since the shrine is essentially a foothold of the deity in this world and a battery that collects and stores up their abundant life energy that is produced during manifestation (varying in degree with the level at which that occurs) it is necessary to maintain a clean and orderly shrine and remove perishable objects before they succumb to decay and rot, as these belong to the antithesis of life. (Even if death is what life arises from, they exist on different frequencies and so repulse each other. It is also worth noting that there are Gods and especially Spirits who are not life-aligned and their spaces will naturally require different treatment.)

Since these objects have soaked up the effulgence of divinity, when it comes time to dispose of them one must treat them with special care. In my article "After the Smoke Clears" (found in *Balance of the Two Lands*), I outline a variety of methods for properly disposing of these offerings, but I believe that the most appropriate method is to burn or bury them or add them to composting if that is possible. It is also permissible to expose them provided that they are biodegradable and are not toxic to the animals of the area. Whatever method you employ, be sure to remove the items in a timely fashion so that they do not pollute the shrine through their decay. Even if you are not concerned with the religious purity aspect, it's slovenly and disgusting to let rotten shit just sit there in your home stinking up the place. And while I'm loathe to speak on behalf of the Gods and Spirits I can tell you that I'd be offended if someone claimed to be keeping space sacred for me but couldn't be arsed to look after it or remove stuff before it got all slimy and stinky. But who knows, there could be Gods and Spirits out there who aren't bothered by that sort of thing or hell even require it of their devotees. Y'all know about Demeter's pig pit, right?

The reason I'm so fond of the idea of composting perishable offerings is because it puts them back into the web of life and what's more it does so while those items are imbued with divine potency. Imagine if you raised your own plants which were then offered to your divinities — plants that were nourished on the offerings of the past. That is a powerful chain you are creating there and if you share some of those offerings in a feast with your divinities then you'll be taking even more of that divine potency into you, bringing you yourself more directly into the web. It's like a concrete expression of *charis*, the reciprocal relationship we maintain with the Gods and Spirits. Something that I feel is the heart of true piety.

Cleanliness Is Next To Godliness

I feel weird whenever people come to me with questions about miasma and ritual purity because it really emphasizes how different my spiritual path is from the one that so many others walk. A lot of the advice I end up giving isn't actually stuff that I myself do because, frankly, most people have no business doing the kind of stuff that I do unless they've undergone the sort of initiations that I have. Even then it's a fine line and there are dangerous consequences for straying too far. I've run into some real trouble over the years because of what I've been called to do, the energies I work with — and that has given me a unique perspective on why some of these rules are in place.

These customs provide a buffer between us and the elemental forces of creation which is necessary because too deep or prolonged an exposure to such power warps the soul and diminishes our humanity, making it harder to function in ordinary society. These rules and practices are a way back to regular life and consciousness, a process of reintegration and the reestablishment of order to our personal world. Most forms of miasma, after all, are concerned with the boundaries of mortality: birth, sex, death, madness, etc.

Although contact with these things pollutes us it is important to keep in mind that this pollution carries with it no moral stigma. Miasma is not a state of sin from which we are in desperate need of deliverance — in fact we often have moral and religious obligations to engage in activities that cause pollution as when we conduct the proper ceremonies of mourning for the deceased (which their posthumous fate may depend on) or a soldier doing one's duty for their homeland and people or couples begetting children to ensure that the family line continues and there will be future generations to honor the Gods and ancestors. Even though these acts are right and necessary they still impart miasma and that impurity must be ritually addressed.

Our modern culture has lost its innate sense of the sacred and the rituals by which this territory is navigated. Without them, people have a much harder time finding their way back. Consider how many women suffer from postpartum depression or all the military personnel whose lives are destroyed by PTSD or the folks who years later are still grieving the loss of a loved one. It's because these individuals experienced a violent rupture with the ordinary and yet were thrust right back into the currents of life without anything marking their internal transformation, no means of ritually demarcating this passage from one state to another. They are expected to behave as if everything has gone back to normal even though their experiences have left them feeling as if nothing is the way it was before and never will be again. I do not mean to suggest that miasma and the rituals associated with it are purely psychological, therapy through theater. There's a whole lot more going on there, particularly on an esoteric spiritual level — but it isn't necessary to understand all of that to see the tangible benefits that come with performing these ceremonies.

There also seems to be a lot of misunderstanding about the role of the Gods in all of this. Some people are profoundly bothered by the notion that miasma interrupts our relationship with them. They argue that when we are in such a state we are often most in need of the comforting presence of our divinities, so the idea that they would distance themselves from us is doubly cruel. This often brings up a lot of unresolved mental baggage people have held on to from their Christian upbringing, notions of divine judgment and wrath and never being good enough, pure enough, pious enough to warrant love and acceptance.

First off, I would say that a lot of people don't understand what miasma precluded in antiquity. It was primarily concerned with access to holy places such as groves, mountains, wayside shrines and temples. The temples in particular were regarded as the abodes of the Gods and repositories of their awesome power and consequently for a person to set foot in them required that person to undergo a greater than normal degree of purification, especially since religious functionaries were exposed to this power on a deeper level and a more regular basis than some random pilgrim visiting the site on a festival day. (Think about the extra precautions taken by dentists and x-ray technicians who are daily exposed to radiation. It's such small doses that it won't harm you if you're just getting your teeth fixed but being constantly surrounded by it they have to act more carefully.) In fact most festivals were conducted outside the temple and most people were never permitted past a certain point within it and certainly not where the cult image was housed.

Most of the purity codes and sacred regulations that have come down to us are concerned with access to temples and the proper performance of priestly offices — not the affairs of the average citizen and how they conducted their personal worship in front of their domestic shrine. No matter how deep in a state of miasma one was in they could still pray to their Gods and perform rudimentary ritual actions. Indeed purification would not have been possible without carrying out these ceremonies so it is absurd to suggest that one should cease all religious activity while in this state. Indeed we have accounts of the Gods and Spirits making numerous battlefield epiphanies and coming to the aid of women in distressed labor and all manner of things like that, so just because a playwright used a Goddess abandoning her chosen hero as he expired as a plot device does not mean that we should surmise that the Gods will have nothing to do with us while we are polluted. It can certainly be more difficult to feel their presence or receive communications from them at such times, but I suspect that this has more to do with impurity clouding our perception than it does divinities actively disengaging from us.

However, even if that is the case I would argue that it is their prerogative to do so as Gods. They are not obligated to shower us with attention and blessings and if they do not desire to or cannot because of something within their nature bear witness to such events, it is their right to remove themselves from that situation. They may even be doing so as a boon to us, however much it may not seem like that at the time. Facing such things alone gives us a sort of tragic dignity, allows us to suffer and experience what we must in solitude. While in such a state we are rarely at our best. It can be messy and gross and full of emotional turmoil, our thoughts erratic and perhaps expressing things we would never tolerate from ourselves ordinarily. I'd much rather have Dionysos take a step back, let me get my shit in order and really deal with things the way I need to and then approach him when I'm ready than feel the weight of his presence looming over me, observing the whole sordid and nasty ordeal. I am not actually permitted such grace because of the nature of our relationship, which requires me to be open to him always, in all things in my life — but that's a discussion for another time. Instead of angrily berating the Gods for their perceived absence at such times, we should view it as the kindness it truly is.

Lastly I would say that even if we do not feel that such periods of withdrawal and reintegration marked by our rituals of purification are necessary, we should still do them anyway.

It is a sign of respect, a demonstration of our willingness to be at our best when we come before the holy powers, an extension of hospitality which should govern all of our interactions with others regardless of their place in the great chain of being. If you were going to have an audience with an important person would you show up in filthy, ratty clothes, hair a mess, stinking of the brothel or worse? Hopefully not! (And if you answered yes, consider yourself permanently uninvited to all rituals — and hell, all social engagements — I host. Unless you're a *sadhu* or something similar. Then we're cool.)

Unless you're some kind of stank ass trifling fool (or a *sadhu*) you're going to put some thought and effort into your appearance and be on your best behavior while around them. Certainly the Gods are worthy of the same decorum you would show to a politician or celebrity or your boss at work — indeed I'd say they are due even greater consideration!

More, the act of carrying out these preliminary rites of purification help focus the mind and prepare oneself for the solemnity of the devotion one is about to engage in. Even if it's just taking a couple moments to quietly center and set the tone by sprinkling some sacred water, fumigating with aromatic herbs, or scattering the barley that can be enough to shift from mundane to sacred mode. Those who neglect such attention to detail in their rites often do not have very satisfying religious lives.

So that's my take on all of this. Although I am a lot more comfortable with impurity than most people — indeed much of my work involves activities and cultivating mental and spiritual states that are deeply miasmic, which I won't go into here as it's not relevant to other people's practice — I still observe basic protocol in such matters, especially when I am engaged in worship for divinities other than Dionysos and Arachne or worshiping alongside human people. I do these rites, in fact, for all but my most spontaneous and informal devotional activities because the mental and spiritual benefits they bring about more than make up for the minuscule inconvenience involved in doing them. In fact, I'll go through the steps even when I'm just planning to make standard offerings at my shrine and then spend the evening drinking and smoking while in a loose devotional headspace because this act helps set my intent.

None of this is overly complicated despite people's tendency to over-think everything, which so often is what gets them in trouble. If you wait until you've got it all sorted out you're never going to get anywhere. Just do what has been prescribed and trust that these traditions of our ancestors which flourished for thousands of years are effective and meaningful even if you do not yet understand why. Only by immersing yourself in and directly engaging with these traditions will that understanding come to you, if it is meant to.

I'd like to close with a few words about religious prescriptions or taboos (keeping in mind that the English taboo is quite different from the Polynesian *tapu*.) You can tell a lot about the path a person is on and the Powers they serve through the taboos they observe, which is why one of the first conversations I have with other devotees, priests, god-spouses or spirit-workers is a rundown of what is tabooed to them.

Taboos serve a number of vitally important functions. To begin with they are a kind of perpetual sacrifice and I do not mean sacrifice in the modern sense of "to give up something of value" although that is certainly a component of this, but rather in the original sense of the Latin which is "to make sacred" or "to give over to the Gods." Adhering to taboos blurs the artificial boundaries we set up between mundane and spiritual existence. It is saying that my religion is so deeply woven into the fabric of my life that it influences my choices about what I wear, what I eat and drink, what I purchase, what activities I engage in and so forth. I am mindful of the Gods and Spirits always, not just when I'm standing before their shrine in worship. It is saying that they matter more to me than my own desires and convenience.

Taboos also strengthen the bonds of solidarity that one shares with one's co-religionists, assuming that one's taboos are communal in nature and not personally imposed by one's Gods and Spirits. For instance it was common among ancient Dionysians to abstain from wool garments and avoid certain animal foods. Other Greeks did not have these restrictions and so it marked the Dionysians off as a separate people, sometimes subject to mockery by society at large. In order to maintain their unique identity some Dionysians went so far as to establish their own private cemeteries so that the blessed initiates need not spend eternity in the company of the impure. Likewise it was only by scrupulously observing the customs of their ancestors that the Jews managed to preserve their autonomy in the face of such prolonged and bitter attempts to assimilate and eradicate them.

Cleansing and Consecration of the Diviner

As part of your preparation for a divination session, you may want to run yourself a bath (to which may be added wine, milk, honey or appropriate herbs) or a shower.

Once you feel appropriately calm and cleansed, pour water over your head and say:

> My Lord Dionysos, cleanse and prepare my mind that I may think only holy thoughts appropriate to work of *mantike*, and of you.

Pour water into each ear and say:

> My Lord Dionysos, remove all obstacles that I may hear your voice and your voice only.

Pour water over your eyes and say:

> My Lord Dionysos, permit me to see only what you would reveal to me.

Swish some water in your mouth and say:

> My Lord Dionysos, bind my tongue that it may speak only your words, truly and clearly.

Wash your hands and say:

> My Lord Dionysos, I consecrate these hands to your service, especially so that you may move the tools of divination as you need to.

Wash your body and say:

> My Lord Dionysos, strengthen my body and soul that I might bear the terrible grace of your spirit upon and within me.

Dress appropriately, preferably crowning yourself with ivy, and be earnest and focused in your activities until it is time to begin the session.

THE ORACLE BOOK OF SANNION THE ORPHEOTELEST

This problem affects the doctrine in the so-called Orphic poems as well; for he says that the soul, being carried by the winds, enters from the universe into living creatures when they inhale. (Aristotle, *De Anima* 410b)

When you are ready to begin a session, hold two coins in your hand and blow upon them. Toss the coins and:

If **both** should land **face up**, Dionysos is satisfied with your preparations and you may proceed.

If the **right** should land **face up** but the left face down, then make offerings to the Ancestors and toss the coins again.

If the **left** should land **face up** but the right face down, then make offerings to the Gods and toss the coins again.

If **both** should land **face down**, then something is out of alignment and Dionysos will not answer your questions at this time.

The one who greatly hunts, as the writer of the *Alkmeonis* said "Mistress Earth, and Zagreus highest of all the Gods." That is, Dionysos. (*Etymologicum Gudianum* s.v. *Zagreus*)

The Net of Zagreus is woven as follows. First draw a large circle and then divide it into eight sections, labeling each thusly:

Σ   Ψ   Θ   Π   Ο   Α   Φ   Μ

You can make a permanent Net (with wood, cloth, or on laminated paper) or weave it anew for each reading.

The letters refer to the different areas of one's life and the blessings or obstacles that may arise within that sphere of manifestation:

Σ = Σωμα (Soma): Body, health, the material realm
Ψ = Ψυχη (Psuche): Soul, subconscious, the person within
Θ = Θεοι (Theoi): Gods, divine order, religious matters
Π = Πατρικως (Patrikos): Ancestors, tradition, what is inherited
Ο = Οικος (Oikos): Home, family, private matters
Α = Αγορα (Agora): Marketplace, finances, public matters
Φ = Φιλια (Philia): Relationships, connections, the exterior person
Μ = Μουσικη (Mousike): Creativity, the intellect, work

May be used in conjunction with other divination systems (the Toys, the Leaves, the Olbian or Alphabet oracles, etc.) or by dropping beans, pebbles or seeds into the Net.

The Net is particularly useful if you want a general overview or the client isn't certain of what questions to ask or what area to focus on.

Pay attention not only to where the object or items fall but also where in each section, and the spatial relationship they have if you involve more than one.

The answer to all your questions can be found in these words written on bone by the Orphic initiates on the Black Sea:

Βιος
Θανατος
Διονυσος

Crown your heart with their meaning, and you will be wise in all things:

Life is an **affirmation** of possibility;
death its **negation** and completion.
Dionysos hears the **prayer** of the pious and can help.

Inscribe the Greek on pieces of bone or stones that you have painted red, black and white and then keep them in a pouch. When you need guidance, draw one out.

This form of divination was loaned to Dionysos by Hermes, God of currency. For it you will need three coins (ideally coins or ancient replicas with images of Dionysos on them, but in a pinch any will work) which you have formally consecrated to him. They should be, if not the same denomination, of a similar size and value so as not to skew their statistical probability or your interpretation. As part of the consecration you can decorate them (for instance by inscribing a sigil or blackening out the reverse) or anoint them with *chernips* or his holy oil.

Pray to Dionysos for guidance, state your question as carefully and simply as possible, and then throw the coins, interpreting their fall as follows:

3 heads — Emphatic yes.
2 heads — Yes, but it will require effort and thought.
1 head — You should probably reconsider your plans.
No head — You don't have a chance in hell.

This system can be used to get answers from Gods and Spirits other than Hermes or Dionysos — indeed, because of its simplicity it can be employed by beings who might have difficulty with systems of greater or more specific symbolism — though you should confirm that they are willing and able to communicate through it first. When doing so I either throw coins that have not been consecrated to Hermes or Dionysos, or ask them to act as intermediaries and interpreters for the other party. In addition to answering questions, this system can be used to corroborate the results you get through other forms of divination or direct oracular messages.

The Oracle of Meilichios and Bakcheios

And the Naxians, according to Andriskos and again Aglaosthenes, record that Dionysos is called Meilichios (Gentle) because he bestowed the fruit of the fig. For this reason, also, among the Naxians the face of the God called Dionysos Bakcheios is made of the vine, whereas that of Dionysos Meilichios is of fig-wood. For, they say that figs are called *meilicha* (mild fruit). (Athenaios, *Deipnosophistai* 3.78a)

Roll two dice, a black for Bakcheios signifying no and a white for Meilichios signifying yes. Whichever has the higher number indicates your answer. You can gain further information by interpreting the number accordingly. A tie signifies that offerings must be made before proceeding or another system of divination needs to be consulted.

Meilichios
1 —Yes, but there is too much that you don't know to be comfortable. Ask more questions to gain clarity.
2 — Yes, but that is contingent on other things falling into place.
3 — Yes, through great effort on your part.
4 — Yes, and there's nothing further that you need to do.
5 — You know that this is certain — why are you even asking about it?
6 — You have the favor of the Gods with regard to this. All obstacles shall be removed from your path.

Bakcheios
1 — No but only because you don't know enough about the situation to properly formulate your question.
2 — It should, but it won't because of circumstances beyond your control.
3 — No, because of something that you've messed up.
4 — No, and you should begin preparing for that because it's inevitable.
5 — Are you stupid? Of course not!
6 — Hell no! And there's serious miasma around this. Reparations need to be made post haste.

Take four dice that have been consecrated to Dionysos and cast them. Adding the numbers together you will arrive at the epithet which represents the portion of his domain that you need to focus on for a successful resolution.

Alternate method: one may write the names on tiles, pebbles, pieces of wood or scraps of paper and draw them as needed, rather than using dice. This method permits one to employ additional or different epithets.

4. Θυρεπανοίκτης (Thyrepanoiktes) = "Opener of the Door"
5. Σαωτης (Saotes) = "Savior"
6. Βακχειος (Bakcheios) = "Who Howls With Frenzy"
7. Αγυιευς (Agyieus) = "Of the Road"
8. Μειλίχιος (Meilichios) = "Gentle"
9. Προτρυγαιος (Protrygaios) = "Of the First Harvest"
10. Μουσηγετης (Mousegetes) = "Leader of the Mousai"
11. Ἔσχατος (Eschatos) = "The Beyond"
12. Ανθροπορραιστος (Anthroporraistos) = "Man-slayer"
13. Ειραφιωτης (Eiraphiotes) = "Insewn"
14. Λυαιος (Lyaios) = "Who Brings Release"
15. Αισυμνητης (Aisymnetes) = "Tyrant"
16. Αυξιτης (Auxites) = "Giver of Increase"
17. Διμητωρ (Dimetor) = "Of Two Mothers"
18. Πρόσωπον (Prosopon) = "The Mask"
19. Σπουδογέλοιον (Spoudogeloion) = "Of Tearful Laughter"
20. Ανθιον (Anthion) = "Flowering"
21. Μαινολης (Mainoles) = "Insane"
22. Πατρωιος (Patroios) = "Ancestral"
23. Ἀστερίων (Asterion) = "Starry"
24. Ερεβινθινος (Erebinthinos) = "Chickpea"

This is the method of prescribing cleansings.

You will need four stones, a die, and a pouch to keep them in.

The four stones represent the *rizomata panton*, the "roots of all things" or primordial elements which Empedokles described as follows:

> Now hear the fourfold roots of everything:
> shining Zeus, enlivening Hera, Aidoneus,
> and Nestis, moistening mortal springs with her tears.

The stones should either have their Greek name inscribed on them or be of an appropriate color, as derived from the Galenic humours:

- Fire = (πῦρ *pur*) = hot and dry = yellow = bile (χολή, *chole*)
- Air = (ἀήρ *aer*) = hot and wet = red = blood (αἷμα, *haima*)
- Earth = (γῆ *ge*) = cold and dry = black = black bile (μέλαινα χολή, *melaina chole*)
- Water = (ὕδωρ *hudor*) = cold and wet = white = phlegm (φλέγμα, *phlegma*)

Draw the stone out to determine where the root cause of the problem lies and then roll the die to determine the nature of the cleansing that needs to be prescribed.

FIRE
1. Pass fire over the body.
2. Walk on coals.
3. Write your afflictions down on scraps of paper and then give them to the fire.
4. Burn an effigy of your enemy.
5. Keep a flame burning for a month.
6. Wear red clothing for a week and work on cultivating the fire within.

AIR
1. Fumigate with bay or other purifying herbs.
2. Cleanse using music.
3. Cleanse through prayer, singing or intoning epithets and words of power.

4. Burn incense every day for a month.
5. Devote yourself to intellectual study and practice mindfulness and meditation.
6. Cover your head, especially when you're outside the home.

EARTH
1. Apply sacred ash.
2. Cover with mud and sit upon the bare earth for three hours.
3. Make offerings to the ancestors.
4. Make offerings to the land-spirits.
5. Ground and center.
6. Thoroughly clean and put your home in order.

WATER
1. Fast.
2. Cleanse with *chernips*.
3. Take a cleansing bath, with milk and appropriate herbs.
4. Bathe in a river.
5. Cleanse through tears.
6. Wear all white for a week.

Inscribe each letter of the Greek alphabet on a stone, tile, piece of wood, etc., and draw one out when you need an answer. Five words are provided to show the letter's range of meaning.

A (Alpha)
Aeiro (ἀείρω) to lift, raise up, rise above
Aigle (αἴγλη) radiance, glory, splendor
Aparche (ἀπαρχή) dues, first-fruits, preliminary offerings
Aphiemi (ἀφίημι) discharge, loose, set free
Aoton (ἄωτον) the flower of its kind, prime, fairest

B (Beta)
Baino (βαίνω) walk, dance, advance
Bakaion (βακάϊον) measure, evaluate, rule
Biaios (βίαιος) full of life, strength, force
Brephos (βρέφος) babe in the womb, potential, outflow
Bromeo (βρομέω) buzz, roar, boil

Γ (Gamma)
Gamos (γάμος) wedding, union, connections
Gaster (γαστήρ) belly, womb, wide part of a bottle
Gelao (γελάω) joy, laughter, silliness
Genea (γενεά) race, family, offspring
Geitneo (γειτνέω) to share the earth, neighbor, community

Δ (Delta)
Daizo (δαΐζω) rend, cleave, divide
Deire (δειρή) throat, gully, a flow-through channel
Diacheo (διαχέω) scatter, disperse, spread
Doke (δοκή) vision, opinion, expectation
Doleros (δολερός) ruse, deceit, entrapment

E (Epsilon)
Eao (ἐάω) leave alone, be done with, quit
Ezomai (ἔζομαι) seat oneself, sink to the earth, collapse
Eimi (εἰμί) exist, essence, reality

Eleutheria (ἐλευθερία) autonomy, liberality, freedom
Elpis (ἐλπίς) hope, expectation, desire

Z (Zeta)

Zelos (ζῆλος) zeal, fervor, spirit
Zemia (ζημία) loss, damage, penalty
Zeteuo (ζητεύω) seek, search, inquire
Zeo (ζέω) boil, seethe, ferment
Zopureo (ζωπῠρέω) quickening of life, kindle into flame, blazing up

H (Eta)

Egeomai (ἡγέομαι) guide, command, lead the way
Ethos (ἦθος) custom, character, way of life
Epios (ἤπῐος) gentle, rich, soothing
Etrion (ἤτριον) warp, stretch, extend
Eothen (ἠῶθεν) beginning, dawn, eastern

Θ (Theta)

Theiasmos (θειασμός) divine possession, an inspired utterance, given over to the Gods
Thera (θήρα): hunting of wild beasts, the chase, a game
Theoreo (θεωρέω) behold, observe, perceive
Thura (θύρα) door, the other side, entrance
Thuo (θύω) sacrificial offerings, consumed by fire, burning with divine longing

I (Iota)

Iaino (ἰαίνω) cheer, heal, save
Ierizo (ἱερίζω) purify, consecrate, make holy
Ithus (ἰθύς) straight, upright, just
Iketeia (ἱκετεία) supplication, entreat, beg
Iluo (ἱλύω) to conceal, cover with clay, dirty

K (Kappa)

Katharsios (κᾰθάρσιος) cleansing, purging, release of the unnecessary and harmful
Kairos (καιρός) vital part, in season, the exact or critical time
Kentro (κεντρο) core, center, point
Krasis (κρᾶσις) mixing, blending, tempering
Krima (κρίμα) decision, judgment, decree

Λ (Lambda)

Lekithos (λέκῑθος) the yoke of an egg
Lethargeo (ληθαργέω) drowsiness, forgetting, sinking down
Lousis (λοῦσις) washing, bathing, cleansing
Lumeo (λῡμέω) to grieve, distress, or cause pain
Luo (λύω) unbind, dissolve, release

M (Mu)

Mauroo (μαυρόω) darken, blind, make obscure
Medeon (μεδέων) guardian, protector, ruler
Meli (μελί) gentle, sweet, honey
Memneo (μέμνεο) to remind, put in mind, call to mind
Moira (μοῖρα) portion, faction, destiny

N (Nu)

Nama (νᾶμα) flowing, rushing, bursting forth
Neeo (νηέω) build, heap, pile up
Neikos (νεῖκος) quarrel, strife, feud
Noeros (νοερός) think, perceive, reflect
Nusso (νύσσω) stab, pierce, nudge

Ξ (Xi)

Xanthias (Ξανθίας) yellow, foreign, servile
Xeraino (ξηραίνω) parch, wither, dry up
Xenos (Ξενος) guest, stranger, wanderer
Xunos (ξῦνός) common, public, general
Xuston (ξυστόν) scraped, trimmed, cropped

O (Omicron)

Ozos (ὄζος) offspring, offshoot, branch
Olbos (ὄλβος) happiness, prosperity, fulfilment
Opora (ὀπώρα) fruitful, ripe, summer-swollen
Ormos (ὅρμος) harbor-giver, chain, connection
Opheltreuo (ὀφελτρεύω) sweep, change, turn

Π (Pi)

Palai (πάλαι) aged, venerable, of long ago
Peitho (πείθω) persuade, seduce, make obedient
Perao (περάω) pass through, traverse, penetrate
Pistis (πίστις) trust, faith, confidence
Pompos (πομρός) conductor, escort, guide

P (Rho)

Rabasso (ῥαβάσσω) to make a noise by dancing or beating time with the feet

Radis (ῥάδις) cyclical, whirling, rotation

Riza (ῥίζα) root, element, outflow

Rimma (ῥιμμα) throw, cast, swing

Roomai (ῥώομαι) to move with speed or violence, to rush on, forceful

Σ (Sigma)

Sebas (σεβας) reverential awe, worship, terror

Skambos (σκαμβός) crooked, bent, twisted

Semeion (σημεῖον) a sign from the Gods, an omen, an indication of what is or is to be

Schazo (σχάζω) open up, escape, let go

Sophrosune (σωφροσύνη) prudence, sanity, moderation

T (Tau)

Talanton (τάλαντον) weight, scale, balance

Teichos (τεῖχος) wall, boundary, end

Teleio (τελειόω) make perfect, complete, consummate

Timao (τίμάω) honor, acclaim, what is due one

Tonos (τόνος) cord, stretch, tension

Y (Upsilon)

Ugeios (ὕγειος) healthy, sound, unbroken

Upenerthe (ὑπένερθε) beneath, under the earth, in the netherworld

Us (ὗς) maternal, receptive, female genitalia

Uphaino (ὑφαίνω) create, contrive, weave

Uo (ὕω) rain, flow, water

Φ (Ph)

Phantasma (φαντᾰσμα) apparition, phantom, mental image

Phatizo (φᾰτίζω) tell of, express, promise

Phiale (φῐάλη) offering dish, urn for funeral ashes, bowl for administering medicines

Phobos (φόβος) dread, terror, fearful flight

Phuo (φύω) bring forth, produce, formed by nature

X (Chi)

Chairo (χαίρω) rejoice, take pleasure in, celebration

Chasko (χάσκω) yawn, gap, chasm

Cheima (χεῖμα) cold, frost, winter

Choikos (χοϊκός) of earth or clay, funeral libations, of an age to take part in the Choes festival

Chreos (χρεός) debt, obligation, fate

Ψ (Psi)

Psammos (ψάμμος) crumbling, sandy, inconstant

Psaros (ψᾱρός) speckled, dappled, discolored

Psausis (ψαῦσις) brush, touch, graze

Pseudo (ψεύδω) fake, lie, deceive

Psophos (ψόφος) sound, noise, especially by that which cannot be seen

Ω (Omega)

Ode (ᾠδή) dirge, joyful songs, songs of praise

Ope (ὠπή) sight, unobstructed vision, full view

Orai (ὧραι) timely, seasonal, fitting produce

Osis (ὦσις) thrusting, pushing, to bring forth

Opheleia (ὠφέλεια) assistance, advantage, source of gain or profit

My interest in divination predates my polytheism, even if my relationship with Dionysos has it beat by a couple of years. As a Christian, I justified this interest by the example of Jesus' inner circle who used divination to resolve the issue of succession after one of their number committed suicide:

> They nominated two men: Joseph called Barsabbas (also known as Justus) and Matthias. Then they prayed, "Lord, you know everyone's heart. Show us which of these two you have chosen to take over this apostolic ministry." Then they cast lots, and the lot fell to Matthias; so he was added to the eleven apostles. (*Acts* 1.23-26)

I would interpret the shapes formed by dripping hot wax into water, open the Bible at random for guidance, count the seconds between thunderclaps, consult a Magic 8-Ball and pay attention to dreams as well as numerous other folk customs I'd managed to collect. After converting to neopaganism, I progressed to things like palmistry, I Ching, the Runes and Geomancy — though I only gained true proficiency with the Tarot, eventually forgetting most everything I'd learned about the other systems. I got so good with Tarot cards, in fact, that during high school I usually had a large group of classmates gathered around me at lunch, eager to have their fortunes told. Often there were teachers, custodians, administrative personnel and sometimes even the principal in the crowd as well.

When my relationship with Dionysos deepened and I came to practice Hellenic reconstructionism, I became dissatisfied with the Tarot, wanting to practice a more authentic form of ancient Greek divination. So I set myself to learning scrying, bird omens, the Limyran alphabet oracle and a form of bibliomancy found in the Greek Magical Papyri that utilizes verses from Homer's *Iliad* and *Odyssey*. I proved just as adept with these methods as I had the Tarot and the other systems I'd studied in my youth, gaining a solid reputation as a *mantis* or diviner in the Hellenic community. Many people sought my advice on a wide range of topics, religious and otherwise. I came to view the work I did as a holy vocation under the auspices of my God Dionysos. It was a way to serve both him and the community and I felt that much of what came out through my readings was inspired by the God's prophetic spirit.

I was not content, however, with the tools at my disposal. While it was certainly possible to get good results with Dionysos employing the ancient Greek methods, and even Tarot and systems developed in cultures and time periods completely unrelated to him, there was nothing particularly Dionysian about any of them. I wanted something that belonged wholly to him, which spoke his language through his symbols and associations. So I asked the God for his assistance in devising such a method of divination.

Working closely with Dionysos it took me the better part of a year to flesh out the details of the system. The heart of it had been revealed in a flash of sudden divine inspiration but then I had to sort out what each of the elements meant and how the system would actually function in practice. There were a couple of false starts, some things that had to be revised or omitted altogether, but considering how long it took for the Tarot to be codified into the system we recognize today — to say nothing of the I Ching or Runes — a year is scarcely any time at all.

I tried the system out for the first time on July 10th, 2006 and got stunningly accurate results. It had been effective in readings I'd done for myself and a handful of others before that, but I had no idea if it would work on strangers and especially people with no prior Dionysian history. It worked so well, in fact, that I immediately had people requesting further readings. In particular people were impressed — and shocked — by the intimacy and private nature of the information that came through. Things that they hadn't confessed to anyone else, ever, were laid bare by the God through his oracular leaves.

When Dionysos revealed this system to me back in late 2004 he informed me that I would one day share his gift with the world, although I had to fully master it before I could do so. Starting around 2007, when I had progressed to possessionary oracles, I began asking if I could share the system with others. To each inquiry he would respond, "The time is not yet right." I would wait another five or six months to ask again, but always I got the same response. Then in late 2010 while I was putting the final touches on *Ecstatic* (a collection of all my Dionysian themed writings up to that point) I thought to ask one more time and he surprised me by saying, "Now it is ready."

So, with the God's blessing, I present to you The Oracular Leaves from the Tree of Dionysos.

Before we delve into the system itself I would like to provide some of its background.

The genesis of this system lies in a pair of anecdotes found in Pseudo-Kallisthenes' *Alexander Romance*:

> Then came some of the townspeople who said, 'We have to show thee something passing strange, O King, and worth thy visiting; for we can show thee trees that talk with human speech.' So they led me to a certain park full of priests. And in the midst of the park stood the two trees of which they had spoken, like unto cypress

97

trees; and round about them were trees like the myroliolans of Egypt, and with similar fruit. And I addressed the two trees that were in the midst of the park, which were clothed with the skins of animals. And at the setting of the sun, a voice speaking in the Indian tongue came forth from the tree; and I ordered the Indians who were with me to interpret it. But they were afraid and would not. (3.17)

And Philostratos' *Life of Apollonios of Tyana*:

They were now in the country in which the mountain of Nysa rises, covered to its very top with plantations [...], and you can ascend it, because paths have been made by cultivators. They say then that when they ascended it, they found the shrine of Dionysos, which it is said Dionysos founded in honor of himself, planting round it a circle of laurel trees which encloses just as much ground as suffices to contain a moderate sized temple. He also surrounded the laurels with a border of ivy and vines; and he set up inside an image of himself, knowing that in time the trees would grow together and make themselves into a kind of roof; and this had now formed itself, so that neither rain can wet nor wind blow upon the shrine. And there were sickles and wine-presses and their dedications to Dionysos, as if to one who gathers grapes, all made of gold and silver. And the image resembled a youthful Indian, and was carved out of polished white stone. (2.8)

I had a vision in which these two incidents were combined. I saw Alexander the Great enter the verdant temple of Dionysos, a structure made entirely out of leaves, vines and ivy encircling a crude, primitive wooden idol of the God. Alexander approached the image and sacrificed to Dionysos by pouring out a libation of wine at his feet. The image then came to life and addressed Alexander, telling him to ask the question he had traveled so far to learn the answer to. When Alexander did so a multitude of leaves from the canopy overhead rained down upon him. He caught several of these in his hand and the God ordered him to read them for his answer was written upon the leaves. And that is the essence of the system as it was revealed to me and as I now share it with you.

There are 28 different leaves, each of which references a figure from the myths of Dionysos, a symbol or attribute or something else associated with the God. Twenty-eight is a number of deep mystical significance for Dionysos as well as his Egyptian counterpart Osiris. I leave it to you to unravel why this number of leaves was chosen, but know that there can be no more or less than 28 in this system. Likewise there is a great density of meaning behind each of the leaves, things that only a devout Dionysian

98

who has worked very closely with the God for a great length of time and is well-versed in his myths and lore could ever fully hope to comprehend. One could fill a volume many times the size of this present collection with speculation on their nuances. I have presented only the most basic and superficial level of interpretation for each of the leaves in the following commentary. If you are going to use this system effectively you must consider this only a starting point. It is incumbent upon you to search out their true and deeper meaning, to let the God guide you in understanding their mysteries and to open your ears to what each leaf has to say. Keep in mind that the meaning can change significantly depending on the context of the question as well as what leaves are drawn with it. You should spend many hours meditating on the complexities inherent in the leaves before you begin to use them in a divinatory capacity for yourself, let alone others.

In the beginning the only place where the leaves may be consulted is the verdant temple of Dionysos. (Later on, when you've established a relationship with them, you can use them less formally.) Every time that you wish to seek their wisdom you must visit this place. Whether or not it once existed in the distant land of India and was actually visited by Alexander and Apollonios, know that it is a real place and dwells on the periphery between this and other worlds. Those whom the God wishes to use his oracle will be able to find their way to the temple. The path begins in the mind but it leads to a land far from there. Let your imagination form an image of the temple based on the accounts I have provided and what the God himself shows you. Carefully dwell on every branch and vine and leaf that forms the structure, the light shining through the lattice, the smell of damp earth and vegetation, the shadows covering the ancient idol of the God, the fragrant incense and offerings left by past visitors and all of the other sense perceptions that flood your mind. But never forget that the image you construct is only a replica, a phantom of the true temple of the God. It is a real place and the image you construct is the door that leads into it. To properly consult the oracle of the leaves you must pass from illusion into reality — but illusion is how you find your way there.

When you have arrived, make the proper offerings to Dionysos and spend time basking in his presence. The words spoken and the offerings presented to the God will differ from person to person, and necessarily so for this is a highly personal operation. But one thing that must always be present is the sacrifice of wine. You must share the wine with Dionysos, pouring a cup for him to drink and consuming some yourself as well. You need not drink to intoxication, although that can help loosen your mind and allow you to hear the words of the God more clearly, but there can be no true oracle without first exchanging the gift of wine and taking the God's spirit, through the wine, into yourself. This may only be a token sip, but it still has to be done, just as the Pythia had to drink the pure spring water before she could experience the prophetic inspiration of the Lord Apollon.

After you have done this, spend time letting the God's wine settle into you, freeing your mind for the holy work ahead of you. When you feel yourself ready to proceed, ask Dionysos if he is willing to give answer to your questions. You must not rush this part or blurt out your request until he has granted you permission. It is rude and disrespectful and the God may well have good reasons of his own for not wanting to proceed. If he declines your request ask if there is something more you need to do in preparation or if the consultation is better reserved for another time. Sometimes, no matter how ready we think we are for his revelation, the God knows that we are not. The God always knows best and if you cannot trust him utterly then you should not be seeking his oracular guidance. If he says that he will not answer your question under any circumstances take him at his word and do not try it again, no matter how important and pressing the circumstances may seem to you.

Should the God grant you his blessing to proceed, then ask your question and await Dionysos' sign to continue. This may manifest in him telling you to draw the leaves, a nod of his head or smile, or the image of leaves falling around you. At that point you may then draw out the leaves.

There is no set number required to answer a question. Sometimes a single leaf will suffice. Sometimes you will need three or five or even a dozen. Allow the God to inspire you with the proper number. Meditate on what each leaf means alone and in connection with the others. Although each leaf has a specific meaning — or rather layers upon layers of meaning — do not limit yourself just to what is there. Sometimes the true meaning is not immediately apparent but only arrived at intuitively, through suggestion and analogy and irrational leaps of connection. Open yourself up to the story the leaves have to tell, mindful of the broad network of associations they possess, the myths they allude to, and your past history with them. Sometimes once we've been working with the system for awhile, a leaf will become an indicator of a person, a particular situation or feeling, regardless of what it originally may have meant. Understanding it in this way is far more important than a literal reading.

If you cannot properly interpret the leaves, do not hesitate to draw more of them or shuffle the set and start again by drawing a new batch. Also, if it seems like more than the initially indicated number of leaves wish to be present — for instance you draw out four instead of three or a couple extras fall into the pile — include them as part of the reading and give them special consideration, for the God may be indicating something important through them. Likewise pay attention to the spatial relationship of the leaves. If two or more of them are touching or laid down closely together in contrast to the rest of the leaves that are scattered about this can be significant. Also, pay attention to how they fall. If a leaf is upside down or reversed this can have a very different meaning than when it is regular side up. It can, for instance, indicate a blockage in this area or that the worst aspects of the leaf are dominant or even that its negativity is diminished or counteracted by one of the other leaves. The only exception to this is the wine leaf. Belonging to Dionysos in a way that none of the others do, it has no negative aspects. Indeed it transforms everything around it into a positive and indicates the ultimate success of a situation.

There are other tips and tricks involved with this system, but you'll learn them the more you practice and develop the ability to hear what the leaves have to tell you. This system isn't for everyone and it requires hard work and dedication — as well as a strong relationship with Dionysos — to master.

You will need to make your own set. You can do this a number of different ways. You can inscribe the words on tiles or pieces of wood or pebbles or even actual leaves. You can make cards with them by printing the words or collaging images and other representations of the symbols and concepts onto paper or board. You could also assign numerical values to each of the leaves and use dice to get your answers, though I don't really recommend this course of action.

Once you have created your set of leaves you should consecrate them to Dionysos and treat them with the utmost respect and reverence. The more you use them the more energy and life and Dionysian spirit they will acquire. Merely handling them can become a powerful way to connect with the God. And you may find other uses for them beyond just divination. They can be great for meditation, magical operations, devotional activities and even aids to the creative process. Several times now I've been working on a story and run into writer's block, unsure of how to proceed. I asked the leaves for help, dug a couple out and sure enough they provided me with the answer. In fact a couple of the pieces in this collection were finished that way.

I believe that this is everything you need to know to get started with them. Hopefully they will be as beneficial to you as they have been for me.

THE LEAVES

Ακοιτης (Akoites)
You're on the right path, a divine calling or higher purpose, commitment, fidelity, doing what's necessary to attain one's goals even when one has to make tough choices and sacrifices, clarity, honesty, seeing through deception.
Reversed: blindness, aimless wandering, uncertainty, lack of dedication, shirking one's responsibilities, willful ignorance, pursuing things that are bad for you even when you realize it, letting fear get the better of you.

Αμπελος (Ampelos: The Vine)
Growth, unfolding, the process of a thing, connection, binding together, strength, nature and everything related to earthiness, cultivating the gifts of the Gods, having a solid foundation, heat and passion.
Reversed: Entanglement, unhealthy relationships, being smothered or overpowered by something, decay, a need to cut things out of one's life or minimize obligations.

Αριαδνη (Ariadne)
Love, marriage, unity, redemption, wholeness, fulfillment, mysterious feminine power, help from an unexpected source, the unraveling of understanding, a journey through the maze, transformation to a higher state.
Reversed: Loneliness, abandonment, being lost in the dark, unable to find one's way, cruelty, a need to discover one's own power and purpose, denigration of the feminine.

Αστρον (Astron: The Star)
Illumination, revelation, guidance, destiny, insight from a heavenly or unexpected source, hidden things brought to light, have patience and the answer will present itself to you.
Reversed: Doubt, uncertainty, losing one's way, ulterior motives, deception, caution before proceeding and a call to introspection.

'Ερμης (Hermes)
Friendship, divine assistance, communication, luck, magic, thinking your way out of a tight spot, seek the aid of this God.
Reversed: A misunderstanding, a breakdown in communication, bad luck, trouble, someone is conspiring against you, you *really* need the aid of this God.

Ἥρα (Hera)

Relationships, marriage, the home, wealth, concern with material or domestic matters, a powerful, domineering woman, conflict arising from these sources.

Reversed: You've pissed off a woman in your life and now she's out to get you, unfair persecution, vengeance pursued beyond justifiable measure, a serious problem involving relationships and the home.

Ηριγονη (Erigone)

Loyalty, faithfulness, devotion to others even at the cost of one's own self, trials, ultimate vindication even if opinion is currently against you, a difficult or melancholy atmosphere.

Reversed: Failure, depression, a situation outside of one's control, a tendency for morbid thoughts and self-harming, seeing things as worse than they actually are, a cry for help, the need for outside intervention.

Ἥφαιστος (Hephaistos)

Work, doing what's necessary to get the job done, attention to detail, absorption in one's calling, beauty found in unexpected places or coming from unlikely sources, the workplace and everything related to it.

Reversed: Laziness, lack of skill, more effort is required of you, the failure of something you were trying to accomplish, problems in the workplace, holding on to a grudge even when it hurts everyone around you.

Θυρσος (Thyrsos)

Tools, resources, raw potential, the focusing of the will, directing energy towards a specific goal, virility, authority, the conduit through which the miraculous manifests in our lives.

Reversed: Impotency, interruption of flow, lacking what it necessary to accomplish one's goals, not knowing how to use what one has, being cut off from the source.

Κισσος (Kissos: The Ivy)

Protection, nurturing, vitality, the ability to thrive under any conditions, expansion, being emotionally cool and aloof, caring only for one's own self.

Reversed: Selfishness, difficulty dealing with others, too much of a good thing, feeling strangled or smothered, co-dependent relationships, indifference to the suffering of others including when you're the cause of it, a cold-hearted bastard.

Κρατηρ (Krater: The Mixing Bowl)

Balance, synthesis, powerful forces coming together, mixing things up, agitation, fullness, bounty, receptacle for divine blessings, flow, pouring into.

Reversed: Too much of a good thing, imbalance, a need to seek out a complimentary opposite, feeling shaken up or overwhelmed by constant stress, a need to stir the pot and see what happens when things become too settled or stagnant, emptiness, poverty, a lack of divine blessing or presence.

Μαιναδες (Mainades)
Passion, devotion, freedom, throwing off the shackles to follow the desire of one's heart, inability to cope with the daily grind, breaking taboos and conventional roles, doing the unexpected and seemingly impossible, being one's own person regardless of the consequences, an unstable woman.
Reversed: If you don't change your situation right now you're going to go mad — and not in a good way, feeling trapped and overwhelmed, living an inauthentic life, beset on all sides by a host of problems that chase you down and tear you apart mercilessly.

Μαινας (Mainas: Madness)
Intense emotional states, an alternation of consciousness is needed, inspiration, breaking down boundaries, the imagination, disconnect from reality, strange and disturbing behavior, access to wisdom and spiritual gifts unattainable by ordinary means.
Reversed: Delusions, harmful impulses, addiction, paranoia, inability to function, everything you are thinking about the situation is wrong and going to lead to unpleasant consequences, failure of the imagination, healing is called for.

Μιδας (Midas)
Wealth, blessing, the material realm, getting what you want. However, those familiar with the story of Midas will understand that what we want isn't always what's best for us. As such it can also signify lack of understanding, the misuse of what's been given to us, greed, selfishness, being overly concerned with finances and a failure to see the big picture.
Reversed: Money troubles, anxiety, neglecting what's important in life, lack of control and stability, and a warning to stop looking for the easy fix.

Μινυαδες (Minyades)
Arrogance, extremism, control issues, being too driven, a workaholic, failure to enjoy the good things in life, expecting too much out of others, an unfair situation.
Reversed: A crisis is looming because of the above — it may even be too late. Change or dine if it's about you; get out of the way if it's not. Don't even bother trying to talk sense into them, as they won't listen.

Μουσαι (Mousai: The Muses)
Creativity, inspiration, the arts, culture, beauty, charm, fresh ideas, a new way of looking at things, the gifts of the Gods.
Reversed: Frustration, the source of creativity is blocked, stagnation, stupidity, brute force, a need to rekindle the flame or look at things in a different way.

Νηος (Neos: Ship)
A journey which can be physical or metaphorical, transformation, a change of scenery and with it a new perspective on things, strangeness, the unexpected, bounty, divine gifts, cutting ties, the start of a new phase of life.
Reversed: Stagnation, going nowhere, set adrift without moorings, feeling trapped, a desperate need for the positive qualities of the lead in one's life.

Οινος (Oinos: Wine)
Success, abundance, joy, the gift of Dionysos — it makes everything better. It cannot be reversed and cancels out any negativity in the other leaves that are drawn with it.

Οινοτροφοι (Oinotrophoi: The Winegrowers)
Cultivating the gifts you have, doing the seemingly impossible, utilizing your resources to help others, generosity, actively working to improve a situation, the favor of the Gods provided you hold up your end of the bargain.
Reversed: Squandering your gifts, negligence, being taken advantage of, failing to live up to your potential or doing what you know is right.

Ορος (Oros: The Mountain)
Ascending the heights, a goal, success after a difficult struggle, resolution, superiority, gaining a better perspective on an issue, solitude, separating oneself from the crowd and ordinary life.
Reversed: You haven't gone far enough or done enough, difficult work lies ahead, being down in the dumps, matter triumphing over the spiritual, failure because of a lack of effort or vision, inability to get away from one's problems.

Ορφευς (Orpheus)
Creativity, inspiration, hidden wisdom, initiation, descent, depths, a heroic quest, journeys both literal and metaphorical, overcoming obstacles, a time of testing to see what one is made of, introspection and transformation, maturity and power gained through suffering.
Reversed: The journey is incomplete. One must go back down and truly face

their fears. Brashness and foolishness, egotism masquerading as concern for others, being cut off from the source of creativity.

Οφις (Ophis: The Snake)
Transformation, shedding one's skin, adopting a new identity or perspective on things, subtlety, secret wisdom, chthonic forces, cold, alien, a lack of emotion, doing what's necessary regardless of what others think, the unknown and unfamiliar.
Reversed: Danger, deception, unexpected problems seemingly arising out of nowhere, a need to go deeper and cultivate the positive qualities of this leaf.

Πενθευς (Pentheus)
Conflict, overbearing personality, failure to understand nuance, stubbornness, control freak, refusal to listen to other sides in an argument, haughty or abusive language, delusion, spiritual blindness, blundering into situations you aren't prepared to deal with, holding onto outmoded ideas even when they bring you nothing but trouble, unthinkingly perpetuating cycles of violence.
Reversed: Can either mean that the person is beginning to see the error of their ways and is leaving all that behind them or else it's a dire warning of immanent doom.

Προσωπον (Prosopon: The Mask)
Mystery, a hint that things may not be what they seem and one should continue peeling back the layers, an indication that the issues has to do with perception, identity and psychology; it may also indicate that the Gods are behind an encounter or situation, even if one does not fully understand how or why.
Reversed: Delusion, active deception, be wary of a person or situation, dissonance between what one does and feels, being trapped in a false and unfulfilling role.

Σατυροι (Satyroi: Satyrs)
Mirth, freedom, sexual rapaciousness, connection with the vital forces of existence, instincts, animality, a reminder to enjoy life and spend less time worrying about what others think and the roles they try to force us into, a crude, rude and uncivilized person.
Reversed: Overindulgence, lack of discipline, misfortune caused by an inability to take things seriously, a call to change one's ways before that happens. Alternately, sterility, being too much in one's head, a need to cultivate one's more foolish qualities.

Σεμελη (Semele)
Maternal, nurturing, self-sacrifice, intensity, being consumed by

something, closeness to the Gods regardless of the cost, destruction brought about by foolish choices.

Reversed: Being smothered, holding back too much, emotional entanglements, a martyr complex, being taken advantage of or deceived.

Ταυρος (Tauros: The Bull)

Fertility, masculinity, power, rushing headlong into a situation, trampling the obstacles in one's path, stubborn commitment to a cause or idea.

Reversed: Being too focused on the material, refusal to listen to others or give a situation the thought it deserves, lack of virility or passion.

Τιτανοι (Titanoi: The Titans)

Obstacles, conflict, destructive forces whether internal or external, the odds are stacked against you, feeling trapped or persecuted no matter what you attempt to do to fix the situation, being torn apart or pulled in different directions.

Reversed: Most of the time it has the same meaning only to a much worse extent. However if all of the accompanying leaves are positive it can mean triumphing over obstacles or a crisis is coming to an end. However one should still be cautious as the negative influence may linger on undetected for a while.

How To Make Your Very Own
Bibliomantic System

I'm going to show you how to make your very own bibliomantic system on the model of the Homeromanteion found in the *Papyri Graecae Magicae*. (The same approach can be applied to adapt several of the other systems in this book.)

The Homeromanteion was, as Raquel Martín-Hernández writes in *Using Homer for Divination: Homeromanteia in Context*:

> a certain divinatory text that uses a selection of Homeric verses for offering automatic oracular answers by lot. The text was preserved in three different manuscripts: *P.Lond.* 121 (i. e. *PGM* VII), *P.Oxy.* 56.3831, and *P.Bon.* 3, listed here by the quantity of text preserved. The name Homeromanteion is already attested as the title for the text in the copy of *PGM* VII, but according to the Oxyrhynchus papyrus, it could be also called 'the Scimitar.' [...] According to the instructions for use, the Homeromanteion was performed in the following way: firstly, the practitioner has to consult the table of days and hours in which the oracle can be performed. When the day and hour are favourable for divination, the consultant has to utter a prayer addressed to Apollo (preserved in *P.Oxy.* 3831 and fragmentarily in *PGM* VII) composed indeed by five Homeric verses (the last one modified). While reciting the prayer, the consultant is supposed to think about the question he/she wants answered. Then a dice has to be thrown three times. This process gets as a result a number of three digits that must be located throughout the ordered series of numbers followed by a Homeric verse. The numbers are arranged in a series of six numbers of three digits each, separated by lectional signs, a system that covers all the possibilities of throwing a dice three times. The number obtained by the consultant leads him/her to the Homeric verse that would be the oracular answer. As in other different lot divination texts, like the well known *Sortes Astrampsychi,* and the Christian lot-divination books like the *Sortes Sanctorum, Sortes Sangallenses, Sortes Apostollorum,* etc., the mechanism of the oracle is based on chance by a mediating element that led the consultant to the oracular answer.

Needless to say, this method was not without its critics, as we see in

Then, again, collecting a set of expressions and names scattered here and there in Scripture, they twist them, as we have already said, from a natural to a non-natural sense. In so doing, they act like those who bring forward any kind of hypothesis they fancy, and then endeavour to support them out of the poems of Homer, so that the ignorant imagine that Homer actually composed the verses bearing upon that hypothesis, which has, in fact, been but newly constructed; and many others are led so far by the regularly-formed sequence of the verses, as to doubt whether Homer may not have composed them. Of this kind is the following passage, where one, describing Hercules as having been sent by Eurystheus to the dog in the infernal regions, does so by means of these Homeric verses—for there can be no objection to our citing these by way of illustration, since the same sort of attempt appears in both:

Thus saying, there sent forth from his house deeply
    groaning.— Od., x. 76.
The hero Hercules conversant with mighty deeds.— Od.,
    xxi. 26.
Eurystheus, the son of Sthenelus, descended from
    Perseus.— Il., xix. 123.
That he might bring from Erebus the dog of gloomy
    Pluto.— Il., viii. 368.
And he advanced like a mountain-bred lion confident of
    strength.— Od., vi. 130.
Rapidly through the city, while all his friends followed. —
    Il., xxiv. 327.
Both maidens, and youths, and much-enduring old men.—
    Od., xi. 38.
Mourning for him bitterly as one going forward to death.
    — Il., xxiv. 328.
But Mercury and the blue-eyed Minerva conducted him.—
    Od., xi. 626.
For she knew the mind of her brother, how it laboured
    with grief.— Il., ii. 409.

Now, what simple-minded man, I ask, would not be led away by such verses as these to think that Homer actually framed them so with reference to the subject indicated? But he who is acquainted with the Homeric writings will recognise the verses indeed, but not the subject to which they are applied, as knowing that some of them were spoken of Ulysses, others of Hercules himself, others still of Priam, and others again of Menelaus and Agamemnon. But if he takes them and restores each of them to its proper position, he at once destroys the narrative in question.

Why must we assume intent to deceive? Who is to say that the bricoleur did not feel himself inspired in the arrangement of these random scraps of text, especially when a new story seemed to emerge almost of its own bidding from the disparate fragments? As Burroughs said, "When you cut into the present the future leaks out."

At any rate, these methods have deep resonance for me because of Dionysiac *sparagmos*:

> Dionysos, when he saw his image reflected in the mirror, began to pursue it and so was torn to pieces. But Apollon put Dionysos back together and brought him back to life because he was a purifying God and the true savior. (Olympiodoros, *Commentary on Plato's Phaedo* 67c)

Now, I could get into some of my theories of how divination works but who wants a bunch of psychobabble and quantum physics jargon spewed at them?

Yeah, I didn't think so.

Words are magic. That magic creates a portal between our world and that of the Gods. By manipulating seemingly random phenomena such as the shape of a liver or the fall of dice they can communicate with us. Sometimes inert matter is acted upon; sometimes a Spirit indwells and thus controls the object's movements. Not everyone can understand the divine language, and that's when the diviner steps in as translator and sometimes also as interpreter. This is but one of many forms of information we may access; the querent must still make their own life choices.

That, in a walnut shell, is all you need to know about how divination works.

Now onto making your own system!

Items you will need:

o A blank bibliomantic template (going from 1-1-1 all the way through to 6-6-6.) Once you've made one, save a copy so you don't have to recreate it with each system, as that's a long and annoying process.
o A book or large collection of quotes.
o A pen or keyboard.
o 3 dice.

Traditionally one die was thrown three times, but I find it more economical — and fun! — to throw three dice once. Also, the ancients were content with a single verse as their answer, but I find you get a more nuanced oracle with around 3 to 7 verses.

The first step is to set your intent.

- o For what purpose are you creating this system?
- o Who do you intend to use it to communicate with?
- o What sorts of questions do you anticipate it answering?

For instance, I have systems for determining taboos, for general life questions, for matters pertaining to the Starry Bull tradition, and so forth. I have systems I use for general clients, others reserved for colleagues, and some I only read for myself with.

The Who on the other end is really important. Too many novice diviners just lay down their cards or throw the bones and expect an answer from the Universe — problem is, when you leave the line open like that anything can answer, and not all Spirits are obligated to tell the truth or have our best interests at heart. Not only can that be misleading for the client, it can be dangerous for the diviner. Which is why I encourage folks to have opening and closing rites for their divination sessions, as well as some degree of connection with the being they are consulting so they can recognize if the message is authentic or not. As important as this is when divining, it's doubly so when creating a divinatory tool.

Once you have decided who you'll be using the system with, you should confirm that they are able and willing to communicate through it. I generally employ another system of divination for this, unless I'm in direct contact with them.

As you begin constructing the system, consecrate it to the divinity and ask them to seal it as their own, so that none other may use it without their permission. You may add any other wards or protections you deem necessary, though that usually covers it as the Gods and Spirits are quite capable of looking after their own.

At this point you will begin going over the source material. This should be chosen either because the writing is about the divinity or similarly connected to them (e.g., Aphrodite = Sappho, Dionysos = Jim Morrison), or because it is personally meaningful to you and conjures strong associations with them in your mind. I generally prefer to use material from dead people, and particularly dead people who were known to be devotees of the God, so that I can involve them in the oracle, but these systems can work even when that rule of thumb is not observed.

Now there are a couple different ways to select which lines will be used:

1) Sift through the material for appropriate lines. These would be passages which are evocative, enigmatic or capable of being interpreted in multiple ways or clipped answers which may or may not provide specific direction. You'll want a mixture of both to give the divinity as diverse a range of expression as possible.
2) Just start picking lines at random.
3) Use a pendulum or other system of divination to help you decide.
4) Open yourself up to the divinity and allow them to direct your hand as you choose.

I generally employ several of these methods together when coming up with a system.

Once I have finished stitching it together, I make an offering to the divinity (and the author, if they are deceased) thanking them, and then dedicate the physical dice and spiritual substance of the oracular verses to their service.

I then take it out for a test drive, asking them for a significant message if I don't have any pressing concerns at the moment.

Each system, I've discovered, can develop a personality of its own. Sometimes this is a reflection of the author, the divinity, the author plus divinity, or something totally out of left field. It will take some time and practice to familiarize yourself with its quirks and preferences, but this will make you a better diviner.

How formal your divination sessions are is up to you but I like to make offerings to the divinity and the tool itself before each session (even if it's as simple as a puff of smoke and a thanks) as well as feed them periodically between sessions.

Finally, I recommend having specially dedicated dice for each system, as well as an "all purpose" or "skeleton key" set that can be used with any and all of them.

The Oracle of Dionysos Bakcheios

[Made from the lines spoken by Dionysos in Euripides' *Bakchai*.]

> The God is a prophet, too, for in his rites — the Bacchic celebrations and the madness — a huge prophetic power is unleashed. When the God fully enters human bodies, he makes those possessed by frenzy prophets. They speak of what will come in future days. (Euripides' *Bakchai*)

1-1-1: The god himself will set me free.
1-1-2: The rituals are no friend of any man who's hostile to the gods.
1-1-3: I'll go inside your house and dress you up.
1-1-4: Surely a god can make it over any wall?
1-1-5: after he made himself so terrifying
1-1-6: But now it's working in you as it should.
1-2-1: he found a bull.
1-2-2: You bear the city's burden by yourself.
1-2-3: I'm the guide who'll rescue you.
1-2-4: Hold out your hand to him.
1-2-5: You refused my rites.
1-2-6: That's what I proclaim.
1-3-1: in your mother's arms.
1-3-2: a guardian.
1-3-3: he'll transform your lives.
1-3-4: who wants to hide himself.
1-3-5: down to your ankle.
1-3-6: stop all that.
1-4-1: Your harmonious wife.
1-4-2: Your form will change.
1-4-3: abandon your city for barbarian lands.
1-4-4: those places where the nymphs all congregate.
1-4-5: I'm leading this young man in your direction.
1-4-6: all by yourself.
1-5-1: I've arrived here in the land of Thebes.
1-5-2: That's true, but in my own way.
1-5-3: Well, you'll win a towering fame, as high as heaven.
1-5-4: The Thebans learned about my powers too late.
1-5-5: events will show, as they occur.
1-5-6: Follow me.
1-6-1: What for?

1-6-2: while I lead him through the city

1-6-3: Before this your mind was not well adjusted.

1-6-4: In that case, you must clothe your body in a dress—one made of eastern linen.

1-6-5: Now it's up to you.

1-6-6: Maybe you'll capture them, unless you're captured first.

2-1-1: The tasks that have been specially set for you.

2-1-2: you'll have become someone to celebrate.

2-1-3: I fixed it.

2-1-4: A thyrsus to hold and a dappled fawn skin.

2-1-5: He was what he wished to be, not made to order.

2-1-6: In this business I was playing with him.

2-2-1: He came to Thebes with nothing but good things.

2-2-2: A suitable name. It suggests misfortune.

2-2-3: Sacred lord of earthquakes, shake this ground.

2-2-4: But first you'd better listen to this man.

2-2-5: We go by deserted streets.

2-2-6: I watched him, sitting quietly nearby.

2-3-1: you're not far away.

2-3-2: or did you miss that part?

2-3-3: Get up now. Be brave. And stop your trembling.

2-3-4: That will be his punishment.

2-3-5: Before his attitude was not so kind.

2-3-6: But here, this strand of hair is out of place.

2-4-1: I applaud you for it.

2-4-2: That information cannot be passed on to men like you.

2-4-3: Are you ready to take the trip?

2-4-4: Now you're seeing just what you ought to see.

2-4-5: Pan plays his music on his pipes.

2-4-6: He's dropped his sword, worn out, exhausted.

2-5-1: Well, I'll deal with him quite gently.

2-5-2: You'll find just the sort of hiding place.

2-5-3: Perhaps.

2-5-4: That sounds like a wise way to proceed.

2-5-5: mincing as he moves along in women's clothing

2-5-6: Did you feel despair when I was sent away?

2-6-1: outside the palace.

2-6-2: You must lift your right foot in time with it.

2-6-3: Your mind has changed.

2-6-4: Your work is waiting there.

2-6-5: So I've driven those women from their homes in a frenzy.

2-6-6: so desperately eager to see.

3-1-1: He's made a pact with us.

3-1-2: I'll take you.

3-1-3: and there he'll die.
3-1-4: he kept panting in his rage, dripping sweat.
3-1-5: When you return someone else will bring you back.
3-1-6: On your way to horrific suffering.
3-2-1: you too must endure your lot.
3-2-2: That polluted creature.
3-2-3: But you can be sure of this.
3-2-4: Do you lie there on the ground prostrate with fear?
3-2-5: for the great confrontation
3-2-6: Io! Io! I'm calling out again.
3-3-1: If you have desire, you'll have the power.
3-3-2: you'll consider me your dearest friend.
3-3-3: with all those earlier threats
3-3-4: Shadows confer solemnity.
3-3-5: Now you must leave.
3-3-6: As Zeus' oracle declares.
3-4-1: slashing away at nothing but bright air.
3-4-2: What sort of trick, if I want to save you in my own way?
3-4-3: There's more.
3-4-4: I have myself completely covered it.
3-4-5: But he'll do it, if you make him mad.
3-4-6: As you wish.
3-5-1: It's only right.
3-5-2: Hold on. Calm down. Don't be so angry.
3-5-3: You'll rule barbarians.
3-5-4: My hair is sacred. I grow it for the god.
3-5-5: What will he say, I wonder, after this?
3-5-6: If you had understood how to behave as you should have.
3-6-1: you earn the penalty.
3-6-2: You've lost your wits.
3-6-3: Yes, that's true.
3-6-4: too large to count.
3-6-5: I'll rearrange it for you.
3-6-6: Yes, I've changed my form from god to man.
4-1-1: But Ares will guard you and Harmonia.
4-1-2: Why postpone what necessity requires?
4-1-3: Dishonoring me.
4-1-4: my name received no recognition.
4-1-5: you'd now be fortunate.
4-1-6: You've heard what I had to say.
4-2-1: fleeing the thyrsoi of those Bacchic women!
4-2-2: Hunt down evil by committing evil.
4-2-3: Why do you wish to see something that will only cause you pain?

4-2-4: But if you go fighting with these mad women, you'll cause bloodshed.
4-2-5: those things you should not look upon.
4-2-6: You can't see him, because you don't believe.
4-3-1: I'll still be here for you. I won't run off.
4-3-2: consume it all!
4-3-3: You'll confront something you don't expect.
4-3-4: Why then delay?
4-3-5: and dreadfully.
4-3-6: a mere mortal daring to fight a god.
4-4-1: Straighten up your head.
4-4-2: I have made some arrangement with the god.
4-4-3: they'll have a painful journey back again.
4-4-4: I was born a god, and you insulted me.
4-4-5: It seems you feel Dionysos' power, as he rattles Pentheus' palace.
4-4-6: Yes.
4-5-1: My father Zeus willed all this long ago.
4-5-2: Your girdle's loose.
4-5-3: he'll not agree.
4-5-4: But their laws are very different, too.
4-5-5: After all, a wise man ought to keep his temper.
4-5-6: Bacchic women acting modestly.
4-6-1: you'll raze many cities.
4-6-2: But even if you go there secretly, they'll find you out.
4-6-3: Wait! It seems to me I hear marching feet—
4-6-4: Why is that?
4-6-5: most terrifying and yet most kind to men.
4-6-6: There's still a chance to end this calmly.
5-1-1: I've made them put on costumes.
5-1-2: crooked, too.
5-1-3: He ran round, here and there.
5-1-4: He goes insane with some crazed fantasy.
5-1-5: So you're prepared?
5-1-6: One can do shameful things in daylight, too.
5-2-1: you should have known.
5-2-2: I've brought you the man who laughed at you.
5-2-3: making known to men my own divinity.
5-2-4: I will triumph.
5-2-5: When I look at you I think I see them.
5-2-6: with their beautifully constructed towers.
5-3-1: I'd sooner make an offering to that god.
5-3-2: To spoil you?
5-3-3: dancing in the mysteries I established.
5-3-4: Now punish him!

5-3-5: The god walks here.

5-3-6: I saw him—he saw me.

5-4-1: with the offspring of Zeus among your allies.

5-4-2: the costume he'll wear when he goes down to Hades.

5-4-3: So it seems to me, but I'm guessing now.

5-4-4: He'll come to acknowledge Dionysos.

5-4-5: that man's now entangled in our net.

5-4-6: along the salt-sea coast.

5-5-1: in my hand.

5-5-2: He sees my suffering now—and from near by.

5-5-3: full of barbarians and Greeks all intermingled

5-5-4: Would you derive pleasure from looking on?

5-5-5: You learn too late.

5-5-6: They boasted aloud.

5-6-1: Once these things here have been made right, I'll move on somewhere else.

5-6-2: You've heard of Tmolus, where flowers grow.

5-6-3: What harsh penalties will you inflict?

5-6-4: Burn Pentheus' palace.

5-6-5: sisters have acted badly.

5-6-6: They're worth knowing, but you're not allowed to hear.

6-1-1: They'll track you down.

6-1-2: Just a minute!

6-1-3: You're quite ignorant of why you live, what you do, and who you are.

6-1-4: sitting together in the mountains.

6-1-5: Why so desperately eager?

6-1-6: What a disgrace!

6-2-1: You look just like one of Cadmus' daughters.

6-2-2: Bromios will not let you.

6-2-3: consumed by the lightning bolt.

6-2-4: Io! Hear me, hear me as I call you.

6-2-5: attributed her bad luck in bed to Zeus

6-2-6: lands of the gold-rich East.

6-3-1: Here I plead the cause of my own mother.

6-3-2: He's made his daughter's shrine a holy place.

6-3-3: take up the drum.

6-3-4: go in person.

6-3-5: I will not compel.

6-3-6: I warn you—you shouldn't tie me up.

6-4-1: he chooses to ignore me.

6-4-2: You were ignorant.

6-4-3: comrades on the road.

6-4-4: prohibiting all sacrificial rites.

6-4-5: Why do you desire it so much?
6-4-6: that's why Zeus killed her
6-5-1: and all for nothing!
6-5-2: I, commander of these Maenads, will fight them.
6-5-3: of all people, should avoid.
6-5-4: Whatever you do, I'm ready.
6-5-5: the old king has just transferred his power.
6-5-6: They said she made the whole story up.
6-6-1: or, at least, all women
6-6-2: underneath green pine trees, no roof overhead
6-6-3: Come out here now.
6-6-4: Persia's sun-drenched plains.
6-6-5: If they see you as a man, they'll kill you.
6-6-6: All the barbarians are dancing in these rites.

[Made from the words of Jim Morrison and The Doors]

> There are things known and there are things unknown, and in between are the doors of perception. (Aldous Huxley)

1-1-1: Then daylight brought wisdom
1-1-2: like lovers feel
1-1-3: free from disguise
1-1-4: the body of his mother rotting in the summer ground
1-1-5: Awake. Shake dreams from your hair my pretty child, my sweet one.
1-1-6: it's how it has to be.
1-2-1: silver and gold and the mountains of Spain.
1-2-2: of our elaborate plans, the end.
1-2-3: revelry with the one that set them free.
1-2-4: he came to a door and looked inside.
1-2-5: To make oneself invisible or small.
1-2-6: I think you know the game I mean
1-3-1: People are strange when you're a stranger.
1-3-2: I don't know if you're aware of it, but this whole evening is being taped for eternity and beyond that too.
1-3-3: Do you dare?
1-3-4: Why did you throw the Jack of Hearts away?
1-3-5: Like a dog without a bone
1-3-6: they got the guns, but we got the numbers.
1-4-1: the chaos and disorder
1-4-2: Keep your eyes on the road, your hands upon the wheel
1-4-3: Well, I've been down so Goddamn long that it looks like up to me
1-4-4: Events take place beyond our knowledge or control.
1-4-5: Learn to forget
1-4-6: ride the snake
1-5-1: Have you forgotten the keys to the kingdom?
1-5-2: Arms in chains.
1-5-3: Fuck Florida, and fuck college, and fuck me!
1-5-4: We could plan a murder ... or start a religion.
1-5-5: I smiled at you.
1-5-6: get in and we'll do the rest.
1-6-1: The program for this evening is not new
1-6-2: [Inarticulate screaming]
1-6-3: Women seem wicked when you're unwanted.

1-6-4: Nothing left to do, but run, run, run

1-6-5: You know that it would be untrue

1-6-6: excitement soon unfolds.

2-1-1: no way to lose

2-1-2: blows cold this season

2-1-3: very softly

2-1-4: You know the day destroys the night; night divides the day.

2-1-5: Give up your vows

2-1-6: will you give it another chance?

2-2-1: Now I have come again to the land of the fair, and the strong, and the wise

2-2-2: I got the poontang blues.

2-2-3: dogs in heat, rabid, foaming

2-2-4: We live, we die

2-2-5: Stronger than dirt.

2-2-6: Well I'll tell you a story

2-3-1: Took a look around me, which way the wind blows.

2-3-2: Is everybody in? The ceremony is about to begin.

2-3-3: may take a week, and it may take longer

2-3-4: Forget the world, forget the people

2-3-5: no safety or surprise

2-3-6: The future's uncertain and the end is always near.

2-4-1: We're trying for something that's already found us.

2-4-2: This is the strangest life I've ever known.

2-4-3: Choose the day and choose the sign of your day.

2-4-4: I had money and I had none

2-4-5: Can't you see what they were at?

2-4-6: lost in a Roman wilderness of pain

2-5-1: To glory in self like a new monster

2-5-2: river flow, on and on it goes

2-5-3: five to one, baby, one in five

2-5-4: Too late, too late.

2-5-5: until the end.

2-5-6: I know your deepest, secret fear

2-6-1: I can't believe this is happening

2-6-2: I'm not hungry

2-6-3: I'll tell you 'bout the heartache and the loss of God.

2-6-4: See me change, you

2-6-5: Her cunt gripped him like a warm, friendly hand.

2-6-6: We'll meet again.

3-1-1: The dark one, Enterprise

3-1-2: like an invalid who has forgotten to walk

3-1-3: No one remembers your name.

3-1-4: Cancel my subscription to the resurrection

3-1-5: To exalt senses and perceive inaccessible images

3-1-6: One for tomorrow, one just for today.

3-2-1: His brain is squirming like a toad

3-2-2: Won't you get down on your knees

3-2-3: I'm getting out of here

3-2-4: trade in your hours for a handful of dimes

3-2-5: A million ways to spend your time

3-2-6: it was easy, try it again

3-3-1: You are dying in a prison

3-3-2: I think it's sufficiently complex and universal in its imagery that it
could be almost anything you want it to be.

3-3-3: κατα τον δαιμονα εαυτου

3-3-4: The blue bus is calling us.

3-3-5: I got this girl beside me, but she's out of reach

3-3-6: And you won't know a thing till you get inside

3-4-1: A wrong gesture. Too long and curious a glance.

3-4-2: the devil was wiser

3-4-3: Blood is the rose of mysterious union.

3-4-4: tried to run, tried to hide

3-4-5: Take a long holiday

3-4-6: red rivers of weeping

3-5-1: Such a long long road to seek it

3-5-2: relax, take a few deep breaths

3-5-3: can't you see the wonder at your feet?

3-5-4: Want the worms to be my friends

3-5-5: Crap, now that's crap!

3-5-6: Celebrate symbols from deep elder forests

3-6-1: Whenever we seek to break this spell of passivity, our actions are
cruel and awkward and generally obscene

3-6-2: We can only try to enslave others.

3-6-3: I'm sick of dour faces

3-6-4: There's blood in the streets, it's up to my knees.

3-6-5: Hordes crawl and seep inside

3-6-6: No eternal reward will forgive us now for wasting the dawn.

4-1-1: Impossible, yes, but it's true.

4-1-2: Ghosts crowd the young child's fragile eggshell mind.

4-1-3: the snake who lives in a well by the side of the road

4-1-4: The face in the mirror won't stop

4-1-5: with all of your charms.

4-1-6: Do you remember when we were in Africa?

4-2-1: slow and mad like some new language

4-2-2: Currents breed tiny monsters

4-2-3: Out here in the perimeter there are no stars

4-2-4: You're lost, little girl.

4-2-5: Death makes angels of us all
4-2-6: Petition the Lord with prayer, petition the Lord with prayer
4-3-1: Indian, Indian what did you die for? Indian says, nothing at all.
4-3-2: The music and voices are all around us.
4-3-3: I want roses in my garden bower
4-3-4: Can you picture what will be?
4-3-5: Come on baby, light my fire
4-3-6: It hurts to set you free
4-4-1: That was the first time I tasted fear.
4-4-2: Your ballroom days are over
4-4-3: What was that promise that you made?
4-4-4: to become gigantic and reach to the farthest things
4-4-5: the fertility of fire
4-4-6: We chased our pleasures here, dug our treasures there.
4-5-1: Cinema has evolved in two paths.
4-5-2: Go out and buy a brand new pair of shoes
4-5-3: give us an hour for magic
4-5-4: no one here gets out alive
4-5-5: events on other worlds
4-5-6: to freak out or be beautiful, my dear.
4-6-1: Tell me, who are you?
4-6-2: or in the minds of others
4-6-3: I need a brand new friend who doesn't trouble me.
4-6-4: summon the dead
4-6-5: But gradually, special perceptions are being developed.
4-6-6: Life goes on absorbing war.
5-1-1: get your guns, the time has come.
5-1-2: Don't you cry, baby, please don't cry.
5-1-3: to change the course of nature
5-1-4: all the children are insane.
5-1-5: Still one place to go
5-1-6: With ravaged limbs and wet souls
5-2-1: People talk about how great love is, but that's bullshit. Love hurts.
5-2-2: Out here we is stoned ... immaculate.
5-2-3: The Lords have secret entrances and they know disguises.
5-2-4: I touched her thigh and death smiled
5-2-5: I will not go
5-2-6: Hey man, you want girls, pills, grass? C'mon ... I show you good
    time.
5-3-1: going to bury all our troubles in the sand
5-3-2: To propagate our lust for life
5-3-3: Wandering, wandering in hopeless night
5-3-4: he took a face from the ancient gallery and he walked on down the
    hall

5-3-5: Reaching your head with the cold, sudden fury of a divine messenger

5-3-6: flee the swarming wisdom

5-4-1: Have you been born yet and are you alive?

5-4-2: take him by the hand, make him understand

5-4-3: But can you still recall the time we cried

5-4-4: Alchemy is an erotic science, involved in buried aspects of reality, aimed at purifying and transforming all being and matter.

5-4-5: the west is the best.

5-4-6: Windows work two ways, mirrors one way.

5-5-1: Deep and wide

5-5-2: I think it's a bunch of bullshit, myself

5-5-3: I sacrifice my cock on the altar of silence.

5-5-4: Night is drawing near.

5-5-5: "Alive!" she cried

5-5-6: She came into town and then she drove away.

5-6-1: The palace of exile

5-6-2: Oh, what can I do?

5-6-3: Strange days have found us.

5-6-4: Very near yet very far

5-6-5: a feast of friends

5-6-6: Not to touch the earth

6-1-1: I see first lots of things which dance — then everything becomes gradually connected

6-1-2: it's our time to try.

6-1-3: Desperately in need of some stranger's hand.

6-1-4: The death of all joy

6-1-5: Strange, fertile correspondences the alchemists sensed in unlikely orders of being. Between men and planets, plants and gestures, words and weather.

6-1-6: You cannot petition the Lord with prayer!

6-2-1: Yoga powers.

6-2-2: you know this is it.

6-2-3: Not to suggest that material operations are ever abandoned.

6-2-4: But they give themselves away in minor ways.

6-2-5: the names of the kingdom

6-2-6: As here I lie

6-3-1: The old get older and the young get stronger

6-3-2: with fields full of grain.

6-3-3: First there were women and children obeying the moon

6-3-4: Don't worry, the operation won't take long and you'll feel much better in the morning.

6-3-5: there's danger on the edge of town.

6-3-6: Wake up!

6-4-1: Few would defend a small view

6-4-2: The adept holds to both the mystical and physical work.

6-4-3: Break on through to the other side.

6-4-4: it's following me.

6-4-5: I think that you know what to do.

6-4-6: The voices of singing women call us on the far shore

6-5-1: Memories misused.

6-5-2: Can't you see that I am not afraid?

6-5-3: Not to see the sun

6-5-4: She gets high, yeah.

6-5-5: and gives us wings where we had shoulders smooth as raven's claws

6-5-6: The idea of the "Lords" is beginning to form in some minds.

6-6-1: I'm lost in my own mind's pain

6-6-2: he asked her to give back the money she had spent

6-6-3: Try to set the night on fire.

6-6-4: Do you guys want to see it? I'll show it to ya!

6-6-5: We must try to find a new answer instead of a way

6-6-6: I am the Lizard King. I can do anything!

[Made from the songs of David Bowie]

1-1-1: I'm stepping through the door
1-1-2: We like dancing and we look divine.
1-1-3: There is no other day
1-1-4: They scream my name aloud down into the well below
1-1-5: Now I'm back where I started from
1-1-6: Show me who you are
1-2-1: Cried so much his face was wet, then I knew he was not lying.
1-2-2: All the roads were straight and narrow
1-2-3: You'll lose your mind and play
1-2-4: Come and buy my little toys
1-2-5: Ready, set, go
1-2-6: Hey babe, your hair's alright.
1-3-1: I'll give you television.
1-3-2: You know, you know
1-3-3: I shall always watch you until my love runs dry
1-3-4: Nothing we can't shake
1-3-5: There's never gonna be enough bullets
1-3-6: I'm afraid of the world.
1-4-1: When the kids had killed the man I had to break up the band.
1-4-2: Nothing ever goes away
1-4-3: Dead ones and the living
1-4-4: I'm smiling
1-4-5: Just a small thin chance
1-4-6: There'll be some blood no doubt about it
1-5-1: But her mummy is yelling "No"
1-5-2: No one can blame you for walking away
1-5-3: Sister, sister, please take me down, gotta get underground
1-5-4: I think maybe you feel the same
1-5-5: In search of new dreams.
1-5-6: And even down looks up
1-6-1: Daddy didn't have no toys
1-6-2: And we don't charge nothin' (nothin' at all)
1-6-3: Just as I can be so cruel
1-6-4: He took it all too far
1-6-5: Things that happened in the past only happened in your mind
1-6-6: Life is too easy, a plague seems quite feasible now or maybe a war, or
       I may kill you all

2-1-1: As long as there's sun
2-1-2: Who do? You do.
2-1-3: I move the stars for no one.
2-1-4: Feed me no lies
2-1-5: Your eyes can be so cruel
2-1-6: As long as you're still smiling
2-2-1: Let's dance — put on your red shoes and dance the blues.
2-2-2: I'll ruin everything you are
2-2-3: What kind of magic spell to use?
2-2-4: Can you dig our groovy feelin'?
2-2-5: Battle cries and champagne just in time for sunrise.
2-2-6: We are not your friends
2-3-1: Trap you with their beautiful eyes
2-3-2: I saw my baby, crying hard as babe could cry
2-3-3: She's not sure if you're a boy or a girl.
2-3-4: But we'll come thru don't doubt it
2-3-5: Waiting for something
2-3-6: Remember the dead
2-4-1: It's a broken heart that dreams
2-4-2: I've been waiting for you
2-4-3: All things must pass.
2-4-4: Memories that flutter like bats out of hell
2-4-5: A million dead-end streets
2-4-6: Puts my trust in God and man
2-5-1: I got a better way
2-5-2: Dear when I dance with you, we move like the sea
2-5-3: Mother calls, but we don't hear
2-5-4: There's a starman waiting in the sky
2-5-5: Gone, Gone the water's all gone
2-5-6: I'm not quite sure what you're supposed to say
2-6-1: It's only forever, not long at all
2-6-2: Then they take back everything that you have
2-6-3: I can't answer why
2-6-4: there's no one there
2-6-5: Achtung, achtung, these are your orders
2-6-6: And there's never gonna be enough money
3-1-1: But I won't look at that scar
3-1-2: Don't tell me truth hurts, little girl, 'cause it hurts like hell
3-1-3: Waiting for the first move
3-1-4: You want more and you want it fast.
3-1-5: Open up your heart to me
3-1-6: It produced sounds of wailing, crying
3-2-1: and I'll love her till the day she dies
3-2-2: I'm gonna be so good, just like a good boy should

3-2-3: Man is an obstacle, sad as the clown
3-2-4: They live upon their feet and they die upon their knees
3-2-5: They're quite aware of what they're going through
3-2-6: In the year of the scavenger, the season of the bitch
3-3-1: don't believe in modern love
3-3-2: Show me all you are
3-3-3: Guardians of a loveless isle
3-3-4: In the valley of the dead man walks
3-3-5: Their jealousy's spilling down
3-3-6: How many times does an angel fall?
3-4-1: Slap that baby, make him free
3-4-2: Saying no but meaning yes
3-4-3: I'll place the sky within your eyes.
3-4-4: Oh, we can be heroes just for one day.
3-4-5: And the empty man you left behind
3-4-6: Makes no sense to fall.
3-5-1: creating a macabre shrine of remains
3-5-2: First they give you everything that you want
3-5-3: She's not mine for eternity
3-5-4: it's not your brain, it's just the flame
3-5-5: Wasn't too much fun at all
3-5-6: But you got problems oh-oh-oh-oh
3-6-1: I never lied to you, I hated when you lied
3-6-2: Louder than thunder
3-6-3: You've run so long, you've run so far.
3-6-4: And there's nothing I can do.
3-6-5: As the pain sweeps through, makes no sense for you.
3-6-6: Just look through your window, look who sits outside
4-1-1: As long as there's you
4-1-2: Looking for someone
4-1-3: When your thing gets wild
4-1-4: Turn and face the strange.
4-1-5: Ain't got no clothes to worry about
4-1-6: We can beat them, forever and ever
4-2-1: Every thrill is gone.
4-2-2: This way or no way
4-2-3: t's a god-awful small affair
4-2-4: You and me and nothing more
4-2-5: Just strut your nasty stuff,
4-2-6: Do you remember, the bills you have to pay?
4-3-1: Let the wind blow through your hair, be nice to the big blue sea
4-3-2: I would sit and blame the master first and last
4-3-3: Bad luck heh heh
4-3-4: Heaven is smiling down, heaven's girl in a wedding gown

4-3-5: Everything I've done, I've done for you.

4-3-6: Oh I do believe in you. Yes I do.

4-4-1: In the centre of it all, in the centre of it all

4-4-2: So where were the spiders

4-4-3: Down in the underground you'll find someone true

4-4-4: Became the special man

4-4-5: Like dolphins can swim

4-4-6: Give me money for a change of face

4-5-1: I believe in magic

4-5-2: But don't forget your date with me

4-5-3: And when she's dreaming, I believe

4-5-4: Every time I thought I'd got it made, it seemed the taste was not so sweet

4-5-5: I can stare for a thousand years

4-5-6: Fill your heart with love today

4-6-1: Like a leper messiah

4-6-2: He swallowed his pride and puckered his lips

4-6-3: The writing's on the wall

4-6-4: I know something is very wrong

4-6-5: just for show

4-6-6: We passed upon the stair, we spoke of was and when

5-1-1: She opened strange doors

5-1-2: We're painting our faces and dressing in thoughts

5-1-3: It's all deranged — no control

5-1-4: Fear's just in your head

5-1-5: Please trip them gently, they don't like to fall

5-1-6: Walk out of her heart, walk out of her mind

5-2-1: Ch-ch-ch-ch-Changes

5-2-2: With God given ass

5-2-3: You've gotta have a scheme

5-2-4: But she's a queen, and such are queens

5-2-5: Round and round the rumours fly

5-2-6: So I said "So long" and I waved "Bye-bye"

5-3-1: If she says she can do it, then she can do it

5-3-2: Torture comes and torture goes

5-3-3: Keep your mouth shut, you're squawking like a pink monkey bird

5-3-4: There's nothing more I need

5-3-5: But they think that we're holding a secretive ball.

5-3-6: Full of blood, loving life and all it's got to give

5-4-1: Don't let me hear you say life's taking you nowhere, angel

5-4-2: So it goes

5-4-3: Oh give me the night

5-4-4: Breathing in only doubt

5-4-5: Rebel Rebel, you've torn your dress.

5-4-6: They wore it out but they wore it well
5-5-1: She talked to God
5-5-2: As the world falls down.
5-5-3: And he's always a little late
5-5-4: We're choosing the path
5-5-5: Now she's leading him on
5-5-6: It's the nature of being
5-6-1: What a jolly boring thing to do
5-6-2: I don't see the point at all
5-6-3: Yes, it could have been me
5-6-4: Look at that sky, life's begun
5-6-5: Don't fake it baby, lay the real thing on me
5-6-6: Speaks to the shadows
6-1-1: Take your passport and shoes
6-1-2: Femme fatales emerged from shadows to watch this creature fair
6-1-3: And your prayers they break the sky in two
6-1-4: But her friend is nowhere to be seen
6-1-5: Making love with his ego
6-1-6: I said "Do it again, do it again"
6-2-1: Yes, and I wonder why sometimes
6-2-2: It's got nothing to do with you
6-2-3: Lady Stardust sang his songs of darkness and dismay
6-2-4: Can't tell the bullshit from the lies
6-2-5: I could make it all worthwhile
6-2-6: And I heard a voice that cries
6-3-1: Yea! it was time to unfreeze
6-3-2: But, boy, could he play guitar
6-3-3: He'd like to come and meet us, but he thinks he'd blow our minds.
6-3-4: And the possibilities it seems to offer
6-3-5: Cracking all the mirrors in shame
6-3-6: I'm afraid I can't.
6-4-1: Breathe, breathe, breathe deeply
6-4-2: why didn't I say, no, no, no
6-4-3: Believing the strangest things, loving the alien
6-4-4: But I'll be there for you-ou-ou.
6-4-5: if one can grasp it
6-4-6: And if you say hide, we'll hide.
6-5-1: Every single move's uncertain
6-5-2: For the love of the money
6-5-3: Falls upon dead ears
6-5-4: Back away from the light
6-5-5: So hold on to nothing, and he won't let you down.
6-5-6: Stay away from the future
6-6-1: I've got nothing left to lose

6-6-2: With great expectations I change all my clothes
6-6-3: This ain't rock'n'roll. This is genocide!
6-6-4: Now I'm older than movies
6-6-5: And there's never gonna be enough drugs
6-6-6: Live to your rebirth and do what you will

The Lots of Dionysos the Bridegroom

And golden-haired Dionysos made blonde-haired Ariadne, the daughter of Minos, his buxom wife: and the son of Kronos made her deathless and unageing for him. (Hesiod, *Theogony* 947)

Inscribe the numbers 1 through 28 on pieces of paper, stone or pottery sherds and consult the relevant verse when it is drawn if you wish to inquire of the God concerning matters pertaining to the heart or relationships. The verses are taken from Plutarch's Γαμικα Παραγγελματα or *Conjugal Precepts.*

I. It behooves that man to have his family in exquisite order who will undertake to regulate the failing of his friends or the public miscarriages.

II. It becomes a man and his wife at all times to avoid occasions of quarrelling one with another.

III. For it is natural to some mothers to be jealous that the wife deprives her of that filial tenderness which she expects from her son.

IV. Phidias made the statue of Aphrodite at Elis with one foot upon the shell of a tortoise, to signify two great duties of a virtuous woman, which are to keep at home and be silent.

V. The over-rigid humor of a wife renders her honesty irksome.

VI. Queen Olympias, understanding that a young courtier had married a lady, beautiful indeed, but of no good report, said: Sure, the Hotspur had little brains, otherwise he would never have married with his eyes. For they are fools who in the choice of a wife believe the report of their sight or fingers.

VII. They who refuse to frolic in retirement with their wives, or to let them participate of their private pastimes and dalliances, do but instruct them to cater for their own pleasures and delights.

VIII. It especially behooves those people who are newly married to avoid the first occasions of discord and dissension; considering that vessels newly formed are subject to be bruised and put out of shape by many slight accidents, but when the materials come once to be settled and hardened by time, nor fire nor sword will hardly prejudice the solid substance.

IX. Fire takes speedy hold of straw or hare's fur, but soon goes out again, unless fed with an addition of more fuel.

X. For he that allows himself those pleasures that he forbids his wife, acts like a man that would enjoin his wife to oppose those enemies to which he has himself already surrendered.

XI. But as for quaint opinions and superstitious innovations, let them be exterminated from her outermost threshold.

XII. The question being put by some of his friends to a certain Roman, why he had put away his wife, both sober, beautiful, chaste, and rich, the gentleman, putting forth his foot and showing his buskin, said: Is not this a new, handsome, complete shoe? — yet no man but myself knows where it pinches me.

XIII. However, as in a goblet where the proportion of water exceeds the juice of the grape, yet still we call the mixture wine; in like manner the house and estate must be reputed the possession of the husband, although the woman brought the chiefest part.

XIV. As the woman in difficult labor said to those that were about to lay her upon her bed; How, said she, can this bed cure these pains, since it was in this very bed that my pleasures were the cause of all my throes?

XV. It behooves a husband to control his wife, not as a master does his vassal, but as the soul governs the body, with the gentle hand of mutual friendship and reciprocal affection.

XVI. They who bait their hooks with intoxicated drugs with little pains surprise the hungry fish, but then they prove unsavory to the taste and dangerous to eat.

XVII. Plato asserts those cities to be the most happy and best regulated where these expressions, "This is mine," "This is not mine," are seldomest made use of.

XVIII. On the other side, those young ladies that take a disdain to their husbands by reason of their first debates and encounters may be well compared to those that patiently endure the sting but fling away the honey.

XIX. They will not believe that Pasiphae, the consort of a prince, could ever be enamored of a bull, and yet themselves are so extravagant as to abandon the society of their husbands, — men of wisdom, temperance, and gravity, — and betake themselves to the bestial embraces of those who are given wholly to riot and debauchery as if they were dogs or goats.

XX. It behooves a woman not to make peculiar and private friendships of her own, but to esteem only her husband's acquaintance and familiars as hers.

XXI. It is a common proverb, that the sun is too strong for the north wind; for the more the wind ruffles and strives to force a man's upper garment from his back, the faster he holds it, and the closer he wraps it about his shoulders. But he who so briskly defended himself from being plundered by the wind, when once the sun begins to scald the air, all in a dropping sweat is then constrained to throw away not only his flowing garment but his tunic also.

XXII. Helen was covetous, Paris luxurious. On the other side, Ulysses was prudent, Penelope chaste. Happy therefore was the match between the latter; but the nuptials of the former brought an Iliad of miseries as well upon the Greeks as barbarians.

XXIII. Princes that be addicted to music increase the number of excellent musicians; if they be lovers of learning, all men strive to excel in reading and in eloquence.

XXIV. But altogether different is the humor of our women; for they, unless allowed their jewels, their bracelets, and necklaces, their gaudy vestments, gowns, and petticoats, all bespangled with gold, and their embroidered buskins, will never stir abroad.

XXV. Socrates was wont to give this advice to young men that accustomed themselves to their mirrors: — if ill-favored, to correct their deformity by the practice of virtue; if handsome, not to blemish their outward form with inward vice.

XXVI. Plato observing the morose and sour humor of Xenocrates, otherwise a person of great virtue and worth, admonished him to sacrifice to the Graces.

XXVII. This is an honor conferred upon her, not by the lustre of gold, the sparkling of emeralds and diamonds, nor splendor of the purple tincture, but by the real embellishments of gravity, discretion, humility, and modesty.

XXVIII. They who offer to Hera as the Goddess of Wedlock never consecrate the gall with the other parts of the sacrifice, but having drawn it forth, they cast it behind the altar. Which constitution of the lawgiver fairly implies that all manner of passionate anger and bitterness of reproach should be exterminated from the thresholds of nuptial cohabitation.

The Oracle of Dionysos Mousegetes

As Dionysos is partnered with the Mousai:

> Those who profess the Orphic theology consider a two-fold power
> in souls and in the celestial orbs: the one consisting in knowledge,
> the other in vivifying and governing the orb with which that power
> is connected. Thus in the orb of the Earth, they call the gnostic
> power Pluto, the other Proserpine. In Water, the former power
> Ocean, and the latter Thetis. In Air, that thundering Jove, and this
> Juno. In Fire, that Phanes, and this Aurora. In the soul of the
> Lunar sphere, they call the gnostic power Licnitan Bacchus, the
> other Thalia. In the sphere of Mercury, that Bacchus Silenus, this
> Euterpe. In the orb of Venus, that Lysius Bacchus, this Erato. In
> the sphere of the Sun, that Trietericus Bacchus, this Melpomene. In
> the orb of Mars, that Bassareus Bacchus, this Clio. In the sphere of
> Jove, that Sebazius, this Terpsichore. In the orb of Saturn, that
> Amphietus, this Polymnia. In the eighth sphere, that Pericionius,
> this Urania. But in the soul of the World, the gnostic power,
> Bacchus Eribromus, but the animating power Calliope. From all
> which the Orphic theologers infer that the particular epithets of
> Bacchus are compared with those of the Muses on this account,
> that we may understand the powers of the Muses, as intoxicated
> with the nectar of divine knowledge; and may consider the nine
> Muses, and nine Bacchuses, as revolving round one Apollo, that is
> about the splendor of one invisible Sun. (Marsilio Ficino, *On Plato's
> Theology*)

This form of bibliomancy employs lines from authors who were preeminent
in each of the genres they presided over:

Kalliope (Epic): Homer
Klio (History): Herodotos
Euterpe (Elegy): Archilochos
Erato (Lyric): Sappho
Melpomene (Tragedy): Seneca
Polymnia (Hymns): Orphic
Terpsichore (Dance): Lucian
Thalia (Comedy): Aristophanes
Urania (Astronomy): Aratos

Instructions

In a bag place a representation of each of the Mousai, either one of their traditional symbols or something you personally associate with them. When you need to determine who to consult, reach in and draw one of the tokens out.

Cast four dice that have been consecrated to Dionysos and the Mousai and add the resulting numbers together to receive your message.

Kalliope
4. healing salves, by which he can put an end to the black pains
5. I rejoice at hearing what you say, son of Laërtes
6. For no island is made for driving horses or has broad meadows
7. Would that you not plead with the noble son of Peleus
8. One omen is best, to defend your country
9. Honor then the gods, Achilles, and take pity on me
10. be valiant, that later generations may also speak well of you
11. How then could I forget divine Odysseus?
12. But Zeus causes men's prowess to wax or to wane
13. Talk not like this. There'll be no change before
14. Odysseus has come and reached home, though he was long in coming
15. For mighty Herakles, not even he escaped his doom
16. In no way do I mock you, dear child, nor am I playing tricks
17. For even fair-tressed Niobe turned her mind to food
18. Offer me not honey-tempered wine, honored mother
19. Eurymachos, it will not be so. And even you know it
20. and vow to Lycian-born Apollo the famous archer
21. Bad deeds don't prosper. The slow man for sure overtakes the swift
22. And let him stand up among the Argives and swear an oath to you
23. You would learn what mighty hands I have to back me up
24. Come now, in strict silence, and I shall lead the way

Klio
4. I know that human happiness never remains long in the same place.
5. Force has no place where there is need of skill.
6. Haste in every business brings failures.
7. I am bound to tell what I am told, but not in every case to believe it.
8. If a man insisted always on being serious, and never allowed himself a bit of fun and relaxation, he would go mad or become unstable without knowing it.
9. This is the bitterest pain among men, to have much knowledge but no power.

10. Many very rich men have been unfortunate, and many with a modest competence have had good luck.
11. I am going to talk at some length about Egypt.
12. All think that their own customs are by far the best.
13. In peace sons bury fathers, but in war fathers bury sons.
14. How much better a thing it is to be envied than to be pitied.
15. Circumstances rule men; men do not rule circumstances.
16. Hippocleides doesn't care.
17. Good. Then we will fight in the shade
18. so that the actions of people will not fade with time.
19. It was the fault of the Greek gods, who with their arrogance, encouraged me to march onto your lands.
20. It is better by noble boldness to run the risk of being subject to half of the evils we anticipate than to remain in cowardly listlessness for fear of what might happen.
21. Call no man happy until he is dead.
22. But this I know: if all mankind were to take their troubles to market with the idea of exchanging them, anyone seeing what his neighbor's troubles were like would be glad to go home with his own."
23. When the Many are rulers, it cannot but be that, again, knavery is bred in the state.
24. Look upon this corpse as you drink and enjoy yourself; for you will be just like it when you are dead.

Euterpe

4. The fox knows many things, but the hedgehog knows one big thing.
5. Soul, my soul, don't let them break you, all these troubles.
6. Nothing can be surprising any more or impossible or miraculous, now that Zeus, father of the Olympians has made night out of noonday, hiding the bright sunlight.
7. It was a beautiful shield: life seemed somehow more precious.
8. Be bold! That's one way of getting through life.
9. stood on the edge between sea and wind
10. For I shall no more heal a wound by weeping than make it worse by pursuing joys and feasts.
11. No longer doth thy soft skin bloom as it did; 'tis withering now.
12. Victorious! All hail Lord Herakles!
13. Singing to the fluteplayer's accompaniment.
14. Thou hast taken a cricket by the wing.
15. I'd as soon hump her as kiss a goat's butt.
16. I care not for the wealth of golden Gyges, nor ever have envied him.
17. Whosoever lives is enchanted by song.
18. In that situation feet are the most valuable.
19. I sinned and I won't deny it.

20. I beg you, Mouse, say something to the audience.
21. And much was the wealth which, gathered with long time and labour, he would pour into the lap of a harlot.
22. Aisimides, nobody who considers the censure of the people could enjoy very many pleasurable moments.
23. For all these things are very far from my eyes.
24. For it is at the hands of your friends that you are strangled.

Erato

4. But come now, if ever before you heard my voice
5. If she runs now she'll follow later.
6. They gained great things there, and at sea.
7. But I say it's what you love.
8. He's equal with the Gods, that man.
9. Those I care for best, do me most harm
10. Stand up and look at me, face to face.
11. Nightingale, herald of spring, with a voice of longing.
12. Yet I am not one who takes joy in wounding, mine is a quiet mind.
13. Dear mother, I cannot work the loom.
14. He is dying, Cytherea, your tender Adonis, what should we do?
15. And I say to you someone will remember us in time to come.
16. Hesperus, you bring back again what the Dawn light scatters.
17. The hours flow on.
18. And I would not exchange her for all the riches of Lydia.
19. It's not right, lament in the Muses' house.
20. Like the sweet-apple reddening high on the branch.
21. For the Graces prefer those who are wearing flowers, and turn away from those who go uncrowned
22. Remembering those things we did in our youth. Many, beautiful things
23. Shivering with sweat, cold tremors over the skin, I turn the colour of dead grass, and I'm an inch from dying.
24. The Muses have filled my life with delight.

Melpomene

4. All hail! my house, and portals of my home.
5. What put such desperate thoughts into your heads?
6. Take heart, and no more let the tears stream from your eyes.
7. Great Apollon! What a prelude to thy story!
8. Come, let me veil my head in darkness.
9. For I had been lucky enough to witness the rites of the initiated.
10. Well, I must lead them, taking them by the hand to draw them after me, like a ship when towing.
11. Fly, luckless wretch, from my unholy taint.
12. How glad am I to emerge into the light and see thee.

13. I purposely made my entry by stealth
14. I will do so; the advice is good.
15. When I have beheaded the miscreant, I will throw him to dogs to tear.
16. Farewell my labours!
17. My father weeping o'er some mischance.
18. Aye, and brought to the light that three-headed monster.
19. I will not neglect to greet first of all the gods beneath my roof.
20. Henceforth I shall be called Herakles the Victor.
21. Endurance must have a limit.
22. God help us! What suspicions these dark hints of thine again excite!
23. Which of my friends is near or far to help me in my ignorance?
24. I never remember being mad.

Polymnia
4. Foe to the wicked, but the good man's guide.
5. All-flourishing, connecting, mingling soul.
6. Its secret gates unlocking, deep and strong.
7. With all-devouring force, entire and strong, horrid, untam'd.
8. Mortal destroying king, defil'd with gore
9. So vast thy wisdom, wond'rous, and sublime.
10. Arm bearers, strong defenders, rulers dread.
11. Endless praise is thine.
12. Dire weapon of the tongue.
13. Rejoicing in the chase.
14. For labour pains are thy peculiar care.
15. And glorious strife, and joyful shouts are thine.
16. To every mortal is thy influence known.
17. Secret source of persuasion.
18. Dissolving anxious care, the friend of Mirth, with darkling coursers riding round the earth.
19. Of seed, of fruits abundant, fair, harvest and threshing.
20. Men beneath thy righteous bondage groan.
21. When blust'ring winds in secret caverns pent, by thee excited, struggle hard for vent.
22. Avert your rage.
23. Pleasure abundant and pure belongs to you.
24. 'Tis thine alone to punish.

Terpsichore
4. The best antiquarians, let me tell you, trace dancing back to the creation of the universe.
5. Of dancing then, in the strict sense of the word, I have said enough.
6. You will find that dance is no easy profession, nor lightly to be undertaken.

7. Another essential for the pantomime is ease of movement.
8. Socrates–that wisest of men, if we may accept the judgement of the Pythian oracle–not only approved of dancing, but made a careful study of it.
9. A youth leads off the dance.
10. But in Pantomime, as in rhetoric, there can be too much of a good thing.
11. Pantomimes cannot all be artists; there are plenty of ignorant performers, who bungle their work terribly.
12. Rhythm says one thing, their feet another.
13. I have the authority of Plato, in his Laws, for approving some forms of dance and rejecting others.
14. Indeed, they pride themselves more on their pantomimic skill than on birth and ancestry and public services.
15. The Ethiopians go further, and dance even while they fight.
16. Like Calchas in Homer, the pantomime must know all 'that is, that was, that shall be'; nothing must escape his ever ready memory.
17. Still, it seems to me that we have no right to visit the sins of the artist upon the art.
18. Persons who divulge the mysteries are popularly spoken of as 'dancing them out.'
19. Leaving the rest for poets to celebrate, for pantomimes to exhibit, and for your imagination to supply from the hints already given.
20. Each of them has its own peculiar form of dance; tragedy its emmelia, comedy its cordax, supplemented occasionally by the sicinnis.
21. In old days, dancer and singer were one: but the violent exercise caused shortness of breath; the song suffered for it, and it was found advisable to have the singing done independently.
22. In Delos, not even sacrifice could be offered without dance and musical accompaniment.
23. The choral dance is modeled on that which Daedalus designed for Ariadne.
24. Faithfully to represent his subject, adequately to express his own conceptions, to make plain all that might be obscure;–these are the first essentials for the pantomime.

Thalia
4. There is no honest man!
5. Learn not to contradict your father in anything.
6. Wealth, the most excellent of all the gods.
7. Under every stone lurks a politician.
8. Times change. The vices of your age are stylish today.
9. Ah! the Generals! they are numerous, but not good for much!
10. You will never make the crab walk straight.

11. One must resign oneself to misfortune with good grace.
12. In still waters they catch nothing, but if they thoroughly stir up the slime, their fishing is good
13. I shall not please, but I shall say what is true.
14. We are crying with hunger at our firesides.
15. Tis the Whirlwind, that has driven out Zeus and is King now.
16. And yet you are fool enough, it seems, to dare to war with me, when for your faithful ally you might win me easily.
17. An insult directed at the wicked is not to be censured; on the contrary, the honest man, if he has sense, can only applaud.
18. Do you like Nephelokokkygia?
19. A man may learn wisdom even from a foe.
20. To invoke solely the weaker arguments and yet triumph is a talent worth more than a hundred thousand drachmae.
21. Prudence is the best safeguard.
22. Why do you bite your lips and shake your heads? Why are your faces blanched? Why do you weep?
23. I want all to have a share of everything and all property to be in common.
24. I pained folk but little and caused them much amusement; my conscience rebuked me for nothing."

Urania
4. From Zeus let us begin.
5. On either side the Axis ends in two Poles.
6. Her two feet will guide thee to her bridegroom, Perseus, over whose shoulder they are for ever carried.
7. Andromeda, though she cowers a good way off, is pressed by the rush of the mighty Monster of the Sea.
8. He ever seems to stretch his right hand towards the round Altar.
9. Each crop in turn brings a sign for the sowing.
10. Yonder, too, is the tiny Tortoise, which, while still beside his cradle, Hermes pierced for stings and bade it be called the Lyre.
11. Beneath both feet of Orion is the Hare pursued continually through all time.
12. For dread is the Bear and dread stars are near her.
13. For oft, too, beneath a calm night the sailor shortens sail for fear of the morning sea.
14. For with varying hue from time to time the evening paints her and of different shape are her horns at different times.
15. For men divide the sowing season into three — early, middle, late.
16. It would profit much to mark the last four days of the old and first four of the new month.

17. For thus do we poor, changeful mortals win in divers ways our livelihood.
18. Seek in calm for signs of storms, and in storm for signs of calm.
19. Not useless were it for one who seeks the signs of coming day to mark when each sign of the Zodiac rises.
20. Thrice the mastich buds and thrice wax ripe its berries
21. Nor are dark halos near the Sun signs of fair weather.
22. Here too that Crown, which glorious Dionysos set to be memorial of the dead Ariadne.
23. The anxious husbandman may rejoice in well-being.
24. Make light of none of these warnings.

The Tablets of Orpheus

The oracle of Dionysos was built in Thrace on the so called Haemus where, it is said, there were some writings of Orpheus upon tablets. (Scholia to Euripides, *Alkestis* 968)

This system employs lines from the Gold Leaves.

Cast four dice; by adding the numbers together you will have your oracle.

4. in order that he may find
5. bull you rushed to milk
6. thrice blessed one, on this very day.
7. you have wine as your fortunate honor
8. by you all things are subdued, all things overpowered, all things smitten
9. who are you, and where do you come from
10. peace war truth lie
11. on account of the rite they paid the penalty of their fathers
12. beloved by gods and mortal men
13. charmer of all pains for humans
14. fate and other immortal gods conquered me, the star-smiting thunder
15. and by the law of the river
16. rejoice at the experience
17. do not even go near this
18. thereafter you will reign with the other heroes
19. if the fast can endure, to fast for seven nights and days
20. flew out from the hard and deeply-grievous circle
21. for the initiate is without penalty
22. enter on the right
23. let no uninitiated look on
24. you have become a god instead of a man

The Head of Orpheus

When the Thracian women dismembered Orpheus, they say that his head, together with his lyre, having fallen into the Hebrus, was cast into the Black Gulf and that the head sailed on the lyre, singing a lament for Orpheus, as the story goes, whilst the lyre echoed in answer as the winds fell on the chords. Thus they approached Lesbos to the sound of music, and the Lesbians, taking them up, buried the head where their Bakcheion now is. (Lucian, *Against the Unlettered Bibliomaniac* 11-12)

Consecrate four coins to Dionysos and his prophet Orpheus; you may use them as is or paint one side red (front) and the other black (back). Throw the coins and note how many heads are turned towards (F) or away from (B) you. Then roll a die to determine the verse from the *Rhapsodic Theogony* of Orpheus which you must hear.

I — FFFF
1: Long did he ponder.
2: None has an unchanging destiny laid upon it, but all must go full circles.
3: As we draw in the air we gather to ourselves divine soul.
4: The insolent are brought down below Kokytos to the chilly horrors of Tartaros.
5: These things keep in thy mind, dear son, and in thy heart.
6: Well knowing all the things of long ago.

II — BBBB
1: The souls of beasts and winged birds when they flit away.
2: Conspiring with Kronos and his other brethren.
3: This is now the twelfth voice of those I heard from thee.
4: 'Twas thou that said it.
5: And thee thyself, far shooter, would make my witness.
6: They were born from Earth and from the blood of Heaven.

III — BFFB
1: Throughout the misty darkness.
2: And it moved without slackening in a vast circle.
3: With golden wings moving this way and that.
4: Uttering the voice of a bull and of glaring lion.
5: Female and Father the mighty god Erikepaios.
6: Cherishing in his heart swift and sightless Eros.

IV — FBBF

1: The key of mind.
2: An awful daimon.
3: But all the others marveled when there burst upon their gaze the unlooked-for light.
4: He built for the immortals an imperishable house.
5: The genitals fell down into the sea.
6: A great yawning gulf on this side and on that.

V — FFBB

1: There was no limit to it, no bottom nor foundation.
2: All things were in confusion.
3: Holding in her hands the noble scepter of Erikepaios.
4: He granted to Night to have the gift of prophecy wholly true.
5: He cast them into Tartaros, deep in the earth.
6: Seven fair daughters and seven kingly sons.

VI — BBFF

1: Okeanos who winds about and enfolds the earth with his swirling streams.
2: Titans of evil counsel, with overweening hearts.
3: For powerful though the were they had set themselves against a mightier foe.
4: Burdens to the earth.
5: Whose counsels never perish.
6: Then circling seasons the year brought forth.

VII — FBBB

1: And the spirits of Rivalry and Beguilement together took her up in their arms.
2: At this time Okeanos kept within his halls, debating with himself to which side his intent should lean.
3: He held the body of all things in the hollow of his own belly.
4: Whether he should maim his father's might and do him wanton injury.
5: Then bind him.
6: Of four and twenty measures.

VIII — BBBF

1: And Justice, bringer of retribution, attended him, bringing succor to all.
2: Out of their fatal insolence and reckless pride.
3: With their inexorable hearts and lawless spirit.
4: All things one and each one separate.
5: Drunk with the works of loud-murmuring bees.
6: Zeus is head, Zeus is middle, and from Zeus all things have their being.

IX — FFFB

1: She is called by the noble name of Arete.
2: That she might be for him the accomplisher of great deeds.
3: Therefore together with him all things in Zeus were created anew.
4: A world which has many mountains, cities, and mansions.
5: That it may return in a month as much as the sun in a year.
6: And the honourable works of nature are steadfast.

X — BFFF

1: These things the Father made in the misty darkness of the cave.
2: All that was to come to pass.
3: Thou shalt bear splendid children.
4: And he was called sweet child of Zeus.
5: Only the heart, the seat of thought, did they leave.
6: Seven parts of the child in all did they divide between them.

XI — BFBB

1: All the immortal blessed gods and goddesses rejoiced.
2: He took in his hands the glorious daimon.
3: Perform the mystic rites.
4: With four eyes looking this way and that.
5: Fair Ide and her sister Adrasteia.
6: For he was wroth with his mother, and yet more with his brethren.

XII — BBFB

1: Under the weight of stern necessity.
2: Instead of one stock of wine they put in its place three.
3: Many are the wand-bearers, but few the Bakchoi.
4: How am I to establish my proud rule?
5: Plying the loom, an unfinished toil, flowery.
6: Performing mighty acts.

XIII — FBFF

1: Until Rhea should bear a child to Kronos in love.
2: He lay with his stout neck lolling sideways, and all conquering sleep overtook him.
3: So as the year completed its circling course.
4: Unmarried and all untried in child birth she resolves its issues.
5: He mingled with his own limbs the power and strength of the god.
6: All come out of each other in the succeeding generations.

XIV — FFBF

1: Water is death to soul, and soul to water.
2: Yearning to be set free from their lawless ancestry.

3: Of all the springing herbs with which mortals have to do on the earth.
4: Vain and foolish and improvident.
5: For there is no worse, no more terrible thing than a woman.
6: To cease from the circle and have respite from evil.

XV — FBFB
1: Men will dispatch full hecatombs in all the seasons of the year.
2: He remained sitting in his halls.
3: From water comes earth, and from earth water again.
4: For thou hast power in these things.
5: Set free from grievous pain and endless sting of frenzy.
6: He took and divided.

XVI — BFBF
1: Without wit to perceive the approach of evil.
2: Close the doors, you uninitiated.
3: Mother, highest of the gods.
4: Taking the brazen cymbals and tympanon of goat hide.
5: Counterfeit images.
6: Then great Chronos fashioned in the divine Aither a silvery egg.

Roll three dice and count the numbers that appear.

3: Hybla makes flowers grow for the Girl.
4: Asterion wails in the Labyrinth.
5: Dionysos soothes the anger of Hephaistos and persuades him to return
   to Mount Olympos.
6: Erigone greets the stranger at her door.
7: The daughters of Kadmos gossip about their sister.
8: Seilenos and king Midas talk.
9: Hermes and Aphrodite bless the union of Persephone and Haides.
10: Plump Iakchos shakes a distaff and giggles in the liknon.
11: Ariadne watches the black-sailed ship depart.
12: Hermes is greeted by the Nymphs and Satyrs of Nysa.
13: Orpheus looks back.
14: Herakles and Dionysos clasp hands.
15: Lykourgos is bound by the vines he reviled.
16: Melampos journeys to Egypt.
17: Akoites sees the truth.
18: Dionysos fulfills his pledge beneath a fig tree.

Close your eyes.

Breathe slow and rhythmically, in and out nine times.

Contemplate the reconstructed fragments of Pherekydes:

> Chronos and Zas always were, and also Chthonie. Once Chronos, alone and without a partner, cast forth his seed. From his seed he made fire, air, and water, and deposited these in five hollows. Lo, from the mixtures of fire, air and water in the hollows arose another generation of Gods. The fiery Gods dwelt in Ouranos and gleaming Aither, the Gods of wind in gusty Tartaros, the watery Gods in Chaos, and the Gods of darkness dwelt in black Night.
>
> After the generation of Gods, born of the seed of Time, assumed their habitations, Zas became Eros and married Chthonie. The other Gods built many large palaces for him; they provided all the necessary goods, the banquet tables, servants and maids, and when all the needful things had been accomplished, they performed the wedding.
>
> On the third day of the wedding, Zas fashioned a big and beautiful robe, and on it he embroidered Earth and Ogenos and the mansions of Ogenos. When he had finished his task, he presented the robe to Chthonie and said: 'Because I wish to marry you, I honour you with this robe. Rejoice and be my consort!' This they say was the first feast of unveiling, and hence arose the custom for both Gods and men. And she responded as she received the robe from him: 'I take this as my honour, and henceforth I shall be called Ge...' The Gods celebrated, feasting on ambrosia.
>
> And the Earth was like a winged Oak, strong and mighty; its roots extended into the depths of Tartaros, its trunk was encircled by Ogenos, and its branches reached into Ouranos. The Earth flourished and Zas rejoiced.
>
> But below the Earth, in a hollow of Tartaros, Ophioneus was born. He and his monstrous sons challenged Kronos. The battle-lines were drawn up, with Kronos the commander of one army and

Ophioneus leading the Ophionidai. The terms of the battle were stated: whichever of them fell into Ogenos would be the defeated, while those who thrust them out and defeated them would possess Ouranos. A fierce conflict followed. Kronos had a strong ally in Zas; in single combat he overthrew Ophioneus. So Ophioneus and his brood were cast into Ogenos, and they dwell in the mansions of Ogenos to this day. Kronos, commander of the victorious army, was crowned by the other Gods (from this arose the custom of the wearing of crowns by victors).

Zeus, who is Zas, honoured the victorious Gods and assigned them their domains. Kronos had won Ouranos. These are the shares of the other Gods: below Ouranos is the fiery Aither; below Aither the portion of Earth; below that portion is Tartaros; the daughters of Boreas, the Harpies and Thuella, guard it; there Zeus banishes any of the Gods who behave with insolence. There also are the souls of men who have committed bloodshed. Their souls are borne through the portals and gates of Tartaros on an outflowing river to birth; the river is like the seed that leads to new life. And the souls of men depart from life and enter again the caves and hollows of Tartaros through its portals and gates. Alongside Tartaros is Chaos and the realms of dark Night.

Record yourself reading the *hieros logos*, and play it when you wish to consult the Tree. Let an image form in your mind and when you are ready ask the Spider in the Tree to guide you either up or down to behold visions of the many worlds which intersect with it.

Once you have done this exercise enough times you may dispense with the reading.

Appropriate music playing in the background may be helpful.

Write your question on a grape leaf and then store it in a secure location where it will not be disturbed. Wait 48 hours and then examine it. If it has dried and withered there will be malign influences and obstacles to overcome. If it is normal, you have nothing to worry about.

Pithomanteia

Write devotional activities on scraps of paper and place them in a jar. Add to it as often as you are inspired to. When you need guidance in your practice recite *Orphic Hymn 52*:

> I call upon you, blessed, many-named and frenzied Bakchos,
> Bull-horned Nysian redeemer, God of the wine-press, conceived in fire.
> Nourished in the thigh, O Lord of the Cradle,
> You marshal torch-lit processions in the night,
> O filleted and thyrsos-shaking Eubouleus.
> Threefold is your nature and ineffable your rites,
> O secret offspring of Zeus.
> Primeval, Erikepaios, father and son of Gods,
> you take raw flesh, and, sceptered,
> you lead into the madness of revel and dance
> in the frenzy of triennial feasts that bestow calm on us.
> You burst forth from the earth in a blaze...
> O son of two mothers,
> horned and clad in fawnskin, you roam the mountains,
> O Lord worshiped in annual feasts.
> Paian of the golden spear, nursling, decked with grapes,
> Bassaros, exulting in ivy, followed by many maidens...
> Joyous and all-abounding, come, O blessed one to the initiates.

Then ask Dionysos to assign you a task and draw out one of the scraps.

Some examples

Play a game.
Learn a new divination system.
Write a story.
Leave something valuable in a conspicuous place.
Read poetry.
Go to the outskirts of town.
Learn ten new words in Latin.
Go to the market.
Make an offering of your pain.
Perform magic.
Go to a river.

Abstain from meat for a week.
Abstain from the internet for a week.
Dance as you are moved to.
Go somewhere crowded and listen for a *kledon*.
Go to the coast.
Leave flowers on an untended grave.
Memorize an Orphic Hymn in the original Greek.
Go to the wetlands.
Go to the desert.
Go to a mountain.
Give to a charity.
Keep an all night vigil.
Destroy a mask.
Greet the dawn each morning for a week.
Start keeping a journal.
Give to a homeless person.
Fast from food for three days.
Chant.
Watch some movies.
Read all of the Orphic Hymns from start to finish.
Undertake an ordeal.
Read a fiction book.
Watch dancers.
Leave a glamourbomb.
Wear a mask.
Meditate.
Come up with twenty more devotional activities to add to the jar.
Abstain from doing drugs for a week.
Make a mask.
Go for a run each morning for a week.
Listen to music.
Sing regularly.
Play an instrument.
Memorize an Orphic Hymn.
Delete all of your playlists and start over.
Learn ten new words in Italian.
Make a drink offering.
Search out new music.
Go to a holy place.
Go to a concert.
Go to the movies.
Read a graphic novel.
Go to the shrine of a hero.
Go to a temple.

Go to a cemetery.
Read a non-fiction book.
Make an offering of incense.
Dance a specific dance.
Abstain from drinking alcohol for a week.
Make an offering of your pleasure.
Write a poem.
Go to a park.
Make a chapbook.
Go to the woods.
Write a hymn.
Go to a lake.
Go to the crossroads.
Sing a song.
Drink alcohol.
Go to the theatre.
Put together a devotional playlist.
Take drugs.
Write a song.
Take your shrine apart and completely redesign it.
Make a collage.
Get *really* drunk.
Get even more drunk and give Sannion a large sum of money.
Learn ten new words in Greek.
Pretend to be someone else.
Sacrifice an animal.
Go to the tracks.
Write a book.
Research a random topic.
Go to the library.
Push your boundaries; do something uncomfortable.
Make an offering of your blood.
Perform divination for someone else.
Make a food offering.
Reorganize your shrine.
Come up with ten more devotional activities to add to the jar.

On the Noumenia, boil a pot of water and pour in the white of an egg; the shape it forms will reflect the month to come.

That Dionysos is also the discoverer of the apple is attested by Theokritos of Syracuse, in words something like these: 'Storing the apples of Dionysos in the folds at my bosom, and wearing on my head white poplar, sacred bough of Herakles.' And Neoptolemos the Parian, in the *Dionysiad*, records on his own authority that apples as well as all other fruits were discovered by Dionysos. (Athenaios, *Deipnosophistai* 3.82d)

Hold an apple which still has its stem attached aloft and ask Dionysos your question.

Then take the apple in one hand and begin twisting its stem, with each twist saying either "yes" or "no."

What you say when the stem comes off will be your answer.

The Oracle of the Wheel and Key

To determine the most auspicious date for something, recite *Orphic Hymn* 6:

> Upon two-natured, great and ether-tossed Protogonos I call;
> Born of the egg, delighting in his golden wings he bellows like a
>   bull,
> This begetter of blessed Gods and mortal men.
> Erikepaios, seed unforgettable, attend to my rites,
> Ineffable, hidden, brilliant scion, whose motion is whirring,
> You scattered the dark mist that lay before your eyes,
> and, flapping your wings, you whirled about
> and throughout this world, you brought pure light.
> For this I call you Phanes and lord Priapos and bright-eyed
>   Antauges.
> But, O blessed one of many counsels and seeds,
> Come gladly to the celebrants of this holy and elaborate rite.

And then spin the Key on the Wheel. The Wheel is a circle with a minimum of thirty spaces marked out along its rim and a minimum of thirteen towards the center. Each of the thirty represent a day of the lunar month and each of the thirteen represent a month of the lunar year. Place them on the Wheel in a random order and leave empty spaces so that Dionysos may decline to answer if the undertaking is not at all auspicious. The Key is a key.

Additionally you may use the schedule of offerings of the Starry Bull tradition to determine which God or Spirit is involved in the matter.

Day 1: All of them collectively
Day 2: Leto
Day 3: Persephone
Day 4: Hermes
Day 5: Aphrodite
Day 6: Artemis
Day 7: Apollon
Day 8: Arachne
Day 9: None
Day 10: Hera
Day 11: Melampos

Day 12: Athene
Day 13: Dionysos
Day 14: Ariadne
Day 15: Flora
Day 16: The Mousai
Day 17: The Nymphai
Day 18: The Mountain Mothers
Day 19: The Satyrs
Day 20: Erigone
Day 21: Pasiphae
Day 22: Orpheus
Day 23: Medeia
Day 24: Herakles
Day 25: Semele
Day 26: The Sirens
Day 27: The Dead
Day 28: The Harlequinade
Day 29: Melinoe
Day 30: Hekate

There will be more reason in appealing to the ancient inventors of names, who would never have connected prophecy (*mantike*) which foretells the future and is the noblest of arts, with madness (*manike*), or called them both by the same name, if they had deemed madness to be a disgrace or dishonour;-they must have thought that there was an inspired madness which was a noble thing; for the two words, *mantike* and *manike*, are really the same, and the letter t is only a modern and tasteless insertion. And this is confirmed by the name which was given by them to the rational investigation of futurity, whether made by the help of birds or of other signs-this, for as much as it is an art which supplies from the reasoning faculty mind (*nous*) and information (*istoria*) to human thought (*oiesis*) they originally termed *oionoistike*, but the word has been lately altered and made sonorous by the modern introduction of the letter Omega (*oionoistike* and *oionistike*), and in proportion prophecy (*mantike*) is more perfect and august than augury, both in name and fact, in the same proportion, as the ancients testify, is madness superior to a sane mind (*sophrosune*) for the one is only of human, but the other of divine origin. Next, madness can provide relief from the greatest plagues of trouble that beset certain families because of their guilt for ancient crimes: it turns up among those who need a way out; it gives prophecies and takes refuge in prayers to the Gods and in worship, discovering mystic rites and purifications that bring the man it touches through to safety for this and all time to come. So it is that the right sort of madness finds relief from present hardships for a man it has possessed. The third kind is the madness of those who are possessed by the Muses; which taking hold of a delicate and virgin soul, and there inspiring frenzy, awakens lyrical and all other numbers; with these adorning the myriad actions of ancient heroes for the instruction of posterity. But he who, having no touch of the Muses' madness in his soul, comes to the door and thinks that he will get into the temple by the help of art — he, I say, and his poetry are not admitted; the sane man disappears and is nowhere when he enters into rivalry with the madman. (Plato, *Phaedrus*)

All the wives offer — understood as a loan — handkerchiefs, shawls, scarves, petticoats and linens of every color, pots of basil, lemon verbona, mint and rue, mirrors and baubles, and last but not least a great tub full of water. The surroundings are decorated in this way, and when everything is ready the victim of the bite, dressed in gaudy colors, chooses as she pleases ribbons, handkerchiefs and shoes that remind her of the colors of the tarantula and she adorns herself with them while waiting for the musicians. (Anna Caggiano, *Folklore Italiano* 6.72ff)

You will need eight pieces of woolen cloth of different colors, cut into small squares of uniform size approximately two inches by two inches. Keep them in a box on which a spider has been engraved. These cloths may be used to determine the nature of an obstacle or to determine the type of spiritual mania the client is suffering from.

For the first method, shuffle the cloths, then reach into the box and draw one out.

> **Red** = lack of emotional control
> **Black** = acedia
> **White** = perfectionism
> **Blue** = money troubles
> **Green** = your associates
> **Yellow** = procrastination
> **Purple** = divine opposition
> **Brown** = self-sabotage

And for the second method, draw each of the cloths out in turn and show them to the client. Note their response, whether favorable or averse.

Red = erotic mania, which is overseen by Aphrodite, Ariadne, Arachne, Erigone, Pasiphae, Semele and the Satyrs.

Black = chthonic mania, which is overseen by Dionysos, Persephone, Hekate and Melinoe.

White = telestic mania, which is overseen by Dionysos, Orpheus, Melampos, the Mountain Mothers and Hermes.

Blue = apophenia, which is overseen by Dionysos, Hermes, the Harlequinade and Arachne.

Green = entheogens, which are overseen by Dionysos, Orpheus, the Nymphai, Flora, Medeia, Aphrodite and Ariadne.

Yellow = mantic mania, which is overseen by Dionysos, Apollon, the

Prophets, the Mousai, the Nymphai and Hekate.

Purple = possession, which is overseen by Dionysos, Ariadne, the Mountain Mothers, the Neoi Dionysoi, the Aletides, the Harlequinade and Hekate.

Brown = mountain madness, which is overseen by Dionysos, Ariadne, the Mountain Mothers, the Nymphai, the Satyrs.

The Dead are involved in all forms of madness.

When the moon is new on a **Sunday**, that signifies three things will happen during the month: rain, wind and calm. It also signifies barrenness of cattle and old men's sicknesses — but health and fitness among the young men. Make offerings to the Nurses.

If it is new on a **Monday**, that signifies sorrow for those who are born and young men's heads will ache in that month. Make offerings to Orpheus.

If it is new on a **Tuesday**, that signifies joy for all men, and grief for the young. Make offerings to the Aletides.

If it is new on a **Wednesday**, that signifies that peaceful men will dwell among loyal friends. An end to ancient feuds and generational enmity. Make offerings to Herakles.

If it is new on a **Thursday**, that signifies the health of kings through potent drugs. Make offerings to Medeia.

If it is new on a **Friday**, there will be good hunting that month. Make offerings to king Herla.

If it is new on a **Saturday** that signifies strife, and bloodshed, and whoever begins it with the south wind will have the victory. Make offerings to Achilles.

Icarius' dog returned to his daughter, Erigone; she followed his tracks and, when she found her father's corpse, she ended her life with a noose. Through the mercy of the Gods she was restored to life again among the constellations; men call her Virgo. That dog was also placed among the stars. But after some time such a sickness was sent upon the Athenians that their maidens were driven by a certain madness to hang themselves. The oracle responded that this pestilence could be stopped if the corpses of Erigone and Icarius were sought again. These were found nowhere after being sought for a long time. Then, to show their devotedness, and to appear to seek them in another element, the Athenians hung rope from trees. Holding on to this rope, the men were tossed here and there so that they seemed to seek the corpses in the air. But since most were falling from the trees, they decided to make shapes in the likeness of their own faces and hang these in place of themselves. Hence, little masks are called *oscilla* because in them faces oscillate, that is, move. (*The First Vatican Mythographer* 19)

For this type of divination you'll have to acquire or make a Doll which should be around four to thirteen inches in length. It can be as detailed as you like, and may represent one of the Aletides (Erigone, Arachne, Ariadne, etc.) or Phales, Pinocchio, Arlecchino or some other expression of Paignia Kampesiguia.

Once the Doll is finished, tie a noose around its neck with enough of a "tail" or rope of string left over so that it may hang suspended from your hand.

Consecrate this tool to Dionysos and his Retinue and keep it wrapped in linen when not in use.

Either stand or sit in a comfortable position, completely relaxing your mind and body.

When you are ready, ask the Doll to show you its "Yes" movement.

Wait patiently, as it may take a few moments for it to awaken.

The Doll will begin to swing in a direction, either side to side or in a circular fashion. This will be your "Yes" for the session. (The Doll may have a regular "Yes" or move in recognizable ways depending on who's on the other end, but always establish its movements at the start of each session.)

Once the Doll has stopped moving, do the same for "No."

Now start with simple, easily verifiable questions such as "Am I wearing a red shirt?" or "Is my name Sannion?"

When you feel satisfied that you've established a secure and accurate connection move on to any questions you have for this session. In addition to binary divination the Doll can be consulted to help find lost items, provide directions, choose between several options written on cards, help diagnose blockages and areas to focus on (in conjunction with the Net of Zagreus) determine dates (using the Wheel and Key) or spell out messages (Smoky Words.) Other uses will become apparent the more you play with the Doll.

Alchemy is an erotic science, involved in buried aspects of reality, aimed at purifying and transforming all being and matter. Not to suggest that material operations are ever abandoned. The adept holds to both the mystical and physical work. They can picture love affairs of chemicals and stars, a romance of stones, or the fertility of fire. Strange, fertile correspondences the alchemists sensed in unlikely orders of being. Between men and planets, plants and gestures, words and weather. (Jim Morrison, *The Lords: Notes on Vision*)

Do you know the warm progress under the stars? Do you know we exist? Have you forgotten the keys to the kingdom? Have you been born yet & are you alive? Let's reinvent the Gods, all the myths of the ages, celebrate symbols from deep elder forests. (Jim Morrison, *American Prayer*)

For this system you'll need *astragaloi* or the knucklebones of a sheep, goat or pig, which may be read as follows:

- o   The curved, small side is called "Chian." It counts for one point.
- o   The wide, convex side is called "Belly." It counts for four points.
- o   The wide concave, side is called "Back." It counts for three points.
- o   "Snake," the flat small "S" shaped side counts for six points.

You may either throw five bones once or one bone five times; this will tell you who among the Starry Bull pantheon to focus on, provide you with a Symbol to contemplate, an *Orphic Hymn* to recite, prescribe an Offering to make and a Story to reflect upon. From this you may devise all manner of rites.

I. If you see only Chians:

Honor: Dionysos Opener of the Door.
Contemplate the Symbol: Door.
Recite *Orphic Hymn* 0. Orpheus to Mousaios.
Offering: a bowl of red wine.
Reflect on the Story:

At Athens on the eleventh of the month of Anthesterion they begin drinking new wine, calling the day Pithoigia. And in the old days, it is likely, they poured a libation of wine before drinking, and prayed that the use of the drug be harmless and healthful or saving for them. Among us Boiotians the month is called Prostaterios and it is customary, sacrificing on the sixth to the Agathos Daimon, to taste the wine after a west wind. This wind of all the winds especially moves and changes the wine and wine that has already avoided it seems to remain stable. (Plutarch, *Questiones Convivales* 3.7.1)

II. If you see four Chians and a Back:

Honor: Hermes of the Gates.
Contemplate the Symbol: Kerykeion.
Recite *Orphic Hymn* 28. To Hermes.
Offering: strong spirits.
Reflect on the Story:

> There are sanctuaries of Hermes Kriophoros (Ram-bearer) and of Hermes called Promachos (Champion) at Tanagra in Boiotia. They account for the former surname by a story that Hermes averted a pestilence from the city by carrying a ram round the walls; to commemorate this they made an image of Hermes carrying a ram upon his shoulders. Whichever of the youths is judged to be the most handsome goes round the walls at the feast of Hermes, carrying a lamb on his shoulders. Hermes Promachos (Champion) is said, on the occasion when an Eretrian fleet put into Tanagra from Euboia, to have led out the youths to the battle; he himself, armed with a scraper like a youth, was chiefly responsible for the rout of the Euboians. In the sanctuary of Promachos (the Champion) is kept all that is left of the wild strawberry-tree under which they believe that Hermes was nourished. Nearby is a theater and by it a portico. I consider that the people of Tanagra have better arrangements for the worship of the Gods than any other Greeks. For their houses are in one place, while the sanctuaries are apart beyond the houses in a clear space where no men live. (Pausanias, *Description of Greece* 9.22.1-2)

III. If you see one Belly and four Chians:

Honor: Medeia the Root-Cutter.
Contemplate the Symbol: Snake.
Recite *Orphic Hymn* 3. To Night.
Offering: strange drugs.

Reflect on the Story:

> Medea, an exile from Corinth, came to Athens to the hospitality of Aegeus, son of Pandion, and married him; to him Medus was born. Later the priestess of Diana began to censure Medea, and tell the king that she could not perform sacrifices piously because there was a woman in that state who was a sorceress and criminal. She was exiled then for the second time. Medea, however, with her yoked dragons, returned to Colchis from Athens. On the way she came to Absoros where her brother Absyrtus was buried. There the people of Absoros could not cope with a great number of snakes. At their entreaties Medea gathered them up and put them in her brother's tomb. They still remain there, and if any goes outside the tomb, it pays the debt to nature. (Hyginus, *Fabulae* 26)

IV. If you see two Backs and three Chians:

Honor: Hekate of the Gallows.
Contemplate the Symbol: Key.
Recite *Orphic Hymn* 1. To Hekate.
Offering: three eggs.
Reflect on the Story:

> Dionysos waited for darksome night, and appealed in these words to the circular moon in heaven: 'O daughter of Helios, Mene of many turnings, nurse of all! O Selene, driver of the silver car! If thou art Hekate of many names, if in the night thou doest shake thy mystic torch in brandcarrying hand, come nightwanderer, nurse of puppies because the nightly sound of the hurrying dogs is thy delight with their mournful whimpering.' (Nonnos, *Dionysiaka* 44.198)

V. If you see one Snake and four Chians:

Honor: Apollo Soranus.
Contemplate the Symbol: Fire.
Recite *Orphic Hymn* 34. To Apollon.
Offering: burn a pillar candle.
Reflect on the Story:

> Beyond the Chastiser Stone is an altar of Apollon surnamed Spodios (God of Ashes); it is made out of the ashes of the victims. The customary mode of divination here is from voices (*kledones*), which is used by the Smyrnaians, to my knowledge, more than by

any other Greeks. The Thebans in ancient days used to sacrifice bulls to Apollon of the Ashes. Once when the festival was being held, the hour of the sacrifice was near but those sent to fetch the bull had not arrived. And so, as a wagon happened to be near by, they sacrificed to the God one of the oxen, and ever since it has been the custom to sacrifice working oxen. (Pausanias, *Description of Greece* 9.11.7-12.1)

VI. If you see three Chians, one Back and the fifth a Belly:

Honor: Arachne the Purple-Dyer.
Contemplate the Symbol: Wool.
Recite *Orphic Hymn* 85. To Sleep.
Offering: make art.
Reflect on the Story:

> So Dionysos distributed the spoils of battle among his followers, after the Indian War, and sent returning home the whole host who had shared his labours. The people made haste to go, laden with shining treasures of the Eastern sea and birds of many strange forms. Their return was a triumphal march with universal acclaim to Dionysos the invincible. Leaving the long stretch of Arabia with its deepshadowy forests he measured the Assyrian road on foot, and had a mind to see the Tyrian land, Kadmos' country; for thither he turned his tracks, and with stuffs in thousands before his eyes he admired the manycoloured patterns of Assyrian art, as he stared at the woven work of the Babylonian Arachne; he examined cloth dyed with the Tyrian shell, shooting out sea-sparklings of purple: on that shore once a dog busy by the sea, gobbling the wonderful lurking fish with joyous jaws, stained his white jowl with the blood of the shell, and reddened his lips with running fire, which once alone made scarlet the sea-dyed robes of kings. (Nonnos, *Dionysiaka* 40)

VII. If you see three Bellies, and further two Chians:

Honor: Prosymnos the Guide.
Contemplate the Symbol: Phallos.
Recite *Orphic Hymn* 73. To the Daimon.
Offering: celebrate your desire.
Reflect on the Story:

> Dionysos was anxious to descend into Haides, but did not know the way. Thereupon a certain man, Prosymnos by name, promises

to tell him; though not without reward. It was a favour of lust, this reward which Dionysos was asked for. The God is willing to grant the request; and so he promises, in the event of his return, to fulfil the wish of Prosymnos, confirming the promise with an oath. Having learnt the way he set out, and came back again. He does not find Prosymnos, for he was dead. In fulfilment of the vow to his lover Dionysos hastens to the tomb and indulges his unnatural lust. Cutting off a branch from a fig-tree which was at hand, he shaped it into the likeness of a phallos, and then made a show of fulfilling his promise to the dead man. As a mystic memorial of this passion phalloi are set up to Dionysos in cities. 'For if it were not to Dionysos that hey held solemn procession and sang the phallic hymn, they would be acting most shamefully,' says Herakleitos. (Clement of Alexandria, *Exhortation to the Greeks* 2.30)

VIII. If you see two Backs and three Chians:

Honor: The Nurses.
Contemplate the Symbol: Milk.
Recite *Orphic Hymn* 51. To the Nymphs.
Offering: weave a crown of flowers.
Reflect on the Story:

> Zeus gave Dionysos, born from his thigh, to be nursed by the Dodonian Nymphs, Ambrosia, Koronis, Eudore, Dione, Phaisyle, Polyxos, Phaio. Having nursed Dionysos, they went around with him, bestowing the vine invention by the God upon humankind. And Lykourgos chased Dionysos as far as the sea, but Zeus pitied them and turned them into stars. The story is in Pherekydes. (Scholiast on Homer's *Iliad* 18.486)

IX. If you see one Back, two Chians and two Bellies:

Honor: Friedrich Nietzsche, the Rope.
Contemplate the Symbol: Ox-Goad.
Recite *Orphic Hymn* 39. To Korybas.
Offering: beer.
Reflect on the Story:

> In Turin on 3rd January, 1889, Friedrich Nietzsche steps out of the doorway of number six, Via Carlo Alberto. Not far from him, the driver of a hansom cab is having trouble with a stubborn horse. Despite all his urging, the horse refuses to move, whereupon the driver loses his patience and takes his whip to it. Nietzsche comes

up to the throng and puts an end to the brutal scene, throwing his arms around the horse's neck, sobbing. His landlord takes him home, he lies motionless and silent for two days on a divan until he mutters the obligatory last words, and lives for another ten years, silent and demented, cared for by his mother and sisters. We do not know what happened to the horse. (Béla Tarr, introduction to *A torinói ló*)

X. If you see three Chians, a Snake and the fifth a Belly:

Honor: Achilles Swiftfoot.
Contemplate the Symbol: Mirror.
Recite *Orphic Hymn* 8. To the Sun.
Offering: a race.
Reflect on the Story:

> When Thetis the Nereid knew that Achilles, the son she had borne to Peleus, would die if he went to attack Troy, she sent him to the island of Scyros, entrusting him to King Lycomedes. He kept him among his virgin daughters in woman's attire under an assumed name. The girls called him Pyrrha, since he had tawny hair, and in Greek a redhead is called *pyrrhos*. When the Achaeans discovered that he was hidden there, they sent spokesmen to King Lycomedes to beg that he be sent to help the Danaans. The King denied that he was there, but gave them permission to search the palace. When they couldn't discover which one he was Ulysses put women's trinkets in the fore-court of the palace, and among them a shield and a spear. He bade the trumpeter blow the trumpet all of a sudden, and called for clash of arms and shouting. Achilles, thinking the enemy was at hand, stripped off his woman's garb and seized shield and spear. In this way he was recognized and promised to the Argives his aid and his soldiers, the Myrmidons. (Hyginus, *Fabulae* 96)

XI. If you see three Chians, a Snake and the fifth a Back:

Honor: Aphrodite of Flowers.
Contemplate the Symbol: Dove.
Recite *Orphic Hymn* 55. To Aphrodite.
Offering: fragrant perfume.
Reflect on the Story:

> At Eryx in Sicily, where the holy and venerable temple of Aphrodite stands, the inhabitants of Eryx at a certain season of the

year celebrate with sacrifice the Anagogia (the Embarkation), and they say that Aphrodite departs from Sicily for Libya. At that time the pigeons disappear from the locality as if they were departing with the Goddess. For the rest of the year, however, it is a known fact that a great number of these birds are found at the temple. (Aelian, *Historical Miscellany* 1.15)

XII. If you see one Chian and four Bellies:

Honor: Erigone the Wanderer.
Contemplate the Symbol: Noose.
Recite *Orphic Hymn* 63. To Justice.
Offering: hang a mask or doll.
Reflect on the Story:

> Can you picture what will be, so limitless and free
> desperately in need of some stranger's hand
> in a desperate land.
> Lost in a Roman wilderness of pain
> and all the children are insane, all the children are insane.
> Waiting for the summer rain, yeah;
> there's danger on the edge of town.
> Ride the King's highway, baby.
> Weird scenes inside the gold mine.
> Ride the highway west, baby.
> Ride the snake, ride the snake,
> to the lake, the ancient lake, baby.
> The snake is long, seven miles.
> Ride the snake, he's old, and his skin is cold.
> The west is the best, the west is the best.
> (The Doors, *The End*)

XIII. If you see all Bellies but the last, a Chian:

Honor: The Fairies and Goblins.
Contemplate the Symbol: Fox.
Recite *Orphic Hymn* 38. To the Kouretes.
Offering: leave a glamour bomb.
Reflect on the Story:

> That is no wonder; for 'tis Bacchus himself, the God of wine, and the captain and emperor of drunkards. He is crown'd with ivy and vine leaves. He has a thyrsus instead of a scepter; that is, a javelin with an iron head, encircled by ivy or vine leaves in his hand. He is

carried in a chariot, sometimes drawn by tigers and lions and sometimes by lynxes and panthers. And like a King he has his guards, who are a drunken band of Satyrs, Demons, Nymphs that preside over the wine presses, Fairies of the fountains and priestesses. Silenus sometimes comes after him sitting on an ass that bends under his burden. (Andrew Tooke, *The Pantheon representing the Fabulous Histories of the Heathen Gods and Most Illustrious Heroes*)

XIV. If you see one Chian, three Bellies and one Back:

Honor: Thyone of Golden Memory.
Contemplate the Symbol: Lightning.
Recite *Orphic Hymn* 44. To Semele.
Offering: set out lights.
Reflect on the Story:

> Semele saw her fiery end, and perished rejoicing in a childbearing death. In one bridal chamber could be seen Himeros, Eileithyia, and the Erinyes together. So the babe half-grown, and his limbs washed with heavenly fire, was carried by Hermes to his father for the lying-in. Zeus was able to change the mind of jealous Hera, to calm and undo the savage threatening resentment which burdened her. Semele consumed by the fire he translated into the starry vault; he gave the mother of Bakchos a home in the sky among the heavenly inhabitants, as one of Hera's family, as daughter of Harmonia sprung from both Ares and Aphrodite. So her new body bathed in the purifying fire ((lacuna)) she received the immortal life of the Olympians. Instead of Kadmos and the soil of earth, instead of Autonoe and Agave, she found Artemis by her side, she had converse with Athena, she received the heavens as her wedding-gift, sitting at one table with Zeus and Hermes and Ares and Kythereia. (Nonnos, *Dionysiaka* 8.402 ff)

XV. If you see a Snake, two Chians and a pair of Bellies:

Honor: Harlequin the Leaper.
Contemplate the Symbol: Rhombos.
Recite *Orphic Hymn* 31. Hymn to the Kouretes.
Offering: juggle.
Reflect on the Story:

> Understanding this theatrical device is essential to understanding the harlequinade. Characters established in the main pantomime

story (a young girl, her lover, her father, the servant etc) get into trouble, an impossible situation for which there is no solution, and are transformed by some benign spiritual agent (think fairy godmother, 'the gods', that kind of thing) into the characters of the harlequinade in a strange parallel topsy-turvy world. The purpose of this, dramatically was to introduce the comedy and to move the plot along by creating such chaos that the 'powers-that-be' would acquiesce to the union of the lovers just so that order could be restored. At that point the characters were transformed back and the drama proceeded with the full on happy ending, parades, fireworks, dancing girls, spectacles and general rejoicing. Structurally, it is the act of transforming that is important to remember as this signals the move to the parallel world where things do not behave in the same way. Most comedy has to have an isolating device of this type to contain the strange goings on. The tool for effecting the change is another inheritance — Harlequin has his magic bat or slapstick, but it could be a wand, a magic lamp or a host of other things. Sometimes, the transformation is effected by falling asleep, or love potions, or drunkenness (a favourite of Chaplin's). Chaos must be created (as in *A Midsummer Night's Dream* with the juice of the flower) in order that all are eventually brought to their senses. (Bryony Dixon, *Chaplin and the Harlequinade*)

XVI. If you see three Backs and two Chians:

Honor: Ariadne of the Dancing Ground.
Contemplate the Symbol: Wheel.
Recite *Orphic Hymn* 9. To the Moon.
Offering: honeycomb.
Reflect on the Story:

> Behold the troup of dancers, like the chorus which Daidalos is said to have invented for Ariadne, daughter of Minos; young men and maidens with hands clasped and going about in a circle. (Philostratos the Younger, *Imagines* 10)

XVII. If you see one Chian, two Bellies and two Backs:

Honor: Flora of the Delicate Feet.
Contemplate the Symbol: Triskelion.
Recite *Orphic Hymn* 43. To the Horai.
Offering: make something beautiful.
Reflect on the Story:

Thomas Morton and the Merry-mount colonists set up a May-pole, drinking and dancing about it many days together, inviting the Indian women for their consorts, dancing and frisking together like so many fairies, or furies rather and worse practices. As if they had anew revived & celebrated the feasts of ye Roman Goddess Flora, or ye beastly practices of ye mad Bacchanalians. (William Bradford, *History Of Plymouth Plantation*)

XVIII. If you see three Chians and two Snakes:

Honor: Alexander the Firebrand.
Contemplate the Symbol: Whip.
Recite *Orphic Hymn* 19. To Zeus the Thunderbolt.
Offering: set a goal and achieve it.
Reflect on the Story:

> When Alexander had caught fire at their words, all leaped up from their couches and passed the word along to form a victory procession in honour of Dionysos. Promptly many torches were gathered. Female musicians were present at the banquet, so the king led them all out for the *komos* to the sound of voices and flutes and pipes, Thaïs the courtesan leading the whole performance. She was the first, after the king, to hurl her blazing torch into the palace. As the others all did the same, immediately the entire palace area was consumed, so great was the conflagration. It was remarkable that the impious act of Xerxes, king of the Persians, against the acropolis at Athens should have been repaid in kind after many years by one woman, a citizen of the land which had suffered it, and in sport. (Diodoros Sikeliotes, *The Library of History* 17.72)

XIX. If all you see are Bellies:

Honor: Artemis of the Wilds.
Contemplate the Symbol: Bear.
Recite *Orphic Hymn* 36. To Artemis.
Offering: clean up a park or woods.
Reflect on the Story:

> Aktaion was the child of Autonoe and Aristaios. He was raised by Cheiron and taught to be a hunter, and then later he was devoured on Kithairon by his own dogs. He died in this manner because, as Akousilaos says, he angered Zeus by wooing Semele, but according to the greater number of authorities it was because he saw Artemis

bathing. (Apollodoros, *Bibliotheka* 3.30)

XX. If you see a Back, a Belly, a Snake and two Chians:

Honor: Athene Protector of the Dead.
Contemplate the Symbol: Basket.
Recite *Orphic Hymn* 32. To Athena.
Offering: leave flowers on a veteran's grave.
Reflect on the Story:

> Theseus is represented as coming up from the underworld with
> Athena and Herakles. (Pausanias, *Description of Greece* 1.15.3)

XXI. If you see one Snake, three Bellies and a Chian:

Honor: Herakles the Bird-Slayer.
Contemplate the Symbol: Krotala.
Recite *Orphic Hymn* 12. To Herakles.
Offering: give two bottles of wine.
Reflect on the Story:

> For the sixth labour Herakles was ordered to drive off the
> Stymphalian birds. Herakles was stumped by the problem of
> driving the birds out of the woods, but Athena got some bronze
> noise-makers from Hephaistos and gave them to him, and by
> shaking these from a mountain adjacent to the lake he frightened
> the birds. Not enduring the racket, they flew up in fear, and in this
> manner Herakles reached them with his arrows. (Apollodoros,
> *Bibliotheka* 2.92)

XXII. If you see one Snake, two Backs, and two Chians:

Honor: Melampos Who Hears.
Contemplate the Symbol: Pinecone.
Recite *Orphic Hymn* 53. To the God of the Annual Feast.
Offering: help those who suffer.
Reflect on the Story:

> In the *Great Eoiae* it is related that Melampos, who was very dear
> to Apollon, went abroad and stayed with Polyphantes. But when
> the king had sacrificed an ox, a serpent crept up to the sacrifice and
> destroyed his servants. At this the king was angry and killed the
> serpent, but Melampos took and buried it. And its offspring,
> brought up by him, used to lick his ears and inspire him with

prophecy. And so, when he was caught while trying to steal the cows of Iphiklos and taken bound to the city of Aegina, and when the house, in which Iphiklos was, was about to fall, he told an old woman, one of the servants of Iphiklos, and in return was released. (Scholiast on Apollonios Rhodios, *Argonautika* 1.118)

XXIII. If you see one Back and all the rest bellies:

Honor: Pasiphae of the White Arms.
Contemplate the Symbol: Cave.
Recite *Orphic Hymn* 72. To Tyche.
Offering: milk and honey.
Reflect on the Story:

> From Oitylos to Thalamai in Lakonia the road is about eighty stades long. On it is a sanctuary of Ino and an oracle. They consult the oracle in sleep, and the Goddess reveals whatever they wish to learn, in dreams. Bronze statues of Pasiphae and of Helios stand in the unroofed part of the sanctuary. It was not possible to see the one within the temple clearly, owing to the garlands, but they say this too is of bronze. Water, sweet to drink, flows from a sacred spring. Pasiphae is a title of Selene, and is not a local Goddess of the people of Thalamai. (Pausanias, *Description of Greece* 3.26.1)

XXIV. If you see three Backs, one Chian and the fifth a Belly:

Honor: The Prophets.
Contemplate the Symbol: Cup.
Recite *Orphic Hymn* 78. To Dawn.
Offering: divine for your community.
Reflect on the Story:

> There are many oracles among the Greeks, and many, too, among the Egyptians, and again in Libya and in Asia there are many too. But these speak not, save by the mouth of priests and prophets: this one is moved by its own impulse, and carries out the divining process to the very end. The manner of his divination is the following: When he is desirous of uttering an oracle, he first stirs in his seat, and the priests straightway raise him up. Should they fail to raise him up, he sweats, and moves more violently than ever. When they approach him and bear him up, he drives them round in a circle, and leaps on one after another. At last the high priest confronts him, and questions him on every subject. The God, if he disapproves of any action proposed, retreats into the background;

if, however, he happens to approve it, he drives his bearers forward as if they were horses. It is thus that they gather the oracles, and they undertake nothing public or private without this preliminary. This God, too, speaks about the symbol, and points out when it is the due season for the expedition of which I spoke in connexion therewith. (Lucian, *The Syrian Goddess* 36)

XXV. If you see two Snakes, two Chians and the fifth a Belly:

Honor: Hera the Perfector.
Contemplate the Symbol: Cauldron.
Recite *Orphic Hymn* 16. To Hera.
Offering: tithe the first fruits of your labor for a year.
Reflect on the Story:

> It fell to the lot of Herakles to go mad because of the jealousy of Hera. In his madness he threw into a fire his and Megara's children, as well as two belonging to Iphikles. (Apollodoros, *Bibliotheka* 2.72)

XXVI. If you see a Chian, a Snake, two Bellies and a Back:

Honor: Hermes the Savior.
Contemplate the Symbol: Rose.
Recite *Orphic Hymn* 57. To Chthonic Hermes.
Offering: leave all of your change at the street corner.
Reflect on the Story:

> Brimo, who as legend tells, by the waters of Boebeis laid her virgin body at Mercurius' side. (Propertius, *Elegies* 2. 29c)

XXVII. If you see two Backs and three Bellies:

Honor: Orpheus the Healer.
Contemplate the Symbol: Lyre.
Recite *Orphic Hymn* 58. To Eros.
Offering: use music to induce an altered state of consciousness.
Reflect on the Story:

> Turning our gaze again to the lower part of the picture we see, next after Patroklos, Orpheus sitting on what seems to be a sort of hill; he grasps with his left hand a harp, and with his right he touches a willow. It is the branches that he touches, and he is leaning against the tree. The grove seems to be that of Persephone,

where grow, as Homer thought, black poplars and willows. The appearance of Orpheus is Greek, and neither his garb nor his head-gear is Thracian. (Pausanias, *Description of Greece* 10.30.6)

XXVIII. If you see a single Chian and all the rest are Backs:

Honor: Melinoe the Changeable.
Contemplate the Symbol: Fig.
Recite *Orphic Hymn* 71. To Melinoe.
Offering: go on a nocturnal procession.
Reflect on the Story:

> *Aletis:* Some say that she is Erigone, the daughter of Ikarios, since she wandered everywhere seeking her father. Others say she is the daughter of Aigisthos and Klytemnestra. Still others say she is the daughter of Maleotos the Tyrrhenian; others that she is Medea, since, having wandered after the murder of her children, she escaped to Aigeus. Others say that she is Persephone, wherefore those grinding the wheat offer some cakes to her. (*Etymologicum Magnum* 62.9)

XXIX. If you see two Snakes, two Chians and a Back:

Honor: Leto the Obscure.
Contemplate the Symbol: Water.
Recite *Orphic Hymn* 35. To Leto.
Offering: burn fragrant myrrh.
Reflect on the Story:

> Phoibe came to the desired embrace of Titanic Koios. Through their union she conceived and brought forth dark-gowned Leto, always mild, kind to men and to the deathless Gods, mild from the beginning, gentlest in all Olympos. Also she bare Asteria of happy name, whom Perses once led to his great house to be called his dear wife. And she conceived and bare Hekate. (Hesiod, *Theogony* 404)

XXX. If you see a Chian and a Snake, two Backs and the fifth a Belly:

Honor: Columbina the Wise.
Contemplate the Symbol: Apple.
Recite *Orphic Hymn* 10. To Physis.
Offering: play games of wit and chance.
Reflect on the Story:

The Ariadne myth tells how Prince Theseus of Athens set out for Crete to kill the Minotaur, a creature half man, half bull, who was concealed in a Labyrinth. Princess Ariadne of Crete fell in love with Theseus and gave him a ball of thread that enabled him to find his way out of the Labyrinth after he had killed the Minotaur. When Theseus left Crete, he took Ariadne with him as his bride. During their voyage home they stopped at the island of Naxos. While Ariadne was asleep, Theseus slipped away and continued his journey to Athens without her. The opera Ariadne auf Naxos begins at this point.

Ariadne is alone in front of her cave. Three nymphs look on and lament her fate. Watching from the wings, the comedians are doubtful whether they will be able to cheer her up. Ariadne recalls her love for Theseus ("Ein Schönes war"), then imagines herself as a chaste girl, awaiting death. Harlekin tries to divert her with a song ("Lieben, Hassen, Hoffen, Zagen") but Ariadne ignores him. As if in a trance, she resolves to await Hermes, messenger of death. He will take her to another world where everything is pure ("Es gibt ein Reich"). When the comedians' efforts continue to fail, Zerbinetta finally addresses Ariadne directly ("Grossmächtige Prinzessin!"), woman to woman, explaining to her the human need to change an old love for a new. Insulted, Ariadne leaves. After Zerbinetta has finished her speech, her colleagues leap back onto the scene, competing for her attention. Zerbinetta gives in to Harlekin's comic protestations of love and the comedians exit.

The nymphs announce the approach of a ship: it carries the young god Bacchus, who has escaped the enchantress Circe. Bacchus's voice is heard in the distance ("Circe, kannst du mich hören?") and Ariadne prepares to greet her visitor, whom she thinks must be death at last. When he appears, she at first mistakes him for Theseus come back to her, but he majestically proclaims his godhood. Entranced by her beauty, Bacchus tells her he would sooner see the stars vanish than give her up. Reconciled to a new existence, Ariadne joins Bacchus as they ascend to the heavens. Zerbinetta sneaks in to have the last word: "When a new god comes along, we're dumbstruck." (Synopsis of Richard Strauss' *Ariadne auf Naxos* from the Metropolitan Opera)

XXXI. If you see four Backs and two Bellies:

Honor: The Bacchic Martyrs.
Contemplate the Symbol: Grapes.

Recite *Orphic Hymn* 21. To the Clouds.
Offering: incense, wine and honey.
Reflect on the Story:

> About this time, in Easter week, the parish priest of Inverkeithing,
> named John, revived the profane rites of Priapus, collecting young
> girls from the villages, and compelling them to dance in circles to
> the honour of Father Bacchus. When he had these females in a
> troop, out of sheer wantonness, he led the dance, carrying in front
> on a pole a representation of the human organs of reproduction,
> and singing and dancing himself like a mime, he viewed them all
> and stirred them to lust by filthy language. Those who held
> respectable matrimony in honour were scandalised by such a
> shameless performance, although they respected the parson
> because of the dignity of his rank. If anybody remonstrated kindly
> with him, the priest became worse than before, violently reviling
> him. [Note: he was eventually murdered by a Christian mob.] (*The
> Chronicle of Lanercost* for the year 1282)

XXXII. A Snake and four Bellies together:

Honor: The Nymphai.
Contemplate the Symbol: Tree.
Recite *Orphic Hymn* 46. To Liknites.
Offering: seasonal produce.
Reflect on the Story:

> Tellers of stories say that in the land of the Messapians near the
> so-called Sacred Rocks there appeared the choral troupe of the
> Nymphai Epimelides. Young Messapians left their flocks to view
> them. They declared they themselves could dance better. What
> they said irritated the Nymphai and rivalry arose increasingly over
> their dancing. Because the youths did not know that they were
> competing with deities, they danced as they would in a contest
> with mortals of their own age. Their manner of dancing, being that
> of shepherds, was without art, while that of the Nymphai was
> entirely dedicated to beauty. In their dancing they surpassed the
> youths and they said to them: "Young men, did you want to
> compete against the Nymphai Epimelides? So, you foolish fellows,
> now that you have been beaten, you will be punished." The youths,
> as they stood by the sanctuary of the Nymphai, were changed into
> trees. Even today one hears at night the sound of groans coming
> from the trunks. The place is called that of the Nymphai and the
> Youths. (Antoninus Liberalis, *Metamorphoses* 31)

XXXIII. Two snakes, a Chian and two Bellies:

Honor: The Mousai.
Contemplate the Symbol: Stones.
Recite Orphic Hymn 76. To the Muses.
Offering: do something creative.
Reflect on the Story:

> Now most of the Greeks assigned to Dionysos, Apollon, Hekate, the Mousai, and above all to Demeter, everything of an orgiastic or Bakchic or choral nature, as well as the mystic element in initiations. And branch-bearing, choral dancing, and initiations are common elements in the worship of these Gods. (Strabo, *Geography* 10.3.10)

XXXIV. If you see three Backs, one Snake and the fifth a Chian:

Honor: Dionysos of Good Counsel.
Contemplate the Symbol: Mask.
Recite *Orphic Hymn* 30. To Dionysos.
Offering: tell stories.
Reflect on the Story:

> In the temple of Dionysos at Athens there is a painting of Dionysos bringing Hephaistos up to heaven. One of the Greek legends is that Hephaistos, when he was born, was thrown down by Hera. In revenge he sent as a gift a golden chair with invisible fetters. When Hera sat down she was held fast, and Hephaistos refused to listen to any other of the Gods save Dionysos — in him he reposed the fullest trust — and after making him drunk Dionysos brought him to heaven. (Pausanias, *Description of Greece* 1.20.3)

XXXV. If you see one Belly and four Backs:

Honor: The Sirens.
Contemplate the Symbol: Ribbons.
Recite *Orphic Hymn* 22. To the Sea.
Offering: hold a feast for the dead.
Reflect on the Story:

> *Helen of Troy:* Winged maidens, virgin daughters of Gaia, the Sirens, may you come to my mourning with Libyan flute or pipe or lyre, tears to match my plaintive woes; grief for grief and mournful chant for chant, may Persephone send choirs of death in harmony

with my lamentation, so that she may receive as thanks from me, in addition to my tears, a paean for the departed dead beneath her gloomy roof. (Euripides, *Helen* 167)

XXXVI. If you see three Bellies, a Snake and a Back:

Honor: Rheia the Mountain Mother.
Contemplate the Symbol: Double Axe.
Recite *Orphic Hymn* 14. To Rheia.
Offering: honey.
Reflect on the Story:

> In Crete there is said to be a sacred cave full of bees. In it, as storytellers say, Rheia gave birth to Zeus; it is a sacred place and no one is to go near it, whether God or mortal. At the appointed time each year a great blaze is seen to come out of the cave. Their story goes on to say that this happens whenever the blood from the birth of Zeus begins to boil up. The sacred bees that were the Nurses of Zeus occupy this cave. (Antoninus Liberalis, *Metamorphoses* 19)

XXXVII. If all you see are Backs:

Honor: The Toys.
Contemplate the Symbol: Egg.
Recite *Orphic Hymn* 7. To the Stars.
Offering: watch scary movies.
Reflect on the Story:

> Accept ye my great offering as the payment for my lawless fathers.
> Save me, great Brimo ...
> and Demeter and Rheia ...
> and the armed Kouretes: let us ... and we will make fine sacrifices.
> A ram and a he-goat ... boundless gifts.
> ... and by the law of the river ...
> Taking of the goat ... let him eat the rest of the meat ...
> Let no uninitiated look on!
> Prayer of the ...
> I call on ... Eubouleus, and I call the Maenads who cry Euoi ...
> You having parched with thirst ... the friends of the feast ...
> And let us call upon the Queen of the broad Earth,
> Grant the blessings of Demeter and Pallas unto us.
> O Eubouleus, Erikepaios, save me! Phanes!
> Hurler of Lightning!

THERE IS ONE DIONYSOS.
Tokens … God through the bosom.
Having drunk … ass cowboy …
Password: up and down to the … and what has been given to you.
Consume it, put it into the basket …
… cone, bull-roarer, knucklebones, mirror.
(*Gurôb Papyrus*)

XXXVIII. If you see a Back and a Belly, two Snakes, and the fifth a Chian:

Honor: Persephone the Midnight Dove.
Contemplate the Symbol: Wine.
Recite *Orphic Hymn* 77. To Mnemosyne.
Offering: walk a Labyrinth.
Reflect on the Story:

> Persephone who impairs the mind of mortals and brings them forgetfulness. Once death's dark cloud has enveloped him and he has come to the shadowy place of the dead and passed the black gates which hold back the souls of the dead, no man may return to the world above no matter how much he wails and protests. None there have the pleasure of listening to the lyre or pipes or of raising to his lips the gift of Dionysos. (Theognis, *Fragment* 1. 703; 973)

XXXIX. If you see the Snake alone amid two Bellies, two Backs:

Honor: Mark Antony the Dice-Thrower.
Contemplate the Symbol: Labyrinth.
Recite *Orphic Hymn* 65. To Ares.
Offering: go for a prowl.
Reflect on the Story:

> But Kleopatra, distributing her flattery, not into the four forms of which Plato speaks, but into many, and ever contributing some fresh delight and charm to Antony's hours of seriousness or mirth, kept him in constant tutelage, and released him neither night nor day. She played at dice with him, drank with him, hunted with him, and watched him as he exercised himself in arms; and when by night he would station himself at the doors or windows of the common folk and scoff at those within, she would go with him on his round of mad follies, wearing the garb of a serving maiden. For Antony also would try to array himself like a servant. Therefore he always reaped a harvest of abuse, and often of blows, before coming

back; though most people suspected who he was. However, the Alexandrians took delight in their graceful and cultivated way; they liked him, and said that he used the tragic mask with the Romans, but the comic mask with them.

XL. If you should see three Snakes and two Chians:

Honor: Dionysos Who Raves.
Contemplate the Symbol: Nebris.
Recite *Orphic Hymn* 52. To the God of the Triennial Feast.
Offering: run wild.
Reflect on the Story:

> Now you have died and now you have been born, thrice blessed one, on this very day. Say to Persephone that Bakcheios himself freed you. A bull you rushed to milk. Quickly, you rushed to milk. A ram you fell into milk. You have wine as your fortunate honor. And rites await you beneath the earth, just as the other blessed ones. (*Gold tablet from Pelinna*)

XLI. If you see a pair of Snakes, two Backs, the fifth a Chian:

Honor: The Satyrs.
Contemplate the Symbol: Goat.
Recite *Orphic Hymn* 54. To Silenos, Satyros and the Bakcheia.
Offering: watch comedies while drunk.
Reflect on the Story:

> I am borne on, like daughters of the Bacchic cry driven by the frenzy of their God, and those who shake the timbrel at the foot of Ida's ridge, or those whom Dryads half-divine and Fauni two-horned have touched with their own spirit and driven distraught. (Ovid, *Heroides* 4.47 ff)

XLII. If you see three Backs, a Snake and a Belly:

Honor: The Titans.
Contemplate the Symbol: Titanos.
Recite *Orphic Hymn* 37. To the Titans.
Offering: wine, honey and milk.
Reflect on the Story:

> The struggle having proved sharp and many having fallen on both sides, Kronos finally was wounded and victory lay with Dionysos,

who had distinguished himself in the battle. Thereupon the Titans fled to the regions which had once been possessed by Ammon, and Dionysos gathered up a multitude of captives and returned to Nysa. Here, drawing up his force in arms about the prisoners, he brought a formal accusation against the Titans and gave them every reason to suspect that he was going to execute the captives. But when he got them free from the charges and allowed them to make their choice either to join him in his campaign or to go scot free, they all chose to join him, and because their lives had been spared contrary to their expectation they venerated him like a God. Dionysos, then, taking the captives singly and giving them a libation of wine, required of all of them an oath that they would join in the campaign without treachery and fight manfully until death. (Diodoros Sikeliotes, *Library of History* 3.71.4-6)

XLIII. If you see three Bellies and two Snakes:

Honor: Hybla, Rich in Bees.
Contemplate the Symbol: Honey.
Recite *Orphic Hymn* 26. To Earth.
Offering: mead.
Reflect on the Story:

> Look, the ringing gathers strange aerial things, bees, who trail the sounds of the tinkling brass. Liber collects the swarm, shuts it in a hollow tree and is rewarded by finding honey. When the Satyrs and the bald old man tasted it, they ransacked every grove for yellow combs. The old man hears the swarm buzzing in a rotted elm; he spots the wax and pretends otherwise. Sitting lazily on his donkey's sunken back, he guides it to the elm's hollow bark. He stood on the donkey, assisted by branches, and probed hotly for honey stored in the trunk. Thousands of hornets swarm. They jab his bald head with stingers and freckly his pug-nosed face. He falls headlong and is kicked by the donkey's heel. He shouts to his friends and implores their help. The Satyrs come running and laugh at their father's bloated face; he limps from an injured knee. The god also laughs and shows him how to smear mud; he obeys and spreads dirt over his face. (Ovid, *Fasti* 3.736 ff)

XLIV. If you see one Chian, three Snakes, and a Belly:

Honor: Bacchic Cybele.
Contemplate the Symbol: Drum.
Recite *Orphic Hymn* 27. To the Mother of the Gods.

Offering: cut loose.
Reflect on the Story:

> Coroneted Cybele, with her crown of turrets, invites the eternal
> Gods to her feast. She invites, too, Satyrs and Nymphs, the Spirits
> of the Wild; Silenus is present, uninvited. It's not allowed and too
> long to narrate the Gods' banquet: night was consumed with much
> wine. Some blindly stroll shadowy Ida's dells, or lie down and rest
> their bodies in the soft grass. Others play or are clasped by sleep;
> or link their arms and thump the green earth in triple quick step.
> (Ovid, *Fasti* 6.319)

XLV. If all you see are Backs and a Snake:

Honor: Ariadne of the Masks.
Contemplate the Symbol: Severed Head.
Recite *Orphic Hymn* 86. To Dream.
Offering: dance.
Reflect on the Story:

> By what devious detours of the imagination does this apocryphal
> "Ariachne" find her way into the texture of Troilus and Cressida?
> How subtle is "a point as subtle as Ariachne's broken woof?" What
> are we to make of this pointed figure, sharp enough to penetrate
> the impenetrable, yet obscured by breakage and division? How
> Ariadne, who provided Theseus with the clue of a thread to guide
> him out of the Cretan maze, came to be enmeshed in Arachne's
> web, whether by a printer's carelessness or in an author's slip of
> the pen or daring of the imagination, is probably beyond conclusive
> recovery. "Ariachne" may be an "original," a felicitous neologism
> spun spider-fashion out of the creator's own gut; or she may be no
> more than the accidental issue of a typesetter's clumsy fingers. In
> either event she is a new creation who also carries incontestable
> traces of prior origins. The conflation or confusion of this marginal
> figure of "Ariachne," who is and is not Arachne, is and is not
> Ariadne, points the way into the major Labyrinth of citation and
> the travesty of citation which is the "stuff" out of which Troilus and
> Cressida "makes paradoxes" (I. iii. 184). Yet this fragmentary clue
> proves also the very obstacle which thwarts the expectation of a
> safe conduct through the maze. (Elizabeth Freund, *Companion to
> Shakespeare*)

XLVI. If you see Back and two Bellies, two Snakes:

Honor: Persephone the Underground Girl.
Contemplate the Symbol: Ball.
Recite *Orphic Hymn* 29. To Persephone.
Offering: *incubatio* or dream work.
Reflect on the Story:

> To the First-Born, to Mother Earth, to Cybela, daughter of
> Demeter.
> Zeus, Air, Sun. Fire conquers all.
> Avatars of fortune and Phanes. Moirai that remember all. You, O
> illustrious daimon.
> Father who subdues all. Compensation.
> Air, fire, Mother Nestis, night, day,
> Fasting for seven days. Zeus who sees all. Always. Mother, hear
> my prayer.
> Fine sacrifices. Sacrifices. Demeter. Fire. Zeus. The Underground
> Girl.
> Hero. Light to the intelligence. The Adviser seized the Girl.
> Earth. Air. To the intelligence.
> (*Orphic tablet from Thurii*)

XLVII. If you see one Chian, three Snakes, and the fifth a Back:

Honor: Athena the Toymaker.
Contemplate the Symbol: Doll.
Recite *Orphic Hymn* 33. To Nike.
Offering: make something.
Reflect on the Story:

> Mousa, I will sing for the little maid ... once when Hera was
> celebrating the feast of the seventh day of her daughter's birth, the
> Gods sitting on Olympos quarrelled, who would honour the child
> with the most beautiful gift ... Tritonis brought many toys of
> cunning workmanship shrewdly carved, toys more precious than
> gold. (Kallimachos, *Iambi* Fragment 202)

XLVIII. If you see two Snakes, and two Backs and the fifth is a Belly:

Honor: Asterios the Manslayer.
Contemplate the Symbol: Heart.
Recite *Orphic Hymn* 6. To Protogonos.
Offering: do something transgressive.

Reflect on the Story:

> Theseus son of Aigeus, assigned by lot with the youths, sailed to Crete to be supplied to the Minotaur for destruction. But when he arrived, Minos's daughter Ariadne fell in love with him and gave him a ball of thread that she took from Daidalos the builder. She instructed him, when he entered, to bind the beginning of the ball around the crossbar above the door and to go along unrolling it until he entered the innermost place, and if he overtook him while he was sleeping (text missing) that having vanquished (him) to sacrifice to Poseidon from the hairs on his head, and to return back by rolling up the ball of thread. And Theseus took Ariadne and embarked on his ship with both the youths and maidens not yet served up to be killed by the Minotaur. And when he had done these things, he sailed out in the middle of the night. And when he anchored at the island of Dia, he disembarked to sleep on the shore. And Athena stood beside him and ordered that he abandon Ariadne and come to Athens. He did this and departed immediately. But when Ariadne bewailed her lot, Aphrodite appeared and advised her to be strong, for she would be Dionysos' wife and become famous. Whence the God appeared and mated with her, and gave her a golden crown that moreover the Gods placed among the stars by the grace of Dionysos. And they say that she suffered death at the hands of Artemis for throwing away her virginity. The story is in Pherekydes. (Scholiast on Homer's *Odyssey* 11.322)

XLIX. If you see three Snakes and three Bellies:

Honor: The Hanged Maidens.
Contemplate the Symbol: Ivy.
Recite *Orphic Hymn* 41. To Mother Antaia.
Offering: fast from food or words.
Reflect on the Story:

> The story of Ikarios who entertained Dionysos is told by Eratosthenes in his *Erigone*. The Romans, however, say that Saturnus when once he was entertained by a farmer who had a fair daughter named Entoria, seduced her and begat Janus, Hymnus, Faustus, and Felix. He then taught Icarius the use of wine and viniculture, and told him that he should share his knowledge with his neighbours also. When the neighbours did so and drank more than is customary, they fell into an unusually deep sleep. Imagining that they had been poisoned, they pelted Icarius with stones and killed him; and his grandchildren in despair ended their lives by

hanging themselves. When a plague had gained a wide hold among the Romans, Apollo gave an oracle that it would cease if they should appease the wrath of Saturnus and the Spirits of those who had perished unlawfully. Lutatius Catulus, one of the nobles, built for the God the precinct which lies near the Tarpeian Rock. He made the upper altar with four faces, either because of Icarius's grandchildren or because the year has four parts; and he designated a month January. Saturnus placed them all among the stars. The others are called harbingers of the vintage, but Janus rises before them. His star is to be seen just in front of the feet of Virgo. So Critolaus in the fourth book of his *Phaenomena*. (Plutarch, *Greek and Roman Parallel Stories* 9)

L. If you see three Backs and two Snakes:

Honor: The Labyrinth Dwellers.
Contemplate the Symbol: Distaff.
Recite *Orphic Hymn* 69. To the Erinyes.
Offering: wear a mask while you watch a scary movie.
Reflect on the Story:

> ... they roam together — the night-walkers, the magicians, the Bakchai, the Lenai, the participants in mysteries full of unholy rites. Their processions and phallic hymns would be disgraceful exhibitions if it wasn't for the fact that they are done in honor of Dionysos — that Dionysos who is the same as Haides; it is in his honor that they rave madly and hold their revels. (Herakleitos, *Fragments* 76-77)

LI. If you see one Back, three Snakes and a Belly:

Honor: Artemis the Initiator.
Contemplate the Symbol: Net.
Recite Orphic Hymn 87. To Death.
Offering: dance.
Reflect on the Story:

> Note that a child picked up a golden leaf that fell from the crown of Artemis, but he was spotted. The judges put toys and knucklebones in front of the child alongside the leaf. He again made for the golden object, and for this reason they executed him for sacrilege, not forgiving him on account of his age but exacting the penalty for his action. (Aelian, *Historical Miscellany* 5.16)

LII. If you see four Snakes and a Chian:

Honor: Mr. Mojo Risin.
Contemplate the Symbol: Peacock.
Recite *Orphic Hymn* 56. To Adonis.
Offering: light a dozen candles.
Reflect on the Story:

> *Indians scattered on dawn's highway bleeding*
> *Ghosts crowd the young child's fragile eggshell mind.*
> Me and my mother and father, and a grandmother and a
> grandfather, were driving through the desert, at dawn, and a truck
> load of Indian workers had either hit another car, or just — I don't
> know what happened — but there were Indians scattered all over
> the highway, bleeding to death. So the car pulls up and stops. That
> was the first time I tasted fear. I musta' been about four — like a
> child is like a flower, his head is just floating in the breeze, man.
> The reaction I get now thinking about it, looking back — is that
> the souls of the ghosts of those dead Indians... maybe one or two of
> 'em... were just running around freaking out, and just leaped into
> my soul. And they're still there. (Jim Morrison, *American Prayer*)

LIII. If you see three Snakes and two Backs:

Honor: Those Beneath the Earth.
Contemplate the Symbol: Pillar.
Recite *Orphic Hymn* 13. To Kronos.
Offering: your blood.
Reflect on the Story:

> Now I would have you know, men say that noxious spiders,
> together with the grievous reptiles and vipers and the earth's
> countless burdens, are of the Titans' blood. (Nikander of Kolophon,
> *Theriaka* 8-10)

LIV. If it's all Snakes and one Belly

Honor: Heavenly Aphrodite.
Contemplate the Symbol: Breast.
Recite *Orphic Hymn* 4. To Ouranos.
Offering: express your love.
Reflect on the Story:

> For tell me, if anyone offered to introduce you into a palace, and

show you the king sitting there, would you indeed choose to see the theatre instead of these things? And you leave this and run to the theatre to see women swimming, and nature put to open dishonour, leaving Christ sitting by the well? But you, leaving the fountain of blood, the awful cup, go your way to the fountain of the devil, to see a harlot swim, and to endure shipwreck of the soul. For that water is a sea of lasciviousness, not drowning bodies, but working shipwreck of souls. And while she swims naked, you, as you behold, are plunged into the depths of lasciviousness. For in the first place, through a whole night the devil takes over their souls with the expectation of it; then having shown them the expected object, he has at once bound them and made them captives. If now you are ashamed, and blush at the comparison, rise up to your nobility and flee the sea of hell and the river of fire, I mean the pool in the theatre. And you, when there is a question of precedence, claim to have priority over the whole world, since our city first crowned itself with the name of Christian; but in the competition of chastity, are you not ashamed to be behind the ruder cities? (John Chrysostom, *In Matthaeum Homiliae* 7)

LV. If you see four Snakes on a Back:

Honor: All the rest of the Retinue.
Contemplate the Symbol: Pomegranate.
Recite *Orphic Hymn* 45. Hymn to Dionysos, Bassareus and Triennial.
Offering: lay out a feast.
Reflect on the Story:

> During this night, it is said, about the middle of it, while the city was quiet and depressed through fear and expectation of what was coming, suddenly certain harmonious sounds from all sorts of instruments were heard, and the shouting of a throng which none could see, accompanied by cries of Bacchic revelry and satyric leapings, as if a troop of revelers, making a great tumult, were going forth from the city; and their course seemed to lie about through the middle of it toward the outer gate which faced the enemy, at which point the tumult became loudest and then dashed out. (Plutarch, *Life of Antony* 75)

LVI. If all you see are Snakes:

Honor: Square Hermes.
Contemplate the Symbol: Scorpion.
Recite *Orphic Hymn* 64. To Nomos.

Offering: lamb.
Reflect on the Story:

16. I approve of the remarks about the temple made by those who in the main accept the theories of the Greeks: according to these the Goddess is Hera, but the work was carried out by Dionysos, the son of Semele: Dionysos visited Syria on his journey to Aethiopia. There are in the temple many tokens that Dionysos was its actual founder: for instance, barbaric raiment, Indian precious stones, and elephants' tusks brought by Dionysos from the Aethiopians. Further, a pair of phalli of great size are seen standing in the vestibule, bearing the inscription, "I, Dionysos, dedicated these phalli to Hera my stepmother." This proof satisfies me. And I will describe another curiosity to be found in this temple, a sacred symbol of Dionysos. The Greeks erect phalli in honour of Dionysos, and on these they carry, singular to say, mannikins made of wood, with enormous pudenda; they call these puppets. There is this further curiosity in the temple: as you enter, on the right hand, a small brazen statue meets your eye of a man in a sitting posture, with parts of monstrous size.

28. The place whereon the temple is placed is a hill: it lies nearly in the centre of the city, and is surrounded by a double wall. Of the two walls the one is ancient; the other is not much older than our own times. The entrance to the temple faces the north; its size is about a hundred fathoms. In this entrance those phalli stand which Dionysos erected: they stand thirty fathoms high. Into one of these a man mounts twice every year, and he abides on the summit of the phallus for the space of seven days. The reason of this ascent is given as follows: The people believe that the man who is aloft holds converse with the Gods, and prays for good fortune for the whole of Syria, and that the Gods from their neighbourhood hear his prayers. Others allege that this takes place in memory of the great calamity of Deukalion's time, when men climbed up to mountain tops and to the highest trees, in terror of the mass of waters. To me all this seems highly improbable, and I think that they observe this custom in honour of Dionysos, and I conjecture this from the following fact, that all those who rear phalli to Dionysos take care to place mannikins of wood on the phalli; the reason of this I cannot say, but it seems to me that the ascent is made in imitation of the wooden mannikin.

29. To proceed, the ascent is made in this way; the man throws round himself and the phallus a small chain; afterwards he climbs

up by means of pieces of wood attached to the phallus large enough to admit the end of his foot. As he mounts he jerks the chain up his own length, as a driver his reins. Those who have not seen this process, but who have seen those who have to climb palm trees in Arabia, or in Egypt, or any other place, will understand what I mean. When he has climbed to the top, he lets down a different chain, a long one, and drags up anything that he wants, such as wood, clothing, and vases; he binds these together and sits upon them, as it were, on a nest, and he remains there for the space of time that I have mentioned. Many visitors bring him gold and silver, and some bring brass; then those who have brought these offerings leave them and depart, and each visitor gives his name. A bystander shouts the name up; and he on hearing the name utters a prayer for each donor; between the prayers he raises a sound on a brazen instrument which, on being shaken, gives forth a loud and grating noise. He never sleeps; for if at any time sleep surprises him, a scorpion creeps up and wakes him, and stings him severely; this is the penalty for wrongfully sleeping. This story about the scorpion is a sacred one, and one of the mysteries of religion; whether it is true I cannot say, but, as it seems to me, his wakefulness is in no small degree due to his fear of falling. So much then for the climbers of the phalli. As for the temple, it looks to the rising sun. (Lucian, *The Syrian Goddess*)

The Top of Destiny

Get a Top, mark out three equal sections and then paint them black, red and white. Ask your question, spin the Top and when it stops the uppermost portion will provide your answer.

You can assign whatever random meanings you want to the Top's three colors, just make sure you've defined them within the context of your question before you spin the Top.

Examples

"Will this endeavor meet with success?"
Black: Yes. Red: No. White: The outcome is uncertain. Try back later.

"What is behind this series of unfortunate events?"
Black: Something divine. Red: Stupid humans. White: Shit just happens sometimes.

"Where did that dream come from?"
Black: Within me. Red: Outside me. White: Dear Gods, help me! I'm still dreaming!

And so forth.

The day on which the feast of Liberalia falls (March 17) contains all the months of the year. Watch from noon until midnight and you will discover what each month's weather will be like.

Kottabos was a popular game played at *symposia* from the early Classical to late Hellenistic periods, finally declining and then dying out under the Romans. William Smith, in his *Dictionary of Greek and Roman Antiquities*, describes it as follows:

> (Ionic, κόσσαβος or ὄτταβος), a social game which was introduced from Sicily into Greece, where it became one of the favourite amusements of young people after their repasts. The simplest way in which it originally was played was this:— One of the company threw out of a goblet a certain quantity of pure wine, at a certain distance, into a metal basin, endeavouring to perform this exploit in such a manner as not to spill any of the wine. While he was doing this, he either thought of or pronounced the name of his mistress (Etymol. Mag. s.v. Κοτταβίζω), and from the more or less full and pure sound with which the wine struck against the metal basin, the lover drew his conclusions respecting the attachment of the object of his love. [...] This brief description of four various forms of the *cottabus* may be sufficient to show the general character of this game; and it is only necessary to add, that the chief object to be accomplished in all the various modifications of the *cottabus* was to throw the wine out of the goblet in such a manner that it should remain together and nothing be spilled, and that it should produce the purest and strongest possible sound in the place where it was thrown.

While Athenaios (*Deipnosophistai* 15.666) goes into the game's history:

> Since, then, you are unfamiliar with this branch of study, let me inform you that the game of *kottabos*, in the first place, is a Sicilian invention, the Sicels being the first to devise it, as Kritias, the son of Kallaischros, makes clear in his *Elegiac Verses* in these words: "The *kottabos* is the chief product of Sicily; we set it up as a mark to shoot at with drops of wine (*latages*)." Dikaiarchos of Messenê, pupil of Aristotle, says in his book *On Alcaeus* that the word *latagê* is likewise Sicilian. It means the drop of moisture which is left in the cup after it has been drunk out, and which the players tossed up into the basin with a twist of the hand. One must, indeed, bend the wrist very gracefully in shooting the *kottabos*, as Dikaiarchos says, and Plato, too, in *Zeus Outraged*. In that play someone directs

Herakles not to hold his wrist stiffly when he is going to shoot. That the *kottabos* was popular among the Sicilian Greeks is proved by the custom of constructing rooms especially designed for the game; this is recorded by Dikaiarchos in his treatise *On Alcaeus*. And so, with good reason, too, Kallimachos has called the wine-drop "Sicilian." Dionysios Chalkos in his *Elegies* mentions the wine-drops and the *kottabos*-games in these lines: "We, love-sick, add a third *kottabos* prize to stand for you here in the Wine God's gymnasium; a punching-bag and tester of skill it is. All of you in the company must measure with your eyes the air by your couch and see over how much space the wine-drops must reach."

In addition to answering romantic questions, the game of *kottabos* can provide insight on many other matters. Either ask a question aloud or contemplate it internally, then flick the lees from your wine-cup into a basin set an appropriate distance away. This can be anywhere from a couple feet to a man's span, depending on how drunk the querent is. If the querent should fail to make it into the basin, it's a definite no. The quantity of wine that makes it in, where and how it lands, as well as the quality of sound it makes, etc., should all be interpreted by a *mantis*, a priest of Dionysos, the *symposiarch* or the other attendees if no qualified personnel are on hand.

Another method is to either count the number of wine-drops that make it into the basin, or the number of tosses the querent can get in before missing the mark (though this requires some proficiency with the game.)

The oracular messages are taken from an inscription at Termessos for a system of *astragalomancy* or bone-divination.

2 = Dionysos communicates: "I do not see anything painful among the things about which you ask me; do not think small, go forward with courage; you will find everything you wish: your vow will be fulfilled, and there is a perfect occasion for you."

3 = Dionysos announces: "You kick against the goad, you struggle against the waves, you search for a fish in the sea. It does not help you to force the Gods at the wrong time."

4 = Dionysos utters the oracle: "As wolves overpower sheep and powerful lions overpower broad hoofed oxen, so you too will master all this, and everything about which you ask will be yours, with the help of Zeus' son Hermes."

5 = Dionysos laughs: "To buy and to trade is happiness."

6 = Dionysos tells you: "The woman who has given birth to a child, had both breasts dry, but then she again flourished and has milk in abundance. You too will reap the fruits about which you ask me."

7 = Dionysos proclaims: "A storm will come about your business, but it will turn out well in the end." Also the God announces that he will "free the one who is ill from his suffering, and the Gods will bring safely home the one who is abroad."

8 = Dionysos brings news: "I see something hostile to you, so wait; afterwards, it will be possible, and the God will free you from fear and save you from toil."

9 = Dionysos warns: "Scorpions stand in your way, do not hasten to meet them."

10 = Dionysos says: "The moment has not yet arrived, you make too much haste. Do not act in vain, nor like the bitch that has borne a blind puppy. Deliberate calmly, and the God will lead you."

11 = Dionysos prophecies: "Throwing seeds and writing letters on the sea are both pointless and fruitless doing; since you are mortal, do not force a God to harm you."

12 = Dionysos knows: "Do not put your hand into a wolf's mouth, lest some harm happens to you; the matter about which you ask is difficult and delicate; but you stay quiet, avoiding travel and business transactions."

13 = Dionysos speaks: "Approach with courage the business that you set out to do; do it! You will win, since the Gods have given you these favorable signs, and do not avoid them in your intention: nothing bad will come from it."

Diagnosing the Evil Eye With an Egg

Take the egg of a white hen and rub it over the entirety of the client's body, while reciting this charm:

> And what important services do not the birds render to mortals!
> First of all, they mark the seasons for us:, springtime, winter, and
> autumn. Does the screaming crane migrate to Libya,-it warns the
> husbandman to sow, the pilot to take his ease beside his tiller hung
> up in his dwelling, and Orestes to weave a tunic, so that the
> rigorous cold may not drive him any more to strip other folk.
> When the kite reappears, he tells of the return of spring and of the
> period when the fleece of the sheep must be clipped. Is the swallow
> in sight? All hasten to sell their warm tunic and to buy some light
> clothing. Before undertaking anything, whether a business
> transaction, a marriage, or the purchase of food, you consult the
> birds by reading the omens, and you give this name of omen to all
> signs that tell of the future.
>
> O, prematurely dead bird, reveal to me whether N. the child of N.
> suffers affliction from an eye that is evil?

Then have them place the egg under their bed overnight. Upon rising, crack the egg and examine its contents. If there is blood or anything "hard" in the yoke the client has been evil-eyed.

The wife of Dion, king of Laconia, was Iphitea, daughter of Prognaus, who had kindly received Apollo. In return Apollo rewarded her by conferring upon her three daughters (Orphe, Lyco, and Carya) the gift of prophecy on condition, however, that they should not betray the Gods nor search after forbidden things. Afterwards Bacchus also came to the house of Dion; he was not only well received, like Apollo, but won the love of Carya, and therefore soon paid Dion a second visit, under the pretext of consecrating a temple, which the king had erected to him. Orphe and Lyco, however, guarded their sister, and when Bacchus had reminded them, in vain, of the command of Apollo, they were seized with raging madness, and having gone to the heights of Taygetus, they were metamorphosed into rocks. Carya, the beloved of Bacchus, was changed into a walnut tree, and the Lacedaemonians, on being informed of it by Artemis, dedicated a temple to Artemis Caryatis, "of the Walnut Tree." (Maurus Servius Honoratus, *Commentary on the Eclogues of Vergil* 8.29)

If one has several suitors and wishes to know which of them will prove true, place a row of walnuts amongst the hot embers of the hearth. Before placing the nuts speak the name of the suitor over each of them and say, "If you love me, pop and fly; if not, then silently lie." Should the walnut jump away from the embers, it bodes well for the affair. But if the walnut burns completely, it will go badly.

During the All-night Vigil of Ariadne (July 8), go outside and with eyes closed recite *Orphic Hymn* 7:

> I call forth the sacred light of the heavenly Stars,
> and with devotional prayers I summon the holy Demons.
> Heavenly Stars, dear children of dark Night,
> on circles you march and whirl about,
> O brilliant and fiery begetters of all.
> Fate; everyone's fate,
> you reveal and you determine the divine path for mortals,
> as, wandering in midair you gaze upon the seven luminous orbits.
> In heaven and on earth ever indestructible on your blazing trail,
> you shine upon Night's cloak of darkness.
> Coruscating, gleaming, kindly and nocturnal,
> visit the learned contents of this rite,
> finishing a noble race for works of glory

Then look up, ask the Stars in Ariadne's Crown the question that lies in your heart, and open your eyes.

If the Stars should seem to grow brighter, or one shoots across the heavens, it will come to be. If nothing occurs after an appropriate span of time, or nothing is visible because of clouds or light pollution, it shall not be so.

Prognostic for Thunder by Hours of the Day

In Naples you may see the following in a painting: Bronte (Thunder), stern of face, and Astrape (Lightning) flashing light from her eyes, and raging fire from heaven that has laid hold of a king's house, suggest the following tale, if it is one you know. A cloud of fire encompassing Thebes breaks into the dwelling of Kadmos as Zeus comes wooing Semele; and Semele apparently is destroyed, but Dionysos is born, by Zeus, so I believe, in the presence of the fire. And the form of Semele is dimly seen as she goes to the heavens, where the Mousai will hymn her praises: but Dionysos leaps forth as his mother's womb is rent apart and he makes the flame look dim, so brilliantly does he shine like a radiant star. The flame, dividing, dimly outlines a cave for Dionysos more charming than any in Assyria and Lydia; for sprays of ivy grow luxuriantly about it and clusters of ivy berries and now grape-vines and stalks of thyrsos which spring up from the willing earth, so that some grow in the very fire. We must not be surprised if in honour of Dionysos the Fire is crowned by the Earth, for the Earth will take part with the Fire in the Bacchic revel and will make it possible for the revelers to take wine from springs and to draw milk from clods of earth or from a rock as from living breasts. Listen to Pan, how he seems to be hymning Dionysos on the crests of Kithairon, as he dances an Euian fling. And Kithairon in the form of a man laments the woes soon to occur on his slopes, and he wears an ivy crown aslant on his head–for he accepts the crown most unwillingly–and Megaira causes a fir to shoot up beside him and brings to light a spring of water, in token, I fancy, of the blood of Aktaion and of Pentheus. (Philostratos the Elder, *Imagines* 1.14)

If it thunders at twilight, it signifies the birth of something great. Proceed with confidence.

If in the first hour of the night, it signifies death. Prepare.

If in the second hour of the night, it signifies that you have labored well in the vineyard. Dionysos will reward you.

If in the third hour of the night, it signifies the wrath of Dionysos towards Pentheus. Soften your heart and change your ways before it is too late.

If in the fifth hour in the middle of the night, it signifies king Midas, unable to judge the true worth of a thing, making a foolhardy choice.

If at cock-crow it signifies Dionysos' war with the Indians and the shedding of much blood. Stand firm, and do not back down.

If in the early morning it signifies the birth of Dionysos in flame. Many blessings come from much suffering.

If at the hour of sunrise it signifies the Boukoloi and Mainades coming together in the dance. Put aside your enmity and embrace what is good.

If at the sixth hour of the day it signifies the Etruscan pirates plotting to capture the young God. Beware gossip and scandalous speech.

If it thunders at the seventh hour from any part of the sky, it signifies the Grand Procession of Ptolemy the king. There is fruitfulness and great abundance in your future.

If it thunders at the eighth hour from the southern quarter, it signifies that Herakles' herd has gotten loose. There will be an abundance of bread and oil and destruction among herds and four-footed animals.

If it thunders in the ninth hour from the north, it signifies the Minyades at their loom. Confusion, disorder, wasted labor, factiousness.

If it thunders in the tenth hour from the east, it signifies the fall of Thebes. Thoughtlessness and ancestral guilt will lead one to ruin.

If it thunders in the last hour of the day, it signifies a Triton disrupting Bacchic revels. Tempests in the sea and news of war.

If thunder is made at midnight, it signifies great hunger.

Another Method of Divination by Thunder

... even the sound that wakes to frenzy. Another, with brass-bound cymbals, raises a clang ... the twang shrills; the unseen, unknown, bull-voiced mimes in answer bellow fearfully, while the timbrel's echo, like that of subterranean thunder, rolls along inspiring a mighty terror. (Aischylos, *Edonoi* frag 27)

During a storm, go outdoors, lay face down upon the earth and ask Dionysos Bromios your question.

Once it thunders count the number of times you can say "Dionysos" before the lightning flashes. If it is even the answer will be yes; if the number is odd it is no.

Later, when Octavius was leading an army through the remote parts of Thrace, and in the grove of Father Liber consulted the priests of barbarian rites about his son they made the same prediction; since such a pillar of flame sprang forth from the wine that was poured over the altar that it rose above the temple roof and mounted to the very sky, and such an omen had befallen no one save Alexander the Great when he offered sacrifice at the same altar. (Suetonius, *Augustus* 94)

First recite the choral ode from Sophokles' *Antigone*:

> God of the many names, Semele's golden child,
> child of Olympian thunder, Italy's lord.
> Lord of Eleusis, where all men come
> to mother Demeter's plain.
> Bacchus, who dwell in Thebes,
> by Ismenus' running water,
> where wild Bacchic women are at home,
> on the soil of the dragon seed.
>
> Seen in the glaring flame, high on the double mount,
> with the Nymphs of Parnassos at play on the hill,
> seen by Kastalia's flowing stream.
> You come from the ivied heights,
> from green Euboea's shore.
> In immortal words we cry
> your name, lord, who watch the ways,
> the many ways of Thebes.
>
> This is your city, honored beyond the rest,
> the town of your mother's miracle-death.
> Now, as we wrestle our grim disease,
> come with healing step from Parnassos' slope
> or over the moaning sea.
>
> Leader in the dance of the fire-pulsing stars
> overseer of the voices of night,
> child of Zeus, be manifest,
> with due companionship of Maenad maids
> whose cry is but your name.

Then light a coal on a brazier using a piece of paper on which you have inscribed the choral ode so that the fire will become holy. Sprinkle powdered honey, crushed pomegranate seeds and frankincense on the coal then interpret the smoke as it rises.

If your offering causes the flame to burn with much smoke, then it means Dionysos' army shall triumph against the Indians. You will overcome obstacles and enemies with the assistance of many companions.

If your offering causes the flame to gutter and go out it means that Lykourgos will drive the Nurses into the sea. No amount of companions will help you overcome these obstacles and enemies.

If the smoke comes quickly towards you it means you possess what is necessary to succeed.

If the smoke moves quickly away from you it means you must seek divine assistance before proceeding.

If the smoke goes equally in all directions it means the situation will not change or be swiftly resolved. Endure.

If the smoke clusters like the grape it means a fruitful resolution, especially if new relationships are formed or new ventures tried.

If the upper portion of the smoke is cleft unevenly it betokens madness, chaos and confusion.

If the upper portion of the smoke is cleanly cut off it means you will experience hardship and betrayal from loved ones.

If the smoke resembles a *liknon* basket, it means that unseen things will get the better of you or your secrets will be betrayed to your enemies.

If the smoke gathers like the *narthex* plant, full at the top and narrow at the bottom, it means a little thing will lead to great troubles. Be extremely cautious.

If the smoke resembles a *kantharos*, low at the center with plumes to either side it means that your hard labor will result in joyous celebration and health.

If the smoke resembles a *stephanos* crown, it signifies a happy union and accolades from all.

If the fire should make a single popping sound it means that the Gods have answered your question in the affirmative.

If there should be two popping sounds in quick succession it means that the Gods have answered your question in the negative.

If three popping sounds it means you need to ask your question differently.

The Diagnostic of Philolâus of Tarentum

Philolâus of Tarentum was a fifth century Orphic-Pythagorean who wrote numerous works (including *On the School of Pythagoras*, *On the Universe* and *The Bakchai*) which explored the more mystical and occult currents of his master's teachings. Here are some of his fragments which have come down to us:

> For the nature of Number is the cause of recognition, able to give guidance and teaching to every man in what is puzzling and unknown. For none of existing things would be clear to anyone, either in themselves or in their relationship to one another, unless there existed Number and its essence. But in fact Number, fitting all things into the soul through sense-perception, makes them recognisable and comparable with one another as is provided by the nature of the Gnômôn, in that Number gives them body and divides the different relationships of things, whether they be Non-Limited or Limiting, into their separate groups.

> The Bodies or physical Elements of the Sphere are five: the Fire in the Sphere, and the Water, and Earth, and Air, and fifth, the Vehicle of the Sphere.

> The Four Elements of the rational animal are: Head, Heart, Navel, Genital Organ. The Head is the seat of the Mind, the Heart of the Soul and of feeling, the Navel of the Rooting and Growth of the original (embryo), the Genital Organ of the emission of Seed and of Creation. The Head indicates the ruling factor of Man, the Heart that of the animal, the Navel that of the plant, and the Genital Organ of them all; for they all derive their life and growth from a seed.

> The ancient theologians and seers also bear witness that because of certain punishments the soul is yoked to the body and buried in it as in a tomb.

Sprinkle some sand (Earth) in a pot (Sphere), fill it with water (Water) and place it on the stove (Fire) until it comes to a steamy (Air) boil. This is the Vehicle.

On strips of paper write:

Head
Heart
Navel
Genital Organ

Then roll them into tight cylinders and drop them into a metal strainer which is to be held in the steam rising from the pot, until one of them unrolls.

This will tell you where the client is suffering a spiritual block or attack, the root of an ailment, their natural temperament and devotional style, what qualities they need to cultivate, as well as many other things.

One may also inscribe the Bodies on tiles, pebbles, pieces of wood, bone, etc. and draw them out of a pouch to diagnose.

Are you, then, the companion of the Gods, as a man beyond the common? Are you the chaste one, untouched by evil? I will never be persuaded by your vauntings, never be so unintelligent as to impute folly to the Gods. Continue then your confident boasting, take up a diet of greens and play the showman with your food, make Orpheus your lord and engage in mystic rites, holding the vaporings of many books in honor. For you have been found out. To all I give the warning: avoid men like this. For they make you their prey with their high-holy-sounding words while they contrive deeds of shame. (Euripides, *Hippolytos* 948–957)

Place tiles with letters in a bag. You may either inscribe the letters yourself or use a Scrabble set.

Begin by reciting *Orphic Hymn 30*:

I call upon loud-roaring and reveling Dionysos, primeval, two-
  natured,
Thrice-born Bacchic lord, savage,
ineffable, two-horned and two-shaped.
Ivy-covered, bull-faced, warlike, howling, pure, you take raw flesh,
you have triennial feasts, wrapt in foliage, decked with grape
  clusters.
Resourceful Eubouleus, immortal God sired by Zeus,
When he mated with Persephone in unspeakable union.
Hearken to my voice, O blessed one, and with your fair-girdled
  Nurses,
Breathe on me in spirit of perfect kindness.

Shake the bag, turning to greet each of the Four Winds:

Boreas, to the North	**Notos, to the South**
Euros, to the East	**Zephyros to the West**

At each direction open the bag and blow into it, asking Dionysos to breathe forth his prophetic speech. When you have finished, dump out as many of the tiles as you feel are necessary and any words that appear are to be taken as your answer.

Zeus changed his face and came, rolling in many a loving coil through the dark to the corner of the maiden's chamber, and shaking his hairy chaps he lulled to sleep as he crept the eyes of those creatures of his own shape who guarded the door. He licked the girl's form gently with wooing lips. By this marriage with the heavenly dragon, the womb of Persephone swelled with living fruit, and she bore Zagreus the horned baby, who by himself climbed upon the heavenly throne of Zeus and brandished lightning in his little hand, and newly born, lifted and carried thunderbolts in his tender fingers for Zeus meant him to be king of the universe. But he did not hold the throne of Zeus for long. By the fierce resentment of implacable Hera, the Titanes cunningly smeared their round faces with disguising chalk (*titanos*), and while he contemplated his changeling countenance reflected in a mirror they destroyed him with an infernal knife. There where his limbs had been cut piecemeal by the Titan steel, the end of his life was the beginning of a new life as Dionysos. He appeared in another shape, and changed into many forms: now young like crafty Kronides shaking the aegis-cape, now as ancient Kronos heavy-kneed, pouring rain. (Nonnos, *Dionysiaka* 6.155 ff)

Collect sacrificial ash and pour it into a dish with a depth of at least three inches. Over the ashes recite *Orphic Hymn 37*:

> Titans, glorious children of Ouranos and Gaia, forebears of our
>   fathers,
> who dwell down below in Tartarean homes in the earth's bowels.
> From you stem all toiling mortals,
> the creatures of the sea and of the land,
> the birds, and all generations of this world come from you,
> and upon you I call to banish harsh anger,
> if some earthly ancestor of mine stormed your homes.

Suspend a coffin nail, a sickle or a key from a string over the center of the ash. Close your eyes, reflect on your circumstances as you breathe in and out nine times, and then wait for the signifier to begin to move of its own accord. Once it stops, open your eyes and interpret the signs in the sand.

If you see a **large circle** it means that you will face a great ordeal.

If you see a **small circle** it means that you should watch for signs from the Gods before proceeding.

If you see a **triangle** it means that things will come together for you and you will meet with success.

If you see a **square** it means that you will have good luck and your foundations are strong.

If you see a **long line** it means you will go on a journey.

If you see a **short line** it means you will have an unexpected visitor.

If you see a **heart** it means that you will overcome emotional blockages.

If you see a **broken egg** it means that a relationship will be tested.

If you see the **horns of a bull** it means you have the favor of the Gods.

If you see a **leaf** it means that it is time to start something new.

If you see an **X** it means that you need to make a decision, without delay.

If you see a **zigzag** it means that a judgment will go against you.

If you see a **T** it means your burdens will crush you. Lay them aside.

If you see an **S** it means you still have far to go. Don't give up before the work is done.

If other symbols appear, interpret them with your question in mind.

What wickedness takes place during this feast; fortune-tellings, divinations, deceptions and feigned madnesses. On this day, having been seized up by the furies of their bacchant-like ravings and having been inflamed by the fires of diabolical instigation, they flock together to the church and profane the house of god with vain and foolish rhythmic poetry in which sin is not wanting but by all means present, and with evil sayings, laughing and cacophony they disrupt the priest and the whole congregation applauds for the people love these things. (Richard of St.-Victor, *Sermones centum* 177.1036)

On the Kalends of January or its eve, bake bread in the shape of a phallos. Place a loaf on the horns of a goat and when the animal throws it to the ground, read the phallos.

If the phallos points to the **North** it means you have a hard and cold year ahead.

If to the **South** it means you will have warmth and abundance.

To the **West**, the year will start lean and end well.

To the **East**, it will have a good start but dire end.

If one does not have a goat on hand, have someone dress as a goat and play the part. Feed half to the goat, and eat the rest of the bread yourself.

The Grace of Elais, Spermo and Oino

> Liber gave my girls gifts greater than their pious prayers. For at my daughters' touch all things were turned to corn or wine or oil of Minerva's tree. Rich was that role of theirs! (Ovid, *Metamorphoses* 13. 631)

A drop of olive oil is placed in a glass of *chernips*. If the drop floats you are fine, but if it sinks then it means you have the evil eye on you.

Another method: place two drops of olive oil in the *chernips*; if the drops stay separated, there is no cause for worry. If they cohere, move on to the next stage.

Take a handful of barley groats and say the following while scattering them across your doorstep:

> You, baneful one, cannot afflict me until you have counted every last one of these grains!

> And if you should try, well, I know a spell of Orpheus, a most excellent one, to make the brand enter your skull of its own accord, and set alight the one-eyed son of Earth! What ho! my gallants, thrust away, make haste and burn his eyebrow off, the monster's a guest-devouring foe. Oh! singe and scorch the shepherd of Aetna; twirl the brand and drag it round and be careful lest in his agony he treat thee to some wantonness.

Then wash your hands and face in wine over which the following words have been spoken:

> Nothing can be so firmly bound
> by illness, by wrath or by fortune
> that cannot be released by the Lord Dionysos.

Thusthla

According to Liddell & Scott, *thusthla* (θύσθλα) are wands or other sacred implements used in Bacchic worship, most famously found in Homer's *Iliad* 6.136-37 where Lykourgos:

> drove the Nurses of frenzied Dionysos from the Nyseian land
> and rushing headlong, the women threw their *thusthla* to the ground,
> terrified by the man-slaying ox-goad.

Within the Starry Bull tradition *thusthla* are divining rods similar to those described in Tacitus' *Germania*:

> Augury and divination by lot no people practise more diligently. The use of the lots is simple. A little bough is lopped off a fruit-bearing tree, and cut into small pieces; these are distinguished by certain marks, and thrown carelessly and at random over a white garment. In public questions the priest of the particular state, in private the father of the family, invokes the Gods, and, with his eyes toward heaven, takes up each piece three times, and finds in them a meaning according to the mark previously impressed on them. If they prove unfavourable, there is no further consultation that day about the matter; if they sanction it, the confirmation of augury is still required.

You will need a total of seven *thusthla*, cut from a tree sacred to Dionysos such as pine, fig, grapevine, apple, oak, birch, plane or the like, but in a pinch you can just get dowels from a hardware or art supply store. They may be of any size, though it is best if they are nine to thirteen inches in length. Three of them should be painted red, three painted black and the remaining one painted white with appropriate sigils inscribed on it. These may be magical *charakters* such as are found in the *PGM*, symbols of the Starry Bull tradition, or the letters of the Greek alphabet; personally I recommend the latter as the *thusthla* can then be doubled with the Starry Bull Alphabet Oracle for an even more nuanced reading. When not in use the *thusthla* should be wrapped in a pure white or linen cloth, which is also used as a diviner's mat when consulting them.

The first method of consultation is as follows. Lay the mat upon the ground and make the appropriate offerings and prayers. Then kneel before the mat, place the white branch diagonally across the center of the mat and hold the remaining branches in your right hand (per Dionysos' instruction to Pentheus in Euripides' *Bakchai*.) With eyes closed and contemplating the question, shuffle them until you feel you are ready and then let them go and interpret their fall.

For the second method of consultation do the same except instead of kneeling dance in a circular fashion around the mat until you feel the God's spirit take hold of you and then toss them into the air and interpret their fall.

If there should be more red branches than black branches on the mat then your answer is yes.

If there should be more black branches than red branches on the mat then your answer is no.

If any of the branches lay across the white branch then strong forces are at work. If they are touching one of the letters, symbols or *charakters* it will play a decisive role in the outcome, regardless of the color of the branch.

If all of the branches point toward the white branch then the querent must bring about a satisfactory resolution through their own power. The Gods and Spirits will neither assist nor impede.

If none of the branches point towards the white branch then the situation is outside the querent's control and they should make plentiful offerings to the Gods and Spirits.

If the result is mixed it will require a combination of personal effort and the assistance of the Gods and Spirits.

If all of the branches are off of the mat then circumstances are such that no definite answer can be given. Wait a while before doing any further divination on the matter.

Catoptromancy

On the eve of Chutroi, at midnight, stand naked in front of a mirror and say, "Oh holy Erigone, who knew the joy of the Vine, show to me the one I am to marry." The first name you hear upon waking will be that of your future spouse.

To determine the outcome of a matter, take the egg of a white hen and hold it aloft while reciting the *Orphic Hymn to Protogonos*:

> Upon two-natured, great and ether-tossed Protogonos I call;
> born of the egg, delighting in his golden wings he bellows like a bull,
> this begetter of blessed Gods and mortal men.
> Erikepaios, seed unforgettable, attend to my rites,
> ineffable, hidden, brilliant scion, whose motion is whirring,
> You scattered the dark mist that lay before your eyes,
> and, flapping your wings, you whirled about
> and throughout this world, you brought pure light.
> For this I call you Phanes and lord Priapos and bright-eyed Antauges.
> But, O blessed one of many counsels and seeds,
> come gladly to the celebrants of this holy and elaborate rite.

Then light some myrrh and pass the egg several times through the fragrant smoke while chanting the Greek vowels.

When you are ready, hold the egg close to your heart and recite the following:

> I call upon you, author of all creation, who spread your own wings over the whole world, you, the unapproachable and unmeasurable who breathe into every soul life-giving reasoning, who fitted all things together by your power. Firstborn, founder of the universe, golden-winged, whose light is darkness, who shroud reasonable thoughts and breathe forth dark frenzy, clandestine one who secretly inhabits every soul. You engender an unseen fire as you carry off every living thing without growing weary of torturing it, rather having with pleasure delighted in pain from the time when the world came into being. You also come and bring pain, who are sometimes reasonable, sometimes irrational, because of whom men dare beyond what is fitting and take refuge in your light which is darkness. Most headstrong, lawless, implacable, inexorable, invisible, bodiless, generator of frenzy, archer, torch-carrier, master of all living sensation and of everything clandestine, dispenser of forgetfulness, creator of silence, through whom the light and to

whom the light travels, infantile when you have been engendered within the heart, wisest when you have succeeded; I call upon you, unmoved by prayer, by your great name: AZARACHTHARAZA LATHA IATHAL Y Y Y LATHAI ATHA LLALAPH IOIOIO AI AI AI OUERIEU OIAI LEGETA RAMAI AMA RATAGEL, first-shining, night-shining, night rejoicing, night-engendering, witness, EREKISITHPHE ARARACHARARA EPHTHISIKERE IABEZEBYTH IT, you in the depth, BERIAMBO BERIAMBEBO, you in the sea, MERMERGO U, clandestine and wisest, ACHAPA ADONAIE MASMA CHARAKO IAKOB IAO CHAROUER AROUER LAILAM SEMESILAM SOUMARTA MARBA KARBA MENABOTH EIIA.

Reveal to me the [N Matter], O Manifest God!

And then crack the egg and inspect the yolk.

If it is **whole and smooth**, all will go well for you.

If it is **runny and broken up**, you will not succeed.

If the yolk is **lumpy and malformed, but otherwise intact** you will meet adversity only to triumph over it.

If the yolk is **lumpy and broken up**, your defeat will come from unexpected enemies.

If there is **blood in the yolk**, you will suffer greatly.

If there is **no yolk**, it means nothing will come of this, good or bad.

If **only specks**, it means try again. The necessary materials are not there.

If the egg contains a **partially formed bird**, monstrous things will occur and you should seek further divination.

To determine if a client will recover from an ailment, fill a basin with water, make libations before it and recite the Fate's song, which Orpheus composed:

> Boundless Fates, dear children of dark Night,
> hear my prayer, O many-named dwellers on the lake of heaven,
> where the frozen water by night's warmth is broken inside a sleek
>   cave's shady hollow;
> from there you fly to the boundless earth, home of mortals,
> and, thence, cloaked in purple you march towards men whose aims
>   are as noble,
> as their hopes are vain, in the vale of doom, where glory drives her
>   chariot on,
> all over the earth, beyond the goal of justice, of anxious hope, of
>   primeval law,
> and of the immeasurable principle of order.
> In life Fate alone watches.
> The other immortals who dwell on the peaks of snowy Olympos do
>   not,
> except for Zeus' perfect eye.
> But Fate and Zeus' mind know all things for all time.
> I pray to you to come, gently and kindly,
> Atropos, Lachesis, and Klotho, scions of noble stock.
> Airy, invisible, inexorable and ever indestructible,
> you give and take all, being to men the same as necessity.
> Fates, hear my prayers and receive my libations.
> Gently come to the initiates to free them from pain.

Then drop into the basin three needles, each of which have been threaded with wool. The wool should be black, white and red respectively.

If the **black** needle should sink first, it means that their health will be restored.

If the **white** needle should sink first, it means that they will not make it through.

If the **red** needle should sink first, they are on the precipice. Make plentiful prayers and offerings on their behalf.

A mirror is the bronze of beauty; wine, of the soul. (Aischylos, Frag. 384)

To test the quality of an oath that has been sworn, fill a cup with wine. Hold the cup aloft and ask Dionysos to reveal the truth in the mirror of his wine.

Scatter a quantity of sesame seeds upon the surface of the wine and then swirl the cup. When the wine comes to rest, interpret the placement of the seeds.

If they form a **pattern**, such as a thunderbolt or the form of a fearsome animal, it will be as it appears.

If the bulk of the seeds gather on the **right side**, the oath will prove solid.

If the bulk of the seeds gather on the **left side**, there is deception involved.

If the clump of seeds are **broken**, so will the oath be.

If they **sink** into the wine, there will be no problems.

Drink the cup to show that you accept the results; if any dregs remain, it will not go well for you.

NB: The Toys of Dionysos are a group of Spirits who attend the God and oversee our mysteries within the Starry Bull tradition. They are also great allies when it comes to the work of healing, purification, magic and divination. What follows is information on how to work with them in that capacity. It is recommended that you familiarize yourself with them either by reading *Spirits of Initiation* or taking the Toys of Dionysos course first, though that is by no means requisite.

How To Make Your Very Own Telesterion

During the Toys of Dionysos course, students personally introduce themselves to each of the Toys and begin a direct, working relationship with them. This is done in the *telesterion*, which is both a real place that resides on another plane of existence and a mental construct you form within your mind — a memory palace, as it was called by medieval clerics and philosophers. If done properly, the one bleeds through into the other.

According to Cicero's *De Oratore* the concept of a memory palace was first introduced by the poet Simonides of Keos in the 5th century BCE. Simonides had been invited to a lavish feast by Skopas, king of Thessaly. Forced to retire early because of his advanced age, the poet's life was saved, for shortly after he left a small earthquake brought the palace crashing down upon the drunken revelers' heads. Not only was everyone within killed, but they were crushed so badly in the accident that it made identification and burial next to impossible. Until, that is, Simonides realized that he had preserved a near perfect replica of Skopas' home within his mind, including where each guest had been sitting at the time of his departure, and thus was able to attach a name to each of the mangled bodies.

The technique of building mental structures resembling physical architecture to contain facts and other information which the individual could then access as needed became a central component of the Classical education system, relied upon especially by poets, lawyers and public speakers. Quintilian describes the process in great detail:

> For when we return after a time to certain places, we not only recognize the places themselves, but we even recall those things which we did in these, and persons come to mind and sometimes also unspoken thoughts are recalled. And so a technical science has arisen from experiment: they choose places as expansive as possible, and decorated with great variety, perchance a great house, and one divided into many recessed chambers. Whatever is noteworthy in it, they carefully fix their mind on this, so that without delay or pause their conscious mind is able to run through all its parts. And their first task is not to get stuck in coming upon these parts. For that memory of the architecture of the house must be more firmly-ingrained, seeing as how it will help another memory. Then those things which they have written or embraced in their mind, they demarcate with some sign, whereby they may be reminded... Then, they assign the first impression to some

recess, as it were, the second, e.g., to the atrium, then they go around the impluvium, and entrust them in order not only to bedrooms and parlors, but also to statues and the like. By virtue of this, when the memory must be retrieved, they begin to revisit these places from the beginning and demand back what they entrusted to each object, in order that they may be reminded by their image. (*Institutio Oratoria* 11.2.11-21)

This is the method I discussed in the introduction to the Leaves of Dionysos. In particular I advised:

Carefully dwell on every branch and vine and leaf that forms the structure, the light shining through the lattice, the smell of damp earth and vegetation, the shadows covering the ancient idol of the God, the fragrant incense and offerings left by past visitors and all of the other sense perceptions that flood your mind. But never forget that the image you construct is only a replica, a phantom of the true temple of the God. It is a real place and the image you construct is the door that leads into it. To properly consult the oracle of the leaves you must pass from illusion into reality — but illusion is how you find your way there.

And that's how you're going to construct the *telesterion*, the place where you will meet the Toys.

What is the *telesterion*?

In the simplest of terms it is the chamber of initiation.

Whose initiation?

Dionysos'. Yours. Everyone who has preceded you.

The *telesterion* is a room within the great palace of Zeus where the monsters with ash-smeared faces hunt down the young God and tear him to pieces.

The *telesterion* is the cave of the Nurses, dark and wet and full of life.

The *telesterion* is the innermost chamber of the temple of the Kaberoi in Thebes, with its empty tripod, its ivy-twined pillars and the piles of votive toys pilgrims left over the centuries for the Pais.

The *telesterion* is the tent the Orpheotelestai set up, eerie shadows cast upon its walls as strange masked figures dance around the trembling candidate for initiation on the camp-stool.

The *telesterion* is the forecourt of the Labyrinth whose endlessly twisting corridors echo with the cries of the Starry Bull, the great hunter by night.

Go through the sources I have provided in *Spirits of Initiation*, especially those pertaining to the myth of Dionysos' dismemberment, and record any impressions you receive. Make a list or just start writing free form. Once you have all of that down, let it sit for a while.

When you're ready find a quiet, solitary space where you won't be interrupted. Turn down the lights. Sit in a relaxed, comfortable posture. Light a candle and some incense if you find that helps you enter a properly receptive state. Some people find that music helps them to be more focused and attentive by guiding their mood and thoughts and blocking out distractions such as background noise; others prefer total silence. If you choose to have the accompaniment of music make sure that it is dark, somber, slow and lacking English lyrics which can take hold in the mind and jolt you out of the meditative state. Read over your notes so that they are fresh in your mind. Relax and focus on your breathing. Slowly take in breath and feel it circulate through your body like a calming wave, a coiling serpent, an unraveling ball of thread, before releasing it back out. Bring your breathing into rhythm with your pulse. Feel the heart beating in your chest, controlling the flow of breath. Feel yourself slip deeper and deeper into a relaxed and receptive state. Each beat of your heart takes you further and further down into the recesses of your mind. Let the darkness enfold you, until there is only the beat of your heart and the circulation of your breath. The world outside of you is getting further and further away until only the darkness feels real.

And when you're ready, begin to form the *telesterion* around yourself. Watch it spread out from you — the floor, the walls, the ceiling and everything it contains slowly coming into focus like a movie. Pay close attention to the details, using the impression you've already formed through your readings as a basis, but don't limit yourself to just that — let your mind add new elements as it is inspired to. What size is the room? How is it decorated? If there is light, where is it coming from? Are you warm or cold? How does the floor feel against your feet? Go around and explore the room until you have a sense of everything that its boundaries hold.

And then return to the conscious world. Write down everything you can remember about the *telesterion* in your notebook, so that it will be easier to reconstruct the next time you visit. Especially note if anything happens to you or you meet any presences while there.

Repeat this exercise as often as you can over the next week. With each repetition it should be easier to get there and the *telesterion* should come into sharper focus, seeming more real to you.

An important part of establishing a relationship with the Toys involves better understanding the relationships that exist among them. This group of Spirits are deeply connected, to the point that each Toy contains something of its fellows within itself — and yet it goes further than that, for certain of them tend to compliment and augment and work alongside other Toys more than the others, and you can learn a lot about them by studying these affinities.

The first step in this process is to come up with a master list of keywords for the Toys. Although I think it's more important to use your own personal associations (gained after spending significant time reading about them and working with them), I am providing the following list, compiled by the participants in the first Toys class, as an example to help you come up with yours.

Sphaira/Ball

summons, grace, a message, unseen forces, guidance, evolution, revolution, call to adventure, genesis, possibility, break-through, wake up call, epiphany, opening, trickery, magic, journey, awake!, cosmic, rhythm, force, balance, perfection, movement, eternal/unending, shining/luminous, youthfulness, blue/red/gold, celestial symbolism, love, marriage, death, surprise, seduction, lure, distraction, gentleness, hidden motives

Astragaloi/Knucklebones

impulse, sacrifice, leap of faith, communication, exchange, fate, luck, memory, judgment, transition, ancestral roots, relationships, aletheia, bones, ancestors, voice of the dead, neolithic, wisdom, oracle, prophecy, initiation, caves, hamingja, youth, transformation, death, vision, foresight, divinity, apotheosis, boundary, gate, animals, earth, darkness, femininity, children, others, tripping, dancing, restoration, negotiation, obedience, trust, tradition

Trochos/Wheel

challenge, trials, travel, peripeteia, drive, life, physicality, force for change, preparing the way, work, shift, change, moving one toward initiation, catalyst, the wheel of time, solar wheel, ever moving forward, never able to go backward, vessels of movement (boat and chariot), the liberation of non-confinement to our concept of time, divine liberation, grinding, futility, fruitless motion, blind action, shortsightedness, anxiety, mindfulness, focus, purpose, surrender

Rhombos/Bull-Roarer
madness, epiphany, primal emotions, confrontation, crisis, storm, escalation, power, invocation, elevation, vision, opening up to other worlds, journey, raising of power, shifting space, clean, winds, movement, thunder, roaring, whirling about an epicenter, rising through motion, earth, rain, bulls, fear, revelation, awakening, frenzy, mainadism, fearlessness, retribution, advent, heart

Strobilos/Whip Top
madness, pain, trauma, turmoil, purgation, surrender, clarifying, empowering, exhilarating, keen, fierce, driving, forcing fear, challenge, implacable laughing descent, striking, external force, moved, whirled, fricative, fracturing pinnacle, release, dance, provoked, frenzy, catharsis, choice, dredging

Krotala/Rattle
release, integration, healing, frenzy, powerful, magic, warrior dances, stomping rhythms of the dead, shake the cosmos, shatter the walls, between the worlds, drive us onward to where we will all meet walking as warriors, ecstasy, fierce madness, transformation, spider, dance, militaristic, aggression, passion, seizing, sharp, rising, quickening, venomous, wild, uninhibited, unhinged, mad, predatory, webbing, chaos, order, healing, sex, excitement, transition, therapy, joy, union

Paignia Kampesiguia/Puppet
enthousiasmos, inspiration/prophecy, alignment with the story, expression, trickster, ambiguity, dissociation, inversion/transposition, sneaky, quiet, provocateur, loose of control, manipulation, need, desire, life, fragility, storyteller, vehicle, dancer, servant, hanging, mimicry, lost identity, theatre, suspended belief, transformation, resurrection, possession, atonement, identifying with other, uncanny

Pokos/Tuft of Wool
refinement, rawness, connections, heat, holiness, discernment, manifestation, dismemberment, rendering, sacred, innocence, shield, obscurity, comfort, nurture, safety, guardian, cleansing, tearing, purity, femininely, process, solving, recall, dissolution, absolution, healing destruction

Mela/Apple
growth, vitality, immortality, (genetic) wisdom, nature, nourishment, love, enchantment, purification, doorways, sovereignty, song, voice, harmony, beauty, sweetness, marriage, virility/fertility, peace, joy, victory, procreation, coitus, rebirth, knowledge and advancement, fall, corruption,

dispersion, impulse, abundance, deathlessness, timelessness, mother, altruism, compassion

Esoptron/Mirror
reflection, awareness, plurality, immanence, initiation, mysteries, illusion, glamour, truth, protection, warding, cleverness, memory, forgetfulness, revelation, doorway, liquid, transmutable, reflection, descent, gnosis, identity

The second step is to trace the threads of connection between the various Toys. Pick a quality or action at random and then see how many of the Toys fall under that heading. For instance: How many of them are musical instruments? Involve motion? Imitation? Were once part of an animal? Etc. Be as specific with this as you can — for instance, by breaking down the type of motion or musical instrument to which they belong. And map them onto whatever structures you wish, for instance by giving their elemental correspondences, their place on the Kabalistic Tree of Life, what Gods and Spirits you associate them with both in and out of the Starry Bull pantheon, and so forth.

Finally, analyze all of this information and compare and contrast your findings. Just because two Toys fall into the same category doesn't mean that they necessarily manifest that quality in the same way.

Spend a couple weeks performing this analysis. While you're doing that, hunt down representations for each of the Toys — both a personal set and one that you'll be using with clients should you seek a vocation as a *crepundiamantis* or Toy diviner.

The Consecration Ceremony

[Can also be adapted to consecrate other divination tools]

Lay out each of the Toys on a linen sheet, either all together or in succession.

Sprinkle the Toy with sacrificial ash, saying "I prepare you to become [Toy]."

Chant the Toy's name three times.

Sprinkle them with pure water, saying "Remember who you are. Your name is [Toy] of the Toys."

Chant the Toy's name three times.

Smudge them with incense or blow smoke on them, saying "May you breathe and move and see all in this world [Toy]."

Chant the Toy's name three times.

Prick your finger and touch it to them, saying "Given manifestation through me, my [Toy]."

Chant the Toy's name three times.

Sprinkle them with *chernips*, saying "To be my guide and ally in this and the other realms [Toy]."

Chant the Toy's name three times.

Take a sip of wine and spray it over them and then say, "Always mindful of a gift for a gift."

Chant the Toy's name three times.

Wipe them clean with a linen cloth and then move on to the next Toy.

Proper Care of Your Toys

Now that you have collected representations of each of the Toys (both a set for personal use and one for the public), it is time to begin deepening your relationship with them.

The first step is to help them become more than just symbolic representations of the Toys — to make them into living creatures and consecrated vessels through which the Spirits of initiation become manifest in the material realm. After the ceremony on the previous page has been performed, you are to treat them as sentient beings not mere objects or things — that means you must be willing to commit time, energy and resources to their care.

What follows are some general rules of thumb that I've developed over the couple of years that I've been working with them, and should be regarded as nothing more. The *telesterion* where you first meet the Toys is established within you, and it is through your experiences and engagement with them that they are being brought forth; consequently each person's Toys will be slightly different from anyone else's, though the majority of their power and personality come from the original Toys themselves and so remain unfiltered through you. If it helps, imagine a beam of light refracting different colors through a prism. There is Sphaira, and there are all the ways that Sphaira is shown to us.

The Toys should be fed regularly on offerings. In my experience they tend to favor smoke, alcohol, blood and music, though you may find they want something more substantial. Experiment and see how your Toys respond — as you will no doubt discover, these Spirits are not shy about making their wills known.

I left "regularly" vague because the Toys seem to go through phases where they require different levels of sustenance. As a rule of thumb, the more work you're doing with them the more you should feed them, with a bare minimum being once a month. When you're first building up a relationship with the Toys I'd suggest making offerings at least twice a week, and more if you are so moved.

Another way that you can feed them is by giving them your attention. You can go back through the information in *Spirits of Initiation*, do creative projects involving them, chant their names and reflect on their powers and attributes, have an informal conversation with them, put together playlists for them, hunt for them in movies, videos, art and in the world around you, try to engage them through dreamwork, trance and spirit-journeys and any other methods you come up with.

Depending on the personality of your Toys and the type of relationship you develop with them, how you ritualize the offering process can vary widely. In dealing with these Spirits some people come up with elaborate ceremonial procedures and formulae while others tend more towards a causal hospitality — there's no wrong way except the one that doesn't work. Personally I tend to favor a middle course, letting what feels right in the moment dictate the degree of protocol I adopt.

Over the years I've noticed some patterns that may prove helpful. They either like to be prominently displayed — for instance with their own shrine or incorporated into Dionysos' — or else they want to be kept out of sight, in their own special container such as a *kiste* (chest) or *liknon* (woven basket) or a sack, preferably one made of linen or goatskin. You may also place a linen shroud over the container to give them added protection.

Aside from its shielding properties, linen seems to have a soothing effect on the Toys, so if one of them gets "hot" — particularly after difficult work with a client — you may want to wrap it in linen to cool its head. This hotness can come across in a variety of ways — a feeling of agitation radiating out from it, the Toy continuously appearing to you through random media, things breaking or falling off a shrine, etc.

Like all living creatures the Toys can be affected by miasma, which can especially be a concern if you are using them to divine or do healing and cleansing work with clients. I recommend sprinkling them with *chernips* (water that has been consecrated with fire or salt), passing them through sacrificial smoke, vibrating their names and purifying epithets of Dionysos over them and then wrapping them in linen for a couple hours or even days on a monthly basis as well as after any session with a client. Additionally you can place your client set next to your personal set so that they can recalibrate, but this should only be done after the preliminary cleansings so that you don't risk contamination. Different Toys can also be used to cleanse their fellows, particularly Strobilos and Pokos.

That said, the Toys have a strange relationship with miasma, as it is one of the things that they eat. You'll find that the more you use them, especially for healing and cleansing, the stronger they become. But just as food that is too rich or spicy can produce indigestion, too much pollution can harm the Toys or at least dull their effectiveness and perceptivity, so do keep that in mind when working with them. Also keep in mind that miasma is not just a psychospiritual or moral substance — dirt and disorder can impart it as well, so be sure to dust off your Toys from time to time. (And don't forget to scrub behind Paignia's ears, if they exist!)

It has generally fallen out of favor to speak of "working with" Gods or Spirits in devotional polytheist circles, as this tends to suggest the sort of exploitative relationships one finds in certain forms of ceremonial magic. If you sincerely believe that you're going to get the upper hand on a group of Spirits who played a role in the deception, torture and murder of none other than Dionysos you are more than welcome to try but that's not an avenue that I would necessarily recommend taking. On the other hand the Toys aren't looking for the sorts of things that other Gods and Spirits are. The Toys are clever and curious and hungry and enjoy playing games, so interactions with them tend to be transactions of one sort or another. They will happily dispense wisdom and guidance and assist us in various ways — for a price. The more willing you are to pay, the less they tend to ask in return, for this ensures that you will consult them more readily and thus end up owing them more in the long run. If you are hesitant or negligent they may ask more of you in return for their help. But keep in mind that they will always ask something, for that is their nature.

The Toys were old even when Dionysos learned their mysteries; they have seen much in this world and know even more. There are few areas where they cannot provide insight or assistance, especially if you know how to ask them properly. (And learn the right things to bribe them with.) I am going to share a couple methods of consulting them as divinatory tools though this should be considered suggestions only. Feel free to improvise and collaborate on new methods of consultation with them as your relationship with the Toys deepens.

To begin with you must learn to ask the right questions. Think hard about what it is you want to know and then phrase that as clearly as you can. Remember that these are particularly tricky Spirits and they enjoy playing with ambiguity and nuance. They may be aware of what your true intent is but choose to answer the question precisely as you asked it, with dire consequences for you. This is hardly unique to the Toys; the examples of Xenophon and king Kroisos should come immediately to mind.

Perhaps as important as asking the right question is rightly interpreting the answer you receive. When consulting with the Toys this can be challenging since you've got the Toys as Spirits, the Toys as processes, the Toys as concepts and the whole range of associations and histories that each has within the Dionysian tradition to consider. This can require a lot of unpacking, and that is unfortunately not something that can be taught but must be learned through considerable practice, study and engagement with the Spirits. Allow them to direct the process and assist you in interpretation. In other words, when you are doing a reading, open yourself up to the Toys and ask them to help you understand what it is they are trying to communicate instead of going solely by what's written down in a little booklet. This is why I have provided no official "explanations" and give the correspondences that the first Toys class came up with only as an example — in the end you should develop your own personal meanings for each Toy and be able to communicate directly with them to access even higher levels of knowledge.

Conversely, you may wish to have more or less elaborate rituals around consulting them for divination and all the protocols that go with that. This is going to be different for each person so I hesitate to provide a generic template, but as an example so you can begin coming up with your own I will share my procedures.

I tend to spend about twenty minutes to an hour preparing myself for a session. This usually consists of cleansing, making offerings, putting on special jewelry or ritual attire, prayer, reflection, listening to music, reading certain texts, and if I feel it's called for, ingesting entheogens. When I'm ready I'll make sure that the entities I'll be consulting are willing and able to assist either through prayer or preliminary divination and then I set out my tools, take several deep breaths to center and focus myself and begin.

That's my medium level. Sometimes I add more ritual elements (usually spoken parts) and sometimes I shrink it down to the basics, depending on what I feel is called for in a particular session. Sometimes a lot of bells and whistles are called for and sometimes they've got such an urgent message to convey that they're all but bowling you over with it. Let your intuitive sense guide you — though it's important to have a set of procedures built up and to stick to them as much as you can, because they grow in power with each repetition. At one point I had a set of practices that could take me from total mundane headspace to ecstatic gnosis-dump just by going through them, but then all the parameters of my practice got redefined and it stopped working so I had to move on to something else.

So what sorts of questions can you ask the Toys? Pretty much any-thing if you ask it the right way. Obviously anything having to do with madness, initiation, life changes, the human condition, creativity, the realm of Dionysos and the specific domains that each of the Toys preside over. They're good at diagnosing ailments, especially those of a religious or psychological nature, and at offering constructive solutions to problem situations. However, you would do well to keep in mind that you are seeking guidance from the Toys (who possess unique perspectives on things, to say the least) and whatever answer you're receiving is coming mediated through them. In other words, they have an agenda and no obligation to give advice contrary to it. Their agenda tends to align fairly well with that of Dionysos and they're quite astute, meaning that it is usually to your benefit to follow the path they set down for you — but never forget who you're dealing with.

My general method for consulting the Toys is as follows. First I read off the question or have the client ask it and then I open my mind as the pouch containing the Toys is shaken. When I feel the time is right one of the Toys is drawn out or spilled onto the ground and I interpret accordingly. Whether you do the drawing or have your clients is something you'll need to determine as part of your protocols in working with the Toys.

As a test case, suppose that you have a client who is asking about a series of weird dreams she's had and whether Dionysos or her ancestors are behind them. How would you answer if Astragaloi turned up? How about Trochos? Or Esoptron? (Pro tip: For extra information to go on you might want to ask if she can elaborate on what happened in the dreams.)

This basic method is also good as a meditative aid or if you're looking for some general direction or areas to focus on in your work.

Another method for consulting the Toys is the Tau spread, so named because three Toys are drawn and arranged in a rough capital T pattern. The bottommost Toy represents the root cause of the problem and the obstacles to be faced, the rightmost Toy the most effective solution and the left Toy what will happen as a consequence of not taking the proper steps.

So, for example, suppose that your client is having trouble finding work and he drew the following Toys — B: Sphaira R: Trochos L: Rhombos. How would you interpret?

The Toys can also be consulted in conjunction with other methods of divination to tease out nuance or gain corroboration, whether that's a simple binary system involving coins or dice, something more elaborate such as the Leaves of Dionysos or one of the numerous bibliomantic methods. However the system they work best with is the Net of Zagreus.

You can get some really complex readings by combining the latter technique with the Toys, either by dropping a single Toy into the Net or letting the whole pouch spill out. This is particularly useful if you want a general overview or the client isn't certain of what questions to ask or what area to focus on. Pay attention not only to where the Toys fall but also where in each section and the spatial relationship they have if you involve more than one Toy. I could provide a bunch of examples and inter-pretations of layouts, but this is something best learned through doing.

Likewise there are a number of other methods of consulting the Toys that I'm aware of, but these examples are sufficient to get you started. Once you've fully mastered them you can move on to others.

If you'd like more practice, volunteer to read for friends and family. Explain that you are still in the process of learning, and if you need to, do something to ritually mark the fact that this is not an "official" reading and thus should not carry with it the binding weight that normal divination has. Do not charge for readings until you have received permission from the Toys to do so and have properly negotiated the price that they will be asking for working with you in this capacity.

Circles, etc.

APPENDIX:
Miscellaneous Sources on Bacchic Orphic Purity Regulations

Apollodoros, *Bibliotheka* 1.9.12
Bias wooed Pero, daughter of Neleus. But as there were many suitors for his daughter's hand, Neleus said that he would give her to him who should bring him the kine of Phylakos. These were in Phylake, and they were guarded by a dog which neither man nor beast could come near. Unable to steal these kine, Bias invited his brother to help him. Melampos promised to do so, and foretold that he should be detected in the act of stealing them, and that he should get the kine after being kept in bondage for a year. After making this promise he repaired to Phylake and, just as he had foretold, he was detected in the theft and kept a prisoner in a cell. When the year was nearly up, he heard the worms in the hidden part of the roof, one of them asking how much of the beam had been already gnawed through, and others answering that very little of it was left. At once he bade them transfer him to another cell, and not long after that had been done the cell fell in. Phylakos marvelled, and perceiving that he was an excellent soothsayer, he released him and invited him to say how his son Iphiklos might get children. Melampos promised to tell him, provided he got the kine. And having sacrificed two bulls and cut them in pieces he summoned the birds; and when a vulture came, he learned from it that once, when Phylakos was gelding rams, he laid down the knife, still bloody, beside Iphiklos, and that when the child was frightened and ran away, he stuck the knife on the sacred oak, and the bark encompassed the knife and hid it. He said, therefore, that if the knife were found, and he scraped off the rust, and gave it to Iphiklos to drink for ten days, he would beget a son. Having learned these things from the vulture, Melampos found the knife, scraped the rust, and gave it to Iphiklos for ten days to drink, and a son Podarces was born to him. But he drove the kine to Pylos, and having received the daughter of Neleus he gave her to his brother. For a time he continued to dwell in Messene, but when Dionysos drove the women of Argos mad, he healed them on condition of receiving part of the kingdom, and settled down there with Bias.

Apollonios Rhodios, *Argonautika* 1.1132–1141
Jason supplicated Rheia with many prayers to turn away the tempest, as he poured libations on the blazing sacrifices. At the same time, upon Orpheus' command, the young men leapt as they danced the dance-in-armor and beat

their shields with their swords, so that any ill-omened cry of grief, which the people were still sending up in lament for their king, would be lost in the air. Since then, the Phrygians have always propitiated Rheia with rhombus and tambourine. The amenable goddess evidently paid heed to their holy sacrifices, for fitting signs appeared.

Apuleius, *Apologia* 56

Could anyone who has any idea of religion still find it strange that a man initiated in so many divine mysteries should keep at home some tokens of recognition of the cults and should wrap them in linen cloth, the purest veil for sacred objects? For wool, the excrescence of an inert body extracted from a sheep, is already a profane garment in the prescriptions of Orpheus and Pythagoras.

Areios Didymos, *Epitome of Stoic Ethics* 3.604-3.662

The Stoics say that only the wise man can be a priest, while no worthless person can be one. For the priest needs to be experienced in the laws concerning sacrifices, prayers, purifications, foundations, and the like. In addition to this he needs ritual, piety, and experience in the service of the Gods, and to be close to the divine nature. Not one of these things belongs to the worthless; hence, also all the stupid are impious. For impiety as a vice is ignorance of the service of the Gods, while piety is knowledge of that divine service. Likewise they say that the worthless are not holy. For holiness is described as justice with respect to the Gods. The worthless transgress many of the just customs pertaining to the Gods, on account of which they are unholy, impure, unclean, defiled and barred from festive rites. For carrying out festive rites is, they say, the mark of a civilized man, since a festival is a time when one ought to be concerned with the divine for the sake of honor and appropriate celebration. So the person who carries out festive rites needs to have humbly entered with piety into this post.

Aristophanes, *The Frogs* 1030-33

For consider how useful our noble-minded poets have been from the beginning. Orpheus revealed to us the mysteries and abstinence from murder, Musaeus taught us cures from illnesses and oracles.

Aristophanes, *Peace* 959

To purify I take this fire-brand first and plunge it into the water.

Athenaios, *Deipnosophistai* 9.78

However there is a unique use of the word *aponimma* [normally 'dirty water'] among the Athenians, where it is applied to the ritual actions in honor of the dead, or to the purification of those who are *enageis*, as

Kleidemos says in the work called the *Exegetikon*. For, having made remarks 'on sacrifices for the dead', he writes as follows, "Dig a trench on the west side of the grave. Next, standing right next to the trench, look toward the west. Pour water down, saying the following, 'For you the water of purification, to whom it is necessary and for whom it is right.' Then immediately pour down the perfumed oil." Dorotheus also cites this, alleging that such things are written down in the ancestral laws of the Eupatridai, concerning the purification of suppliants, "Next, after you yourself and the other persons taking part in the sacrificial ritual have received the water of purification, take water and purify; clean off the blood-guilt of the one being purified, and after that, having shaken off the water of purification, pour it into the same place."

Aulus Gellius, *Attic Nights* 10.15

Ceremonies in great number are imposed upon the priest of Jupiter and also many abstentions, of which we read in the books written *On the Public Priests*; and they are also recorded in the first book of Fabius Pictor. Of these the following are in general what I remember: It is unlawful for the priest of Jupiter to ride upon a horse; it is also unlawful for him to see the 'classes arrayed' outside the pomerium, that is, the army in battle array; hence the priest of Jupiter is rarely made consul, since wars were entrusted to the consuls; also it is always unlawful for the priest to take an oath; likewise to wear a ring, unless it be perforated and without a gem. It is against the law for fire to be taken from the flaminia, that is, from the home of the flamen Dialis, except for a sacred rite; if a person in fetters enter his house, he must be loosed, the bonds must be drawn up through the impluvium to the roof and from there let down into the street. He has no knot in his head-dress, girdle, or any other part of his dress; if anyone is being taken to be flogged and falls at his feet as a suppliant, it is unlawful for the man to be flogged on that day. Only a free man may cut the hair of the Dialis. It is not customary for the Dialis to touch, or even name, a she-goat, raw flesh, ivy, and beans. The priest of Jupiter must not pass under an arbour of vines. The feet of the couch on which he sleeps must be smeared with a thin coating of clay, and he must not sleep away from this bed for three nights in succession, and no other person must sleep in that bed. At the foot of his bed there should be a box with sacrificial cakes. The cuttings of the nails and hair of the Dialis must be buried in the earth under a fruitful tree. Every day is a holy day for the Dialis. He must not be in the open air without his cap; that he might go without it in the house has only recently been decided by the pontiffs, so Masurius Sabinus wrote, and it is said that some other ceremonies have been remitted and he has been excused from observing them. The priest of Jupiter must not touch any bread fermented with yeast. He does not lay off his inner tunic except under cover, in order that he may not be naked in the open air, as it were under the eye of Jupiter. No other has a place at table above the flamen Dialis, except the *rex sacrificulus*. If the Dialis has lost his wife he abdicates his office. The marriage of the priest cannot be dissolved except by death. He never enters a place of burial, he never touches a dead body; but he is not forbidden to attend a funeral. The ceremonies of the priestess of Jupiter are about the same; they say that she observes other separate ones: for example, that she wears a dyed robe, that she has a twig from a fruitful tree in her head-dress, that it is forbidden for her to go up more than three rounds of a ladder, except the so called Greek ladders; also, when she goes to the Argei, that she neither combs her head nor dresses her hair. I have added the words of the praetor in his standing edict concerning the flamen Dialis and the priestess of Vesta: 'In the whole of my jurisdiction I will not compel the flamen of Jupiter or a priestess of Vesta to take an oath.' The words of Marcus Varro about the flamen Dialis, in the second book of his *Divine Antiquities,* are as follows: He alone has a white cap, either because he is the greatest of priests, or because a white victim should be sacrificed to Jupiter.

Celsus, *Alethes Logos*

If in obedience to the traditions of their fathers they abstain from such victims, they must also abstain from all animal food, in accordance with the opinions of Pythagoras, who thus showed his respect for the soul and its bodily organs. But if, as they say, they abstain that they may not eat along with daimones, I admire their wisdom, in having at length discovered, that whenever they eat they eat with daimones, although they only refuse to do so when they are looking upon a slain victim; for when they eat bread, or drink wine, or taste fruits, do they not receive these things, as well as the water they drink and the air they breathe, from certain daimones, to whom have been assigned these different provinces of nature? We must either not live, and indeed not come into this life at all, or we must do so on condition that we give thanks and first-fruits and prayers to daimones, who have been set over the things of this world: and that we must do as long as we live, that they may prove good and kind. They must make their choice between two alternatives. If they refuse to render due service to the gods, and to respect those who are set over this service, let them not come to manhood, or marry wives, or have children, or indeed take any share in the affairs of life; but let them depart hence with all speed, and leave no posterity behind them, that such a race may become extinct from the face of the earth. Or, on the other hand, if they will take wives, and bring up children, and taste of the fruits of the earth, and partake of all the blessings of life, and bear its appointed sorrows (for nature herself hath allotted sorrows to all men; for sorrows must exist, and earth is the only place for them), then must they discharge the duties of life until they are released from its bonds, and render due honour to those beings who control the affairs of this life, if they would not show themselves ungrateful to them. For it would be unjust in them, after receiving the good things which they dispense, to pay them no tribute in return.

Demosthenes, *On the Crown* 259-60

On attaining manhood, you abetted your mother in her initiations and the other rituals, and read aloud from the cultic writings. At night, you mixed the libations, purified the initiates, and dressed them in fawnskins. You cleansed them off with clay and cornhusks, and raising them up from the purification, you led the chant, 'The evil I flee, the better I find.' And it was your pride that no one ever emitted that holy ululation so powerfully as yourself. I can well believe it! When you hear the stentorian tones of the orator, can you doubt that the ejaculations of the acolyte were simply magnificent? In the daylight, you led the fine thiasos through the streets, wearing their garlands of fennel and white poplar. You rubbed the fat-cheeked snakes and swung them above your head crying 'Euoi Saboi' and dancing to the tune of *hues attes, attes hues*. Old women hailed you as 'Leader', 'mysteries instructor', 'ivy-bearer', 'liknon carrier', and the like.

Derveni Papyrus col. 3 & 6

...Erinyes...of the Erinyes...they honour...are so[uls]...funeral libations in droplets...brings honour...for each receives a bird and...fitted to the music...

... prayers and sacrifices appease the souls, and the enchanting song of the magi is able to remove the daimones when they impede. Impeding daimones are avenging souls. This is why the magi perform the sacrifice, as if they were paying a penalty. On the offerings they pour water and milk, from which they make the libations, too. They sacrifice innumerable and many-knobbed cakes, because the souls, too, are innumerable. Initiates make the preliminary sacrifice to the Eumenides, in the same way as the magi. On account of these, he who is going to sacrifice to the gods, first offers a bird... and the... (they) are... as many as...

Diogenes Laertios, *Lives of Eminent Philosophers* 8.19-21; 23-24

Above all, Pythagoras forbade as food red mullet and blacktail, and he enjoined abstinence from the hearts of animals and from beans, and sometimes, according to Aristotle, even from paunch and gurnard. Some say that he contented himself with just some honey or a honeycomb or bread, never touching wine in the daytime, and with greens boiled or raw for dainties, and fish but rarely. His robe was white and spotless, his quilts of white wool, for linen had not yet reached those parts. He was never known to over-eat, to behave loosely, or to be drunk. He would avoid laughter and all pandering to tastes such as insulting jests and vulgar tales. He would punish neither slave nor free man in anger. Admonition he used to call "setting right." He used to practise divination by sounds or voices and by auguries, never by burnt-offerings, beyond frankincense. The offerings he made were always inanimate; though some say that he would offer cocks, sucking goats and porkers, as they are called, but lambs never. However, Aristoxenus has it that he consented to the eating of all other animals, and only abstained from ploughing oxen and rams. The same authority, as we have seen, asserts that Pythagoras took his doctrines from the Delphic priestess Themistoclea. Hieronymus, however, says that, when he had descended into Hades, he saw the soul of Hesiod bound fast to a brazen pillar and gibbering, and the soul of Homer hung on a tree with serpents writhing about it, this being their punishment for what they had said about the Gods; he also saw under torture those who would not remain faithful to their wives. This, says our authority, is why he was honoured by the people of Croton. Aristippos of Kyrene affirms in his work *On the Physicists* that he was named Pythagoras because he uttered the truth as infallibly as did the Pythian oracle. And he further bade them to honour Gods before demi-gods, heroes before men, and first among men their parents; and so to behave one to another as not to make friends into enemies, but to turn enemies into friends. To deem nothing their own. To support the law, to wage war on lawlessness. Never to kill or injure trees that are not wild, nor even any animal that does not injure man. That it is seemly and advisable neither to give way to unbridled laughter nor to wear sullen looks. To avoid excess of flesh, on a journey to let exertion and slackening alternate, to train the memory, in wrath to restrain hand and tongue, to respect all divination, to sing to the lyre and by hymns to show due gratitude to Gods and to good men. To abstain from beans because they are flatulent and partake most of the breath of life ; and besides, it is better for the stomach if they are not taken, and this again will make our dreams in sleep smooth and untroubled.

Diogenes Laertios, *Lives of Eminent Philosophers* 8.33-35

Pythagoras taught that right has the force of an oath, and that is why Zeus is called the God of Oaths. Virtue is harmony, and so are health and all that is good and God himself; this is why they say that all things are constructed according to the laws of harmony. The love of friends is just concord and equality. We should not pay equal worship to Gods and heroes, but to the Gods always, with reverent silence, in white robes, and after purification, to the heroes only from midday onwards. Purification is by cleansing, baptism and lustration, and by keeping clean from all deaths and births and all pollution, and abstaining from meat and flesh of animals that have died, mullets, gurnards, eggs and egg-sprung animals, beans, and the other abstinences prescribed by those who perform mystic rites in the temples. According to Aristotle in his work *On the Pythagoreans*, Pythagoras counselled abstinence from beans either because they are like the genitals, or because they are like the gates of Hades, as being alone unjointed, or because they are injurious, or because they are like the form of the universe, or because they belong to oligarchy, since they are used in election by lot. He bade his disciples not to pick up fallen crumbs, either in order to accustom them not to eat immoderately, or because they are connected with a person's death; nay, even, according to Aristophanes, crumbs belong to the heroes, for in his *Heroes* he says: Nor taste ye of what falls beneath the board! Another of his precepts was not to eat white cocks, as being sacred to the month and wearing suppliant garb–now supplication ranked with things good– sacred to the month because they announce the time of day; and again white represents the nature of the good, black the nature of evil. Not to touch such fish as were sacred; for it is not right that gods and men should be allotted the same things, any more than free men and slaves. Not to break bread; for once friends used to meet over one loaf, as the barbarians do even to this day; and you should not divide bread which brings them together; some give as the explanation of this that it has reference to the judgement of the dead in Hades, others that bread makes cowards in war, others again that it is from it that the whole world begins.

Euripides, *Cretans* fragment 472
Son of the Phoenician princess, child of Tyrian Europa and great Zeus, ruler over hundred-fortressed Crete—here am I, come from the sanctity of temples roofed with cut beam of our native wood, its true joints of cypress welded together with Chalybean axe and cement from the bull. Pure has my life been since the day when I became an initiate of Idaean Zeus. Where midnight Zagreus roves, I rove; I have endured his thunder-cry; fulfilled his red and bleeding feasts; held the Great Mother's mountain flame; I am set free and named by name a Bakchos of the Mailed Priests. Having all-white garments, I flee the birth of mortals and, not nearing the place of corpses, I guard myself against the eating of ensouled flesh.

Euripides, *Helen* 868-870
Lead on, bearing before me blazing brands, and, as sacred rites ordain, purge with incense every cranny of the air, that I may breathe heaven's breath free from taint; meanwhile do thou, in case the tread of unclean feet have soiled the path, wave the cleansing flame above it, and brandish the torch in front, that I may pass upon my way.

Euripides, *Hippolytos* 948–957
Are you, then, the companion of the Gods, as a man beyond the common? Are you the chaste one, untouched by evil? I will never be persuaded by your vauntings, never be so unintelligent as to impute folly to the Gods. Continue then your confident boasting, take up a diet of greens and play the showman with your food, make Orpheus your lord and engage in

mystic rites, holding the vaporings of many books in honor. For you have been found out. To all I give the warning: avoid men like this. For they make you their prey with their high-holy-sounding words while they contrive deeds of shame.

Gold tablet from Rome
A: I come pure from the pure, Queen of the Underworld, Eukles and Eubouleus, noble child of Zeus! I have this gift of Memory, prized by men! B: Caecilia Secundina, come, made divine by the Law!

The Gurôb Papyrus
... in order that he may find
... on account of the rite they paid the penalty of their fathers. Save me, Brimô, Demeter, Rhea and armed Curêtês!
So that we may perform beautiful sacrifices ...
Goat and bull, limitless gifts ...
And by the law of the river ...
... of the goat, and let him eat the rest of the flesh. Let no uninitiated look on!
... dedicating to the ...
... prayer ...
I call on ... Eubouleus, and I call the Maenads who cry Euoi ...
You having parched with thirst ... the friends of the feast ...
... of Demeter and Pallas for us ...
King Irekepaigos, save me, Phanes!
... top, rattle, dice-bones, mirror ...

Herodotos, *The Histories* 2.49
Melampos was the one who taught the Greeks the name of Dionysos and the way of sacrificing to him and the phallic procession; he did not exactly unveil the subject taking all its details into consideration, for the teachers who came after him made a fuller revelation; but it was from him that the Greeks learned to bear the phallus along in honor of Dionysos, and they got their present practice from his teaching. I say, then, that Melampos acquired the prophetic art, being a discerning man, and that, besides many other things which he learned from Egypt, he also taught the Greeks things concerning Dionysos, altering few of them; for I will not say that what is done in Egypt in connection with the god and what is done among the Greeks originated independently: for they would then be of an Hellenic character and not recently introduced. Nor again will I say that the Egyptians took either this or any other custom from the Greeks. But I believe that Melampos learned the worship of Dionysos chiefly from Kadmos of Tyre and those who came with Kadmos from Phoenicia to the land now called Boiotia.

244

Herodotos, *The Histories* 2.81
The Egyptians wear linen tunics with fringes hanging about the legs, called 'calasiris' and loose white woolen mantles over these. But nothing of wool is brought into the temples, or buried with them; that is forbidden. In this they follow the same rules as the ritual called Orphic and Bacchic, but which is in truth Egyptian and Pythagorean; for neither may those initiated into these rites be buried in woolen wrappings. There is a sacred legend about this.

Hesiod, *Works and Days* 724-745
Never pour a libation of sparkling wine to Zeus after dawn with unwashen hands, nor to others of the deathless Gods; else they do not hear your prayers but spit them back. Do not stand upright facing the sun when you make water, but remember to do this when he has set towards his rising. And do not make water as you go, whether on the road or off the road, and do not uncover yourself: the nights belong to the blessed Gods. A scrupulous man who has a wise heart sits down or goes to the wall of an enclosed court. Do not expose yourself befouled by the fireside in your house, but avoid this. Do not beget children when you are come back from ill-omened burial, but after a festival of the Gods. Never cross the sweet-flowing water of ever-rolling rivers afoot until you have prayed, gazing into the soft flood, and washed your hands in the clear, lovely water. Whoever crosses a river with hands unwashed of wickedness, the Gods are angry with him and bring trouble upon him afterwards. At a cheerful festival of the Gods do not cut the withered from the quick upon that which has five branches with bright steel [i.e. do not cut your fingernails]. Never put the ladle upon the mixing-bowl at a wine party, for malignant ill-luck is attached to that.

Hesiod, *Works and Days* 752-758
A man should not clean his body with water in which a woman has washed, for there is bitter mischief in that also for a time. When you come upon a burning sacrifice, do not make a mock of mysteries, for Heaven is angry at this also. Never make water in the mouths of rivers which flow to the sea, nor yet in springs; but be careful to avoid this. And do not ease yourself in them: it is not well to do this.

***IDelos* 5.2529.21**
They are to enter the temple of Zeus Kynthios and Athene Kynthia with pure hands and soul, with white clothing, barefooted, keeping pure from intercourse with a woman and from meat; and they are not to bring in ... nor a key nor an iron ring nor a belt nor a purse nor weapons of war ...

ILindos 108
You must abstain from the pleasures of sex, from beans, from heart. May you be holy in the temple: not cleansed with water but purified in spirit.

ISmyrna 2.1.728
The theophantes ... son of Menandros dedicated this stele. All who enter the temenos and temples of Bromios: avoid for forty days after the exposure of a newborn child, so that divine wrath does not occur; after the miscarriage of a woman for the same amount of days. If he conceals the death and fate of a relative, keep away from the propylon for the third of a month. If impurity occurs from other houses, remain for three days after the departure of the dead. No one wearing black clothes may approach the altar of the king, nor lay hands on things not sacrificed from sacrificial animals, nor place an egg as food at the Bacchic feast, nor sacrifice a heart on the holy altars ... keep away from the smell, which ... the most hateful root of beans from seed ... proclaim to the mystai of the Titans ... and it is improper to rattle with reeds ... on the days when the mystai sacrifice......, nor bring ...

Jerome, *Against Jovinianus* 2.14
Eubulus who wrote the history of Mithras in many volumes, relates that among the Persians there are three kinds of Magi, the first of whom, those of greatest learning and eloquence, take no food except meal and vegetables. At Eleusis it is customary to abstain from fowls and fish and certain fruits. Euripides relates that the prophets of Jupiter in Crete abstained not only from flesh, but also from cooked food. Xenocrates the philosopher writes that at Athens out of all the laws of Triptolemus only three precepts remain in the temple of Ceres: respect to parents, reverence for the Gods, and abstinence from flesh.

Jerome, *Against Jovinianus* 2.13
Chaeremon the Stoic, a man of great eloquence, has a treatise on the life of the ancient priests of Egypt who, he says, laid aside all worldly business and cares and were ever in the temple, studying nature and the regulating causes of the heavenly bodies; they never had intercourse with women; they never from the time they began to devote themselves to the divine service set eyes on their kindred and relations, nor even saw their children; they always abstained from flesh and wine, on account of the light-headedness and dizziness which a small quantity of food caused, and especially to avoid the stimulation of the lustful appetite engendered by this meat and drink. They seldom ate bread, that they might not load the stomach. And whenever they ate it, they mixed pounded hyssop with all that they took, so that the action of its warmth might diminish the weight of the heavier food. They used no oil except with vegetables, and then only

in small quantities, to mitigate the unpalatable taste. What need, he says, to speak of birds, when they avoided even eggs and milk as flesh. The one, they said, was liquid flesh, the other was blood with the colour changed? Their bed was made of palm-leaves, called by them *baiae*: a sloping footstool laid upon the ground served for a pillow, and they could go without food for two or three days. The humours of the body which arise from sedentary habits were dried up by reducing their diet to an extreme point.

Lampridius, *Vita Alexandri Severi* 29
This was his manner of life: as soon as there was opportunity—that is, if he had not spent the night with his wife—he performed his devotions in the early morning hours in his lararium, in which he had statues of the divine princes and also a select number of the best men and the more holy Spirits, among whom he had Apollonius of Tyana, and as a writer of his times says, Christ, Abraham, and Orpheus, and others similar, as well as statues of his ancestors.

LSCG 94
Do not enter the sanctuary after consuming wine.

Lucian, *The Syrian Goddess*
16. I approve of the remarks about the temple made by those who in the main accept the theories of the Greeks: according to these the Goddess is Hera, but the work was carried out by Dionysos, the son of Semele: Dionysos visited Syria on his journey to Aethiopia. There are in the temple many tokens that Dionysos was its actual founder: for instance, barbaric raiment, Indian precious stones, and elephants' tusks brought by Dionysos from the Aethiopians. Further, a pair of phalli of great size are seen standing in the vestibule, bearing the inscription, "I, Dionysos, dedicated these phalli to Hera my stepmother." This proof satisfies me. And I will describe another curiosity to be found in this temple, a sacred symbol of Dionysos. The Greeks erect phalli in honour of Dionysos, and on these they carry, singular to say, mannikins made of wood, with enormous pudenda; they call these puppets. There is this further curiosity in the temple: as you enter, on the right hand, a small brazen statue meets your eye of a man in a sitting posture, with parts of monstrous size.

28. The place whereon the temple is placed is a hill: it lies nearly in the centre of the city, and is surrounded by a double wall. Of the two walls the one is ancient; the other is not much older than our own times. The entrance to the temple faces the north; its size is about a hundred fathoms. In this entrance those phalli stand which Dionysos erected: they stand thirty fathoms high. Into one of these a man mounts twice every year, and

he abides on the summit of the phallus for the space of seven days. The reason of this ascent is given as follows: The people believe that the man who is aloft holds converse with the Gods, and prays for good fortune for the whole of Syria, and that the Gods from their neighbourhood hear his prayers. Others allege that this takes place in memory of the great calamity of Deukalion's time, when men climbed up to mountain tops and to the highest trees, in terror of the mass of waters. To me all this seems highly improbable, and I think that they observe this custom in honour of Dionysos, and I conjecture this from the following fact, that all those who rear phalli to Dionysos take care to place mannikins of wood on the phalli; the reason of this I cannot say, but it seems to me that the ascent is made in imitation of the wooden mannikin.

29. To proceed, the ascent is made in this way; the man throws round himself and the phallus a small chain; afterwards he climbs up by means of pieces of wood attached to the phallus large enough to admit the end of his foot. As he mounts he jerks the chain up his own length, as a driver his reins. Those who have not seen this process, but who have seen those who have to climb palm trees in Arabia, or in Egypt, or any other place, will understand what I mean. When he has climbed to the top, he lets down a different chain, a long one, and drags up anything that he wants, such as wood, clothing, and vases; he binds these together and sits upon them, as it were, on a nest, and he remains there for the space of time that I have mentioned. Many visitors bring him gold and silver, and some bring brass; then those who have brought these offerings leave them and depart, and each visitor gives his name. A bystander shouts the name up; and he on hearing the name utters a prayer for each donor; between the prayers he raises a sound on a brazen instrument which, on being shaken, gives forth a loud and grating noise. He never sleeps; for if at any time sleep surprises him, a scorpion creeps up and wakes him, and stings him severely; this is the penalty for wrongfully sleeping. This story about the scorpion is a sacred one, and one of the mysteries of religion; whether it is true I cannot say, but, as it seems to me, his wakefulness is in no small degree due to his fear of falling. So much then for the climbers of the phalli. As for the temple, it looks to the rising sun.

Marinus of Samaria, *The Life of Proclus* 18-19

Proclus made use of the noble purificatory practices which woo us from evil, that is lustrations and all of the other processes of purification whether Orphic or Chaldean, such as dipping himself into the sea without hesitation every month, and sometimes even twice or thrice a month. He practiced this discipline, rude as it was, not only in his prime, but even also when he approached his life's decline; and so he observed, without ever failing, these austere habits of which he had, so to speak, made himself a law ... As to the

248

necessary pleasures of food and drink, he made use of them with sobriety, for to him they were no more than a solace from his fatigues. He especially preached abstinence from animal food, but if a special ceremony compelled him to make use of it, he only tasted it, out of consideration and respect. Every month he sanctified himself according to the rites devoted to the Mother of the Gods by the Romans, and before them by the Phrygians; he observed the holy days observed among the Egyptians even more strictly than did they themselves; and especially he fasted on certain days, quite openly. During the first day of the lunar month he remained without food, without even having eaten the night before; and he likewise celebrated the New Moon in great solemnity, and with much sanctity. He regularly observed the great festivals of all peoples, so to speak, and the religious ceremonies peculiar to each people or country. Nor did he, like so many others, make this the pretext of a distraction, or of a debauch of food, but on the contrary they were occasions of prayer meetings that lasted all night, without sleep, with songs, hymns and similar devotions. Of this we see the proof in the composition of his hymns, which contain homage and praises not only of the Gods adored among the Greeks, but where you also see worship of the God Marnas of Gaza, Asklepios Leontukhos of Askalon, Thyandrites who is much worshipped among the Arabs, the Isis who has a temple at Philae, and indeed all other divinities. It was a phrase he much used, and that was very familiar to him, that a philosopher should watch over the salvation of not only a city, nor over the national customs of a few people, but that he should be the hierophant of the whole world in common. Such were the holy and purificatory exercises he practiced, in his austere manner of life.

Marinus of Samaria, *The Life of Proclus* 28

But since, as I said before, by his studies on this subject, Proclus had acquired a still greater and more perfect virtue, namely the theurgic, passing beyond the theoretic step, he did not conform his life exclusively to one of the two characteristics suitable to divine beings, but to both: not only did he direct his thoughts upward to the divine, but by a providential faculty which was not merely social, he cared for those things which were lower. He practiced the Chaldean prayer-meetings and conferences, and even employed the art of moving the divine tops. He was a believer in these practices, in unpremeditated responses, and other such divinations, which he had learned from Asklepigenia, daughter of Plutarch, to whom exclusively her father had confided and taught the mystic rites preserved by Nestorius, and the whole theurgic science. Even before that, according to the prescribed order, and purified by the Chaldean lustrations, the philosopher had, as epoptic initiate, witnessed the apparitions of Hekate under a luminous form, as he himself has mentioned in a special booklet. He had the power of producing rains by activating, at the right time, a particular rite, and was able to deliver Attica from a terrible drought. He knew how to foresee earthquakes, he had experimented with the divinatory power of the tripod, and had himself uttered verses prophetic about his own destiny.

Orphic Argonautika

After I came to the enclosures and the sacred place, I dug a three-sided pit in some flat ground. I quickly brought some trunks of juniper, dry cedar, prickly boxthorn and weeping black poplars, and in the pit I made a pyre of them. Skilled Medea brought to me many drugs, taking them from the innermost part of a chest smelling of incense. At once, I fashioned certain images from barley-meal [the text is corrupt here]. I threw them onto the pyre, and as a sacrifice to honor the dead, I killed three black puppies. I mixed with their blood copper sulfate, soapwort, a sprig of safflower, and in addition odorless fleawort, red alkanet, and bronze-plant. After this, I filled the bellies of the puppies with this mixture and placed them on the wood. Then I mixed the bowels with water and poured the mixture around the pit. Dressed in a black mantle, I sounded bronze cymbals and made my prayer to the Furies.

Orphic Argonautika

When the Sun had severed the sky with his swift horses and the dark Night stretched out, indecision stirred the breast of Aeson's son about whether he should impose an oath of loyalty upon the heroes to seal their faith in him. And I say to you, beloved Musaeus, son of Antiophemus, he ordered me to prepare quickly for an appropriate sacrifice. And so I built an altar of excellent oak on the shore, and putting on a robe, I offered service to the gods on behalf of the men. And then I slit the throat of an enormous bull, bending back the head to the gods, cutting up the fresh meat and pouring the blood around the fire. After I laid the heart on broken cakes, I made a libation of oil and sheep's milk. I then ordered the heroes to spread round the victim, thrusting their spears and their swords furnished with handles into the victim, and into the hide and the viscera shining in my hands. And I set up in the middle a vessel containing kykeon, the sacred drink of water and barley, which I carefully mixed, the first nourishing offering to Demeter. Then came the blood of the bull, and salty sea-water. I ordered the crew wreathed with crowns of olive leaves. Then filling up a golden vessel with kykeon by my hands, I divided it by rank so that every man could have a sip of the powerful drink. I asked Jason to order a dry pine torch to be placed beneath, and with swift motion the divine flame ascended.

Pausanias, *Description of Greece* 1.37.4

It is impossible to attribute the discovery of beans to Demeter; whoever has seen the initiation at Eleusis or has read the so-called Orphica knows what I am talking about.

Plato, *Laws* 6.782

Again, the practice of men sacrificing one another still exists among many nations; while, on the other hand, we hear of other human beings who did not even venture to taste the flesh of a cow and had no animal sacrifices, but only cakes and fruits dipped in honey, and similar pure offerings, but no flesh of animals; from these they abstained under the idea that they ought not to eat them, and might not stain the altars of the gods with blood. For in those days men are said to have lived a sort of Orphic life, having the use of all lifeless things, but abstaining from all living things.

Plato, *Laws* 854ac

And, in accordance with our rule as already approved, we must prefix to all such laws preludes as brief as possible. By way of argument and admonition one might address in the following terms the man whom an evil desire urges by day and wakes up at night, driving him to rob some sacred object– "My good man, the evil force that now moves you and prompts you to go temple-robbing is neither of human origin nor of divine, but it is some impulse bred of old in men from ancient wrongs unexpiated, which courses round wreaking ruin; and it you must guard against with all your strength. How you must thus guard, now learn. When there comes upon you any such intention, betake yourself to the rites of guilt-averting, betake yourself as suppliant to the shrines of the curse-lifting deities, betake yourself to the company of the men who are reputed virtuous; and thus learn, partly from others, partly by self-instruction, that every man is bound to honor what is noble and just; but the company of evil men shun wholly, and turn not back. And if it be so that by thus acting your disease grows less, well; but if not, then deem death the more noble way, and quit yourself of life."

Plato, *Republic* 2.364a–365b

But the most astounding of all these arguments concerns what they have to say about the Gods and virtue. They say that the Gods, too, assign misfortune and a bad life to many good people, and the opposite fate to their opposites. Begging priests and prophets frequent the doors of the rich and persuade them that they possess a God-given power founded on sacrifices and incantations. If the rich person or any of his ancestors has committed an injustice, they can fix it with pleasant things and feasts. Moreover, if he wishes to injure some enemy, then, at little expense, he'll be able to harm just and unjust alike, for by means of spells and enchantments they can persuade the Gods to serve them. And they present a hubbub of books by Musaeus and Orpheus, offspring as they say of Selene and the Muses, according to which they arrange their rites, convincing not only individuals but also cities that liberation and purification from injustice is possible, both during life and after death, by means of sacrifices and enjoyable games to the deceased which free us from the evils of the beyond, whereas something horrible awaits those who have not celebrated sacrifices.

Plotinos, *First Ennead* 6.7

There we must ascend again towards the good, desired of every soul. Anyone who has seen this, knows what I intend when I say it is beautiful. Even the desire of it is to be desired as a good. To attain it is for those who will take the upward path, who will set all their forces towards it, who will divest themselves of all that we have put on in our descent:– so, to those who approach the holy celebrations of the mysteries, there are appointed purifications and the laying aside of the garments worn before, and the entry in nakedness– until, passing on the upward way, all that is other than the God, each in the solitude of oneself shall see that solitary-dwelling existence, the apart, the unmingled, the pure, that from which all things depend, for which all look and live and act and know, the source of life and of intellection and of being.

Plutarch, *Life of Caesar* 93

The Romans have a Goddess whom they call Good, whom the Greeks call the Women's Goddess. The Phrygians say that this Goddess originated with them, and that she was the mother of their king Midas. The Romans say that she was a Dryad Nymph who married Faunus, and the Greeks say that she was the Unnameable One among the mothers of Dionysos. For this reason the women who celebrate her rites cover their tents with vine-branches, and a sacred serpent sits beside the Goddess on her throne, as in the myth. It is unlawful for a man to approach or to be in the house when the rites are celebrated. The women, alone by themselves, are said to perform rites that conform to Orphic ritual during the sacred ceremony.

Plutarch, *Moralia* Frag. 97

Let men not cleanse themselves in the women's bath, nor should men strip in the presence of women. Besides the impropriety, there are certain effluences that proceed from the female body and its excretions with which it is a kind of defilement for men to be infected. Both those who enter into the same air and those who enter into the same water are necessarily affected by them.

Plutarch, *On Isis and Osiris* 353e-c

As for wine, those who serve the God in Heliopolis bring none at all into the shrine, since they feel that it is not seemly to drink in the daytime while their Lord and King is looking upon them. The others use wine, but in great moderation. They have many periods of holy living when wine is prohibited, and in these they spend their time exclusively in studying, learning, and teaching religious matters. Their kings also were wont to drink a limited quantity prescribed by the sacred writings, as Hecataeus has recorded; and the kings are priests. The beginning of their drinking dates from the reign of Psammetichus; before that they did not drink wine nor use it in libation as something dear to the Gods, thinking it to be the blood of those who had once battled against the Gods, and from whom, when they had fallen and had become commingled with the earth, they believed vines to have sprung. This is the reason why drunkenness drives men out of their senses and crazes them, inasmuch as they are then filled with the blood of their forbears. These tales Eudoxus says in the second book of his World Travels are thus related by the priests.

Plutarch, *Roman Questions* 112
Did they regard the ivy as an unfruitful plant, useless to man, and feeble, and because of its weakness needing other plants to support it, but by its shade and the sight of its greenness fascinating to most people? And did they therefore think that it should not be uselessly grown in their homes nor be allowed to twine about in a futile way, contributing nothing, since it is injurious to the plants forming its support? Or is it because it cleaves to the ground? Wherefore it is excluded from the ritual of the Olympian gods, nor can any ivy be seen in the temple of Hera at Athens, or in the temple of Aphrodite at Thebes; but it has its place in the Agrionia and the Nyktelia, the rites of which are for the most part performed at night. Or was this also a symbolic prohibition of Bacchic revels and orgies? For women possessed by Bacchic frenzies rush straightway for ivy and tear it to pieces, clutching it in their hands and biting it with their teeth; so that not altogether without plausibility are they who assert that ivy, possessing as it does an exciting and distracting breath of madness, deranges persons and agitates them, and in general brings on a wineless drunkenness and joyousness in those that are precariously disposed towards spiritual exaltation.

Plutarch, *Sayings of the Spartans* 224d
This is his retort to Philip, the priest of the Orphic mysteries, who was in the direst straits of poverty, but used to assert that those who were initiated under his rites were happy after the conclusion of this life; to him Leotychidas said, "You idiot! Why then don't you die as speedily as possible so that you may with that cease from bewailing your unhappiness and poverty?"

Plutarch, *Symposiacs* 2.3
When upon a dream I had forborne eggs a long time, on purpose that in an

egg (as in a Carian) I might make experiment of a notable vision that often troubled me; some at Sossius Senecio's table suspected that I was tainted with Orpheus's or Pythagoras's opinions, and refused to eat an egg (as some do the heart and brain) imagining it to be the principle of generation. And Alexander the Epicurean ridiculingly repeated, —

> *To feed on beans and parents' heads*
> *Is equal sin;*

as if the Pythagoreans covertly meant eggs by the word κύαμοι (beans), deriving it from κύω or κυέω (to conceive), and thought it as unlawful to feed on eggs as on the animals that lay them. Now to pretend a dream for the cause of my abstaining, to an Epicurean, had been a defence more irrational than the cause itself; and therefore I suffered jocose Alexander to enjoy his opinion, for he was a pleasant man and excellently learned. Soon after he proposed that perplexed question, that plague of the inquisitive, Which was first, the bird or the egg? And my friend Sylla, saying that with this little question, as with an engine, we shook the great and weighty question (whether the world had a beginning), declared his dislike of such problems. But Alexander deriding the question as slight and impertinent, my relation Firmus said: Well, sir, at present your atoms will do me some service; for if we suppose that small things must be the principles of greater, it is likely that the egg was before the bird; for an egg amongst sensible things is very simple, and the bird is more mixed, and contains a greater variety of parts. It is universally true, that a principle is before that whose principle it is; now the seed is a principle, and the egg is somewhat more than the seed, and less than the bird; for as a disposition or a progress in goodness is something between a tractable mind and a habit of virtue, so an egg is as it were a progress of Nature tending from the seed to a perfect animal. And as in an animal they say the veins and arteries are formed first, upon the same account the egg should be before the bird, as the thing containing before the thing contained. Thus art first makes rude and ill-shapen figures, and afterwards perfects every thing with its proper form; and it was for this reason that the statuary Polycletus said, Then our work is most difficult, when the clay comes to be fashioned by the nail. So it is probable that matter, not readily obeying the slow motions of contriving Nature, at first frames rude and indefinite masses, as the egg, and of these moulded anew, and joined in better order, the animal afterward is formed. As the canker is first, and then growing dry and cleaving lets forth a winged animal, called psyche; so the egg is first as it were the subject matter of the generation. For it is certain that, in every change, that out of which the thing changes must be before the thing changing. Observe how worms and caterpillars are bred in trees from the moisture corrupted or concocted; now none can say but that the engendering moisture is naturally before all these. For (as Plato says) matter is as a mother or nurse in respect of the bodies that are formed, and we call that matter out of which any thing that is is made. And with a smile continued he, I speak to those that are acquainted with the mystical and sacred discourse of Orpheus, who not only affirms the egg to be before the bird, but makes it the first being in the whole world. The other parts, because deep mysteries (as Herodotus would say), we shall now pass by; but let us look upon the various kinds of animals, and we shall find almost every one beginning from an egg, — fowls and fishes; land animals, as lizards; amphibious, as crocodiles; some with two legs, as a cock; some without any, as a snake; and some with many, as a locust. And therefore in the solemn feast of Bacchus it is very well done to dedicate an egg, as the emblem of that which begets and contains every thing in itself.

Porphyry, *On Abstinence from Animal Foods* 2.45
That is why even sorcerers have thought such advance protection and purification necessary; but it is not effective in all circumstances, for they stir up wicked daimones to gratify their lusts. So holiness is not for sorcerers, but for godly men who are wise about the Gods, and it brings as a guard on all sides, for those who practice it, their attachment to the divine. If only sorcerers would practice it constantly, they would have no enthusiasm for sorcery, because holiness would exclude them from enjoyment of the things for the sake of which they commit impiety. But, being filled with passions, they abstain for a little from impure foods, yet are full of impurity and pay the penalty for their lawlessness towards the universe: some penalties are inflicted by the beings they themselves provoke, some by the justice which watches over all mortal concerns, both actions and thoughts. Holiness, both internal and external, belongs to a godly man, who strives to fast from the passions of the soul just as he fasts from those foods which arouse the passions, who feeds on wisdom about the Gods and becomes like them by right thinking about the divine; a man sanctified by intellectual sacrifice, who approaches the God in white clothing, with a truly pure freedom from passion in the soul and with a body which is light and not weighted down with the alien juices of other creatures or with the passions of the soul.

Porphyry, *On Abstinence from Animal Foods* 2.50
Priests, diviners and all men who are wise in the ways of religion instruct us to stay clear of tombs, of sacrilegious men, menstruating women, sexual intercourse, any shameful or lamentable sight, anything heard which arouses emotion; for often even unseen impurity disturbs those officiating at the rites, and an improperly performed sacrifice brings more harm than good.

Porphyry, *On Abstinence from Animal Foods* **2.61**
The best offering to the Gods is a pure intellect and a soul unaffected by passion; it is also appropriate to make them moderate offerings of other things, not casually but with full commitment. Honors to the Gods must be like the front seats given to good men, and like standing up for them to sit down, not like paying taxes. If a man can say, 'If you remember my good deeds and love me, long since dear one you repaid my favor, it was for this I showed you favor first' surely a God will be satisfied with this. That is why Plato says (*Laws* 716d; 717a) 'it is right for a good man to sacrifice and always to be in conversation with the Gods by prayer and dedications and sacrifices and all forms of worship' but for a bad man 'great effort about the Gods is in vain.' The good man knows what must be sacrificed, from what one must abstain, what should be eaten and from what offerings should be made; the bad man, bringing to the Gods honors suited to his own disposition and what he wants, acts impiously.

Porphyry, *On Abstinence From Animal Food* **4.16**
In the Eleusinian mysteries, likewise, the initiated are ordered to abstain from domestic birds, from fishes and beans, pomegranates and apples, which fruits are as equally defiling to the touch, as a woman recently delivered, and a dead body But whoever is acquainted with the nature of divinely-luminous appearances knows also on what account it is requisite to abstain from all birds, and especially for him who hastens to be liberated from terrestrial concerns, and to be established with the celestial Gods.

Porphyry, *On Abstinence from Animal Foods* **4.6-8**
Chaeremon the Stoic, therefore, in his narration of the Egyptian priests, who, he says, were considered by the Egyptians as philosophers, informs us, that they chose temples, as the places in which they might philosophize. For to dwell with the statues of the Gods is a thing allied to the whole desire, by which the soul tends to the contemplation of their divinities. And from the divine veneration indeed, which was paid to them through dwelling in temples, they obtained security, all men honouring these philosophers, as if they were certain sacred animals. They also led a solitary life, as they only mingled with other men in solemn sacrifices and festivals. But at other times the priests were almost inaccessible to any one who wished to converse with them. For it was requisite that he who approached to them should be first purified, and abstain from many things; and this is as it were a common sacred law respecting the Egyptian priests. But these philosophic priests having relinquished every other employment, and human labours, gave up the whole of their life to the contemplation and worship of divine natures and to divine inspiration; through the latter, indeed, procuring for themselves, honour, security, and piety; but through contemplation, science; and through both, a certain occult exercise of

manners, worthy of antiquity. For to be always conversant with divine knowledge and inspiration, removes those who are so from all avarice, suppresses the passions, and excites to an intellectual life. But they were studious of frugality in their diet and apparel, and also of continence and endurance, and in all things were attentive to justice and equity. They likewise were rendered venerable, through rarely mingling with other men. For during the time of what are called purifications, they scarcely mingled with their nearest kindred, and those of their own order, nor were they to be seen by anyone, unless it was requisite for the necessary purposes of purification. For the sanctuary was inaccessible to those who were not purified, and they dwelt in holy places for the purpose of performing divine works; but at all other times they associated more freely with those who lived like themselves. They did not, however, associate with any one who was not a religious character. But they were always seen near to the Gods, or the statues of the Gods, the latter of which they were beheld either carrying, or preceding in a sacred procession, or disposing in an orderly manner, with modesty and gravity; each of which operations was not the effect of pride, but an indication of some physical reason. Their venerable gravity also was apparent from their manners. For their walking was orderly, and their aspect sedate; and they were so studious of preserving this gravity of countenance, that they did not even wink, when at any time they were unwilling to do so; and they seldom laughed, and when they did, their laughter proceeded no farther than to a smile. But they always kept their hands within their garments. Each likewise bore about him a symbol indicative of the order which he was allotted in sacred concerns; for there were many orders of priests. Their diet also was slender and simple. For, with respect to wine, some of them did not at all drink it, but others drank very little of it, on account of its being injurious to the nerves, oppressive to the head, an impediment to invention, and an incentive to venereal desires. In many other things also they conducted themselves with caution; neither using bread at all in purifications, and at those times in which they were not employed in purifying themselves, they were accustomed to eat bread with hyssop, cut into small pieces. For it is said, that hyssop very much purifies the power of bread. But they, for the most part, abstained from oil, the greater number of them entirely; and if at any time they used it with pot-herbs, they took very little of it, and only as much as was sufficient to mitigate the taste of the herbs.

It was not lawful for them therefore to meddle with the esculent and potable substances, which were produced out of Egypt, and this contributed much to the exclusion of luxury from these priests. But they abstained from all the fish that was caught in Egypt, and from such quadrupeds as had solid, or many-fissured hoofs, and from such as were not horned; and likewise from all such birds as were carnivorous. Many of them, however, entirely abstained from all animals; and in purifications this abstinence was adopted by all of them, for then they did not even eat an egg. Moreover, they also rejected other things, without being calumniated for so doing. Thus, for instance, of oxen, they rejected the females, and also such of the males as were twins, or were speckled, or of a different colour, or alternately varied in their form, or which were now tamed, as having been already consecrated to labours, and resembled animals that are honoured, or which were the images of any thing that is divine, or those that had but one eye, or those that verged to a similitude of the human form. There are also innumerable other observations pertaining to the art of those who are called mosxofragistai, or who stamp calves with a seal, and of which books have been composed. But these observations are still more curious respecting birds; as, for instance, that a turtle should not be eaten; for it is said that a hawk frequently dismisses this bird after he has seized it, and preserves its life, as a reward for having had connexion with it. The Egyptian priests, therefore, that they might not ignorantly meddle with a turtle of this kind, avoided the whole species of those birds. And these indeed were certain common religious ceremonies; but there were different ceremonies, which varied according to the class of the priests that used them, and were adapted to the several divinities. But chastity and purifications were common to all the priests. When also the time arrived in which they were to perform something pertaining to the sacred rites of religion, they spent some days in preparatory ceremonies, some indeed forty-two, but others a greater, and others a less number of days; yet never less than seven days; and during this time they abstained from all animals, and likewise from all pot-herbs and leguminous substances, and, above all, from a venereal connexion with women; for they never at any time had connexion with males. They likewise washed themselves with cold water thrice every day; viz. when they rose from their bed, before dinner, and when they betook themselves to sleep. But if they happened to be polluted in their sleep by the emission of the seed, they immediately purified their body in a bath. They also used cold bathing at other times, but not so frequently as on the above occasion. Their bed was woven from the branches of the palm tree, which they call bais; and their bolster was a smooth semi-cylindric piece of wood. But they exercised themselves in the endurance of hunger and thirst, and were accustomed to paucity of food through the whole of their life.

This also is a testimony of their continence, that, though they neither exercised themselves in walking or riding, yet they lived free from disease, and were sufficiently strong for the endurance of modern labours. They bore therefore many burdens in the performance of sacred operations, and accomplished many ministrant works, which required more than common strength. But they divided the night into the observation of the celestial bodies, and sometimes devoted a part of it to offices of purification; and they distributed the day into the worship of the Gods, according to which they celebrated them with hymns thrice or four times, viz. in the morning and evening, when the sun is at his meridian altitude, and when he is declining to the west. The rest of their time they devoted to arithmetical and geometrical speculations, always labouring to effect something, and to make some new discovery, and, in short, continually exercising their skill. In winter nights also they were occupied in the same employments, being vigilantly engaged in literary pursuits, as paying no attention to the acquisition of externals, and being liberated from the servitude of that bad master, excessive expense. Hence their unwearied and incessant labour testifies their endurance, but their continence is manifested by their liberation from the desire of external good. To sail from Egypt likewise, was considered by them to be one of the most unholy things, in consequence of their being careful to avoid foreign luxury and pursuits; for this appeared to them to be alone lawful to those who were compelled to do so by regal necessities. Indeed, they were very anxious to continue in the observance of the institutes of their country, and those who were found to have violated them, though but in a small degree were expelled from the college of the priests. The true method of philosophizing, likewise, was preserved by the prophets, by the hierostolistae, and the sacred scribes, and also by the horologi, or calculators of nativities. But the rest of the priests, and of the pastophori, curators of temples, and ministers of the Gods, were similarly studious of purity, yet not so accurately, and with such great continence, as the priests of whom we have been speaking. And such are the particulars which are narrated of the Egyptians, by a man who was a lover of truth, and an accurate writer, and who among the Stoics strenuously and solidly philosophized.

Porphyry, *The Philosophy from Oracles* frags. 314 and 315

(Frag 314) Following after what has been said concerning piety we shall record the responses given by the Gods concerning their worship, part of which in anticipation we have set forth in the statements concerning piety. Here is an oracle of Apollo that also includes a reckoning of the order of the Gods:

Friend who has entered on this heaven-taught path, perform your sacrifices and do not forget the blessed Gods, slaying your sacrifices now to the Gods upon the earth (*epichthonioi*), now again to the Gods of heaven (*ouranioi*); sometimes to the kings of the *aither* themselves and to those of the watery *aer*, and to the kings of of the seas and all those who dwell beneath the earth (*hypochthonioi*). For everything is bound up in the fullness of their nature. I shall sing to you of how it is proper to perform the burnt offerings (*kathagismous*) of living creatures (be sure to write my oracle down on tablets): offerings to the Gods upon the earth (*epi-chthonioi*) and to the Gods of the heavens (*ouranioi*).

– Bright victims are for the Gods of heaven (*ouranioi*); for the Gods of the earth (*chthonioi*) use victims similar to them in color. Divide the sacrifices for the Gods of the earth into three parts when you slay them.

– Bury the victims for the infernal Gods (*nerterioi*) and pour the blood into a pit.

– For the Nymphs, pour out honey and the gift of Dionysos.

– For those Gods who fly around the earth constantly, having filled the flaming altar altogether with the blood of the victim, throw into the fire the body of a winged creature, sacrificing it.

– Then, having mixed honey with Deo's grain, place the mixture in the fire and throw in as well the aroma of frankincense and sprinkle on the barley grains.

– But when you look upon the sandy shore, pouring out grey sea water, offer the victim's head as a sacrifice and cast the rest of the animal, undivided, into the waves of the sea.

– Then, having done all of these things, make your way to the great company of the Gods who live in the heavens (*ouranioi*) and those who live in the *aer*.

– Finally, for all the Gods who dwell in the stars (*astraioi*) and those who dwell in the *aither*, let blood in fullest stream flow from the throat over the sacrifice. Make a banquet for the Gods out of the limbs, giving the extremities to Hephaistos.

– The rest you can eat, filling the liquid *aer* with sweet aromas. When everything is done, send forth your prayers.

(Frag 315) This is the method of sacrifices, which are accomplished according to the reckoning of the Gods that I mentioned earlier. For whereas there are Gods beneath the earth (*hypochthonioi*), and upon the earth (*epichthonioi*), and those beneath the earth are also called infernal Gods (*nerterioi*) and those upon the earth are also called Gods of the earth (*chthonioi*) — for all of these in common Apollon commands the sacrifice of black four-footed victims. But with regard to the manner of the sacrifice he makes distinctions: for to the Gods upon the earth (*epichthonioi*) he commands the victims to be slain upon altars, but to the Gods beneath the earth (*hypochthonioi*) he commands the victims to be slain over pits, and moreover after the offering to bury the bodies therein.

That four-footed animals are appropriate to all these deities, the God himself added, when he was questioned, Four-footed victims must be given only to Gods of the earth (*chthonioi*) and Gods beneath the earth (*hypochthonioi*). For Gods of the earth (*chthonioi*) the new limbs of lambs are appropriate.

But to the Gods of the *aer* Apollon commands us to make holocaust offerings of winged creatures, letting the blood run round upon the altars; winged creatures are also appropriate for the Gods of the sea, but they must be cast alive into the waves and must be black. For he says: Winged creatures for the Gods, but for the sea Gods black.

He names winged creatures for all of the Gods except those of the earth (*chthonioi*), and he names black for the sea Gods only, and therefore he intends white for the other Gods. But to the Gods of the heavens (*ouranioi*) and the Gods of the *aither* he commands us to consecrate the extremities of white victims, and to eat the other parts: for these animals only are appropriate for eating, and not the others. But those whom in his classification he calls Gods of heaven (*ouranioi*), here he calls Gods of the stars (*astraioi*).

Will it then be necessary to explain the *symbola* of the sacrifices, clear as they are to those who are in-the-know? There are four-footed land animals for the Gods of the earth (*chthonioi*) because like rejoices in like. And the sheep is of the earth (*chthonios*) and therefore dear to Demeter, and in heaven the ram, with the help of the sun, brings forth out of the earth its display of fruits. The ram must be black, for the earth is dark in nature. The victim must be divided into three parts because three is the *symbolon* of the corporeal and earthy.

To the Gods upon the earth (*epichthonioi*) one must make sacrifices high upon altars, for these Gods dwell on earth; but to the Gods beneath the earth (*hypochthonioi*) one must make sacrifices in a pit and in a grave, where they abide.

To the other Gods we must offer birds, because all things are in swift motion. For the water of the sea is also in perpetual motion, and dark, and therefore victims of this kind are suitable.

But white victims are appropriate for the Gods of the *aer* because the *aer* itself is filled with light, being of a translucent nature.

For the Gods of heaven (*ouranioi*) and the Gods of the *aither*, the parts of the animals that are lighter in weight are appropriate, and these are the extremities.

With these Gods we must participate in the sacrifice; for they are the givers of good things, but the others are averters of evil.

Porphyry, *Life of Pythagoras* 33
While his friends were in good health Pythagoras always conversed with them; if they were sick, he nursed them; if they were afflicted in mind, he solaced them, some by incantations and magic charms, others by music. He had prepared songs for the diseases of the body, by singing which he cured the sick. He had also some that caused forgetfulness of sorrow, mitigation of anger, and destruction of lust.

Proklos, *Commentary on Hesiod's Works and Days* 808
The ancestral laws of the Athenians devotes the 18th and 19th of the month to purifications and apotropaic rituals, as Philochoros and Kleidemos, both *exegetes* of ancestral law.

Proklos, *Commentary on Plato's Republic* 2.167.17-23
The capacity to hear the voices of daimones is provided to some by the priestly power, to others by their natural constitution … some can even hear things that are inaudible to all mortal hearing and see things invisible to mortal sight.

Suidas s.v. *Ἀποτεθρίακεν*
Meaning plucked, made smooth. But properly pruned fig-trees; for thria ["fig-leaves"] are the leaves of the fig-tree. Aristophanes writes, "which of the Odomanti has unpetalled his prick?" The Odomanti are a Thracian people. The Thracians used to pluck and smooth their genitals and had them circumcised. They say Judaeans are the same. Also attested is the participle ἀποτεθρυωμένοι ["they having gone to pieces"], meaning they having gone savage. This is said in a metaphor from rushes, tethrua, which are wild and sterile plants.

Suidas s.v. *Hêraïskos*
Hence his life also reached such a point that his soul always resided in hidden sanctuaries as he practiced not only his native rites in Egypt but also those of other nations, wherever there was something left of these. Heraiskos became a Bakchos, as a dream designated him and he traveled

widely, receiving many initiations. Heraiskos actually had a natural talent for distinguishing between religious statues that were animated and those that were not. For as soon as he looked at one his heart was struck by a sensation of the divine and he gave a start in his body and his soul, as though seized by the God. If he was not moved in such a fashion then the statue was soulless and had no share of divine inspiration. In this way he distinguished the secret statue of Aion which the Alexandrians worshiped as being possessed by the god, who was both Osiris and Adonis at the same time according to some mystical union. There was also something in Heraiskos' nature that rejected defilements of nature. For instance, if he heard any unclean woman speaking, no matter where or how, he immediately got a headache, and this was taken as a sign that she was menstruating.

Suidas s.v. *Sarapio*

For Isidore said that never in fact could he persuade him to meet another man, especially because when he grew old he no longer came out frequently from his own house; he lived alone in a truly small dwelling, having embraced the solitary life, employing some of the neighbors only for the most necessary things. He said that Sarapio was exceptionally prayerful, and visited the holy places in the dress of an ordinary man, where the rule of the feast led him. For the most part he lived all day in his house, not the life of a man, but to speak simply, the life of a God, continually uttering prayers and miracle-stories to himself or to the divinity, or rather meditating on them in silence. Being a seeker of truth and by nature contemplative, he did not deign to spend time on the more technical aspects of philosophy, but absorbed himself in the more profound and inspired thoughts. For this reason Orpheus was almost the only book he possessed and read, in each of the questions which came to him always asking Isidore, who had achieved the summit of understanding in theology. He recognized Isidore alone as an intimate friend and received him in his house. And Isidore seemed to observe in him the Kronian life of mythology. For that man continued doing and saying nothing else but recollecting himself and raising himself, as far as he could, towards the inward and indivisible life. He despised money so much that he possessed nothing whatever but only two or three books (among these was the poetry of Orpheus); and he despised the pleasures of the body so much that straightway from the beginning he offered to the body only what is necessary and alone brings benefit, but of sexual activity he was pure throughout his life. And he was so little concerned about honor from men that not even his name was known in the city. He would not have been known subsequently, if some one of the Gods had not wished to make him an example for mankind of the Kronian life. He used Isidore as an heir, having no heir from his family, nor supposing that anyone else was worthy of his property, I mean the two or three books.

Sylloge2, 566
Whoever wishes to visit the temple of the Goddess, whether a resident of the city or anyone else, must refrain from intercourse with his wife that day, from intercourse with another than his wife for the preceding two days, and must complete the required lustrations. The same prohibition applies to contact with the dead and with the delivery of a woman in childbirth. But if he has come from funeral rites or from the burial, he shall purify himself and enter by the door where the holy water stoups are, and he shall be clean that same day.

Sylloge2, 653
Concerning sacred men and sacred women. The scribe of the magistrates is to administer the following oath, then and there, to those who have been designated sacred men, who pour the blood and wine when the [offerings] are kindled, that no one may be remiss: "I swear, by the Gods for whom the mysteries are celebrated: I shall be careful that the things pertaining to the initiation are done reverently and in fully lawful manner; I myself shall do nothing shameful or wrong at the conclusion of the mysteries, nor shall I confide in anyone else; rather, I shall obey what is written; and I shall administer the oath to the sacred women and the priest in accordance with the rule. May I, by keeping the oath, experience what is in store for the pious, but may one who breaks the oath experience the opposite." If someone does not wish to take the oath, he is to pay a fine of one thousand drachmai, and in his place he is to appoint by lot another person from the same clan. The priest and the sacred men are to administer the same oath to the sacred women in the sacred area of Karneios on the day before the mysteries, and they are to administer an additional oath as well: "I also have lived purely and lawfully with my husband." The sacred men are to fine one who does not wish to take the oath one thousand drachmai and not allow her to celebrate the things pertaining to the sacrifices or participate in the mysteries. Rather, the women who have taken the oath are to celebrate. But in the fifty-fifth year those who have been designated sacred men and sacred women are to take the same oath in the eleventh month before the mysteries.

Regarding transferral. The sacred men are to hand over, to those appointed as successors, the chest and the books that Mnasistratos donated; they also are to hand over whatever else may be furnished for the sake of the mysteries.

Regarding wreaths. The sacred men are to wear wreaths, the sacred women a white felt cap, and the first initiates among the initiated a tiara.

But when the sacred men give the order, they are to take off their tiara, and they are all to be wreathed with laurel.

Regarding clothing. The men who are initiated into the mysteries are to stand barefoot and wear white clothing, and the women are to wear clothes that are not transparent, with stripes on their robes not more than half a finger wide. The independent women are to wear a linen tunic and a robe worth not more than one hundred drachmai, the daughters an Egyptian or linen tunic and a robe worth not more than a mina, and the female slaves an Egyptian or linen tunic and a robe worth not more than fifty drachmai. The sacred women: the ladies are to wear an Egyptian tunic or an undergarment without decoration and a robe worth not more than two minas, and the [daughters] an Egyptian tunic or a robe worth not more than one hundred drachmai. In the procession the ladies among the sacred women are to wear an undergarment and a woman's wool robe, with stripes not more than half a finger wide, and the daughters an Egyptian tunic and a robe that is not transparent. None of the women are to wear gold, or rouge, or white makeup, or a hair band, or braided hair, or shoes made of anything but felt or leather from sacrificial victims. The sacred women are to have curved wicker seats and on them white pillows or a round cushion, without decoration or purple design. The women who must be dressed in the manner of the Gods are to wear the clothing that the sacred men specify. But if anyone somehow has clothing contrary to the rule, or anything else of what is prohibited, the supervisor of the women is not to allow it, but the supervisor is to have the authority to inflict punishment, and it is to be devoted to the Gods.

Oath of the supervisor of the women. When the sacred men themselves take the oath, they also are to administer the oath to the supervisor of the women, before the same sacred men: "I truly shall be careful concerning the clothing and the rest of the things assigned to me in the rule.

Sylloge2, 939, 2-9
It is not permitted to enter the temple of the Lady Goddess with any object of gold on one's person, unless it is intended for an offering; or to wear purple or bright colored or black garments, or shoes, or a finger ring. But if one enters wearing any forbidden object, it must be dedicated to the temple. Women are not to have their hair bound up, and men must enter with bared heads. No flowers are to be brought in at the mysteries; no pregnant women or nursing mothers are to have any part. If anyone wishes to make an offering, let it be of olive, myrtle, honey, grains of barley clean from weeds, a picture, a white poppy, lamps, incense, myrrh, spice. But if anyone wishes to offer the Lady Goddess sacrificial animals, they must be female and white …

Sylloge3 1218

These are the laws concerning the dead; bury the dead person as follows: in three white cloths, a spread, a garment, and a coverlet — there may be less — worth not more than 300 drachmas. Carry it out on a wedge-footed bed and do not the cover the bier completely with the cloths. Bring not more than three khoes of wine to the tomb and not more than khous of olive oil, and bring back the vessels. Carry the dead man, covered over, up to the tomb in silence. Perform the preliminary sacrifice according to ancestral custom. Bring the bed and its coverings from the tomb indoors. On the following day first sprinkle the house with sea water, then wash it with water having anointed it with earth; when it has been sprinkled throughout, the house is purified and sacrifices should be made on the hearth. The women who go to the funeral are to leave the tomb before the men. Do not carry out the rites performed on the thirtieth day in honor of the deceased. Do not put a kylix under the bed, do not pour out the water, and do not bring the seepings to the tomb. Whenever someone dies, when he is carried out, no women should go to the house other than those polluted by death. The mother and wife and sisters and daughters are polluted, and in addition to these not more than five women, children of the daughters and of the cousins, and no one else. Those polluted washed from head to foot ... a pouring of water are purified ...

Sylloge3 26. 524

The madman shall exit the oracle.

Theon of Smyrna, *Mathematica*

Philosophy may be called the initiation into true sacred ceremonies, and the instruction in genuine Mysteries; for there are five parts of initiation: the first of which is the previous purification; for neither are the Mysteries communicated to all who are willing to receive them; but there are certain persons who are prevented by the voice of the crier [κηρυξ, kerux], such as those who possess impure hands and an inarticulate voice; since it is necessary that such as are not expelled from the Mysteries should first be refined by certain purifications: but after purification, the reception of the sacred rites succeeds. The third part is denominated epopteia, or reception. And the fourth, which is the end and design of the revelation, is [the investiture] the binding of the head and fixing of the crowns. The initiated person is, by this means, authorized to communicate to others the sacred rites in which he has been instructed; whether after this he becomes a torch-bearer, or an hierophant of the Mysteries, or sustains some other part of the sacerdotal office. But the fifth, which is produced from all these, is friendship and interior communion with God, and the enjoyment of that felicity which arises from intimate converse with divine beings. Similar to this is the communication of political instruction; for, in the first place, a certain purification precedes, or else an exercise in proper mathematical discipline from early youth. For thus Empedocles asserts, that it is necessary to be purified from sordid concerns, by drawing from five fountains, with a vessel of indissoluble brass: but Plato, that purification is to be derived from the five mathematical disciplines, namely from arithmetic, geometry, stereometry, music, and astronomy; but the philosophical instruction in theorems, logical, political, and physical, is similar to initiation. But he (that is, Plato) denominates εποπτεια [or the revealing], a contemplation of things which are apprehended intuitively, absolute truths, and ideas. But he considers the binding of the head, and coronation, as analogous to the authority which any one receives from his instructors, of leading others to the same contemplation. And the fifth gradation is, the most perfect felicity arising from hence, and, according to Plato, an assimilation to divinity, as far as is possible to mankind.

Theophrastos, *On The Superstitious Man*

It is apparent that superstition would seem to be cowardice with regard to the spiritual realm. The superstitious man is one who will wash his hands and sprinkle himself at the Sacred Fountain, and put a bit of laurel leaf in his mouth, to prepare himself for each day. If a marten should cross his path, he will not continue until someone else has gone by, or he has thrown three stones across the road. And if he should see a snake in his house, he will call up a prayer to Sabazios if it is one of the red ones; if it is one of the sacred variety, he will immediately construct a shrine on the spot. Nor will he go by the smooth stones at a crossroads without anointing them with oil from his flask, and he will not leave without falling on his knees in reverence to them. If a mouse should chew through his bag of grain, he will seek advice on what should be done from the official diviner of omens; but if the answer is, 'Give it to the shoemaker to have it sewn up,' he will pay no attention, but rather go away and free himself of the omen through sacrifice. He is also likely to be purifying his house continually, claiming that terrible Hecate has been mysteriously brought into it. And if an owl should hoot while he is outside, he becomes terribly agitated, and will not continue before crying out, 'O! Mighty Athena!' Never will he step on a tomb, nor get near a dead body, nor a woman in childbirth: he says he must keep on his guard against being polluted. On the unlucky days of the month— the fourth and seventh— he will order his servants to heat wine. Then he will go out and buy myrtle-wreaths, frankincense, and holy pictures; upon returning home, he spends the entire day arranging the wreaths on statues of the Hermaphrodites. Also, when he has a dream, he will go to the dream interpreters, the fortune-tellers, and the readers of bird-omens, to ask what God or Goddess he should pray to. When he is to be initiated into the Orphic mysteries, he visits the priests every month, taking his wife with him; or, if she can't make it, the nursemaid and children will suffice. It is also apparent that he is one of those people who go to great lengths to sprinkle themselves with sea-water. And if he sees someone eating Hecate's garlic at the crossroads, he must go home and wash his head; and then he calls upon the priestesses to carry a squill or a puppy around him for purification. If he sees a madman or epileptic, he shudders and spits into his lap.

Vergil, 4th *Georgic*

Pick out four choice bulls, of surpassing form, that now graze among your herds on the heights of green Lycaeus, and as many heifers of unyoked neck. For these set up four altars by the stately shrines of the Nymph-Goddesses, and drain the sacrificial blood from their throats, but leave the bodies of the steers within the leafy grove. Later, when the ninth Dawn displays her rising beams, you must offer to Orpheus funeral dues of Lethe's poppies, slay a black ewe, and revisit the grove.

About the Author

The Dionysian poet and clown Sannion organizes religious gatherings, leads public rituals, serves his community as Orpheotelest and *mantis* (diviner) and teaches classes on Bacchic Orphism and the Starry Bull tradition. He is also prolific under the pen-name "H. Jeremiah Lewis," with *Hunting Wisdom* being his XIIIth book published through Nysa Press.

Lucky XIII